"In this meticulously researched and lucidly presented book, Samantha Arnold investigates the implications of the enduring legal disjunction between children's rights and refugee protection norms. At a time when the number of distress child migrants in need of international protection is at an all time high, understanding how children fit into refugee law is a key legal question and an urgent practical necessity. Both legal scholars and child rights advocates stand to gain considerably from this timely study."

Jacqueline Bhabha, *Professor of the Practice of Health and Human Rights, Harvard T.H. Chan School of Public Health*

Children's Rights and Refugee Law

Children make up half of the world's refugees and over 40 per cent of the world's asylum seekers. However, children are largely invisible in historical and contemporary refugee law. Furthermore, there has been very limited interaction between the burgeoning children's rights framework, in particular the Convention on the Rights of the Child (CRC), and the 1951 Convention relating to the Status of Refugees (Refugee Convention). This book explores the possibility of a children's rights approach to the interpretation of the Refugee Convention and within that what such an approach might look like.

In order to construct a children's rights approach, the conceptualisations of children outside the legal discipline, within international children's rights law and then within refugee law and refugee discourse are analysed. The approach taken is socio-legal in nature and the suitability of the Refugee Convention as a framework for the interpretation of child claims is examined. The book analyses to what extent the Refugee Convention is capable of dealing with claims from children based on the modern conceptualisation of children, which is underscored by two competing ideologies: the child as a vulnerable object in law to be protected and the child as subject with rights and the capacity to exercise their agency. The influence each regime has had on the other is also analysed. The work discusses how a children's rights approach might improve outcomes for child applicants.

The book makes an original contribution to child refugee discourse and as such will be an invaluable resource for academics, researchers and policymakers working in the areas of migration and asylum law, children's rights and international human rights law.

Samantha Arnold is a Post-Doctoral Research Fellow within the Irish National Contact Point of the European Migration Network based in the Economic and Social Research Institute and an Adjunct Assistant Professor in the School of Law at Trinity College Dublin. Samantha completed her PhD in the School of Law, Trinity College Dublin. Her research interests include refugee and immigration law and policy and children's rights. She has published on these and related areas.

Law and Migration

Series Editor: Satvinder S. Juss
King's College London, UK

Migration and its subsets of refugee and asylum policy are rising up the policy agenda at national and international level. Current controversies underline the need for rational and informed debate of this widely misrepresented and little understood area.

Law and Migration contributes to this debate by establishing a monograph series to encourage discussion and help to inform policy in this area. The series provides a forum for leading new research, principally from the law and legal studies area, but also from related social sciences. The series is broad in scope, covering a wide range of subjects and perspectives.

A full list of titles in this series is available at:
www.routledge.com/law/series/ASHSER1280

Gender and Migration in Italy
A Multilayered Perspective
Edited by Elisa Olivito
978-1-4724-5575-8

Towards a Refugee Oriented Right of Asylum
Laura Westra, Satvinder Juss and Tullio Scovazzi
978-1-4724-5778-3

The Integration and Protection of Immigrants
Canadian and Scandinavian Critiques
Edited by Paul Van Aerschot and Patricia Daenzer
978-1-4724-3654-2

Asylum – A Right Denied
A Critical Analysis of European Asylum Policy
Helen O'Nions
978-1-4094-0409-5

Regional Approaches to the Protection of Asylum Seekers
An International Legal Perspective
Edited by Ademola Abass and Francesca Ippolito
978-1-4094-4297-4

Immigration, Integration and the Law
The Intersection of Domestic, EU and International Legal Regimes
Clíodhna Murphy
978-1-4094-6251-4

Children's Rights and Refugee Law

Conceptualising Children within the Refugee Convention

Samantha Arnold

Routledge
Taylor & Francis Group
LONDON AND NEW YORK

First published 2018 by Routledge

2 Park Square, Milton Park, Abingdon, Oxfordshire OX14 4RN
52 Vanderbilt Avenue, New York, NY 10017

Routledge is an imprint of the Taylor & Francis Group, an informa business

First issued in paperback 2019

British Library Cataloguing in Publication

British Library Cataloguing in Publication Data
A catalogue record for this book is available from the British Library

Library of Congress Cataloging-in-Publication Data
Names: Arnold, Samantha, author.
Title: Children's rights and refugee law : conceptualising children within the refugee convention.
Description: Abingdon, Oxon [UK] ; New York : Routledge, 2017. | Series: Law and migration | Includes bibliographical references and index.
Identifiers: LCCN 2017009513 | ISBN 978-1-351-68357-9 (adobe reader) | ISBN 978-1-351-68356-2 (epub) | ISBN 978-1-351-68355-5 (mobipocket)
Subjects: LCSH: Refugee children–Legal status, laws, etc. | Children's rights. | Children–Legal status, laws, etc. | Children (International law) | Convention on the Rights of the Child (1989 November 20)–History. | Refugees–Legal status, laws, etc. | Refugees–Protection–International cooperation. | Office of the United Nations High Commissioner for Refugees.
Classification: LCC KZ6530 .A76 2017 | DDC 342.08/3–dc23
LC record available at https://lccn.loc.gov/2017009513

ISBN: 978-1-138-05271-0 (hbk)
ISBN: 978-0-367-28081-9 (pbk)

Typeset in Galliard
by FiSH Books Ltd, Enfield

Contents

Acknowledgements

I would like to thank Trinity College Dublin and my PhD supervisor, Professor Patricia Brazil, who provided me with invaluable guidance and comments. Thanks also to Professor Rosemary Byrne and Dr Ciara Smyth for their comments and suggestions.

I wish to express my gratitude to inspirational friends: Julia Mercier, Benjamin Stevenin, Erik Smith, Carly VanVleet, Sharon Waters, Walt Kilroy and in particular Keith Doyle. Thanks are also due to Lisa Loughrey, my mom, and, in particular, my dad for all the support and encouragement over the years.

1 Introduction

Introduction

In 2015, the United Nations High Commissioner for Refugees (UNHCR) estimated that worldwide there were 21.3 million refugees,[1] 51 per cent of whom were children. While children remain less likely to apply for asylum than their adult counterparts, there has been an increase in both the number of child refugees and child asylum seekers, globally.[2] In 2015, the number of asylum applications submitted by or on behalf of separated or unaccompanied children trebled year on year, from 34,300 in 2014 to 98,400 in 2015.[3] It would be logical to assume, given these numbers, that children would be a highly visible group within refugee law and refugee discourse, in particular in relation to their qualification as refugees. This, however, has not been the case to date.

This book explores the conceptualisation of children within refugee law and refugee discourse. It examines the suitability of the 1951 Convention relating to the Status of Refugees (Refugee Convention) as a framework for the interpretation of child claims. It also analyses to what extent a children's rights approach to the interpretation of the Refugee Convention is possible, while recognising that children's rights violations must not only amount to persecution, but must be characterised by differential impact on the basis of discrimination with a link to a convention ground. This analysis is necessary as there is a significant gap between the two areas of law, not least of all because the Convention on the Rights of the Child (CRC) was adopted by the General Assembly of the United Nations (UN) nearly 40 years after the adoption of the Refugee Convention. The fact that the Refugee Convention was adopted at a time when there was no CRC and international children's rights law was only emerging, poses a challenge to children's rights, refugee discourses and indeed refugee determinations.

Children's rights in international law,[4] including refugee law,[5] have, however, experienced noticeable expansion since the late 1980s. The rapid growth and the near-universal acceptance of the CRC as a formula for protecting the 'period of childhood' were catalysts for this research. The emergence of concerted efforts at bridging the two areas of law provided the impetus to address the hypothesis that a children's rights approach to the interpretation of the Refugee Convention is both possible and needed. Notwithstanding the progress made in children's rights discourse in recent decades, the CRC has had relatively little discernible impact to date on child refugee law. Developments in refugee law prior to and after the adoption of the CRC indicate that such an approach is nevertheless a logical next step in the evolution of child refugee law.

The overarching purpose of this research is to establish that a children's rights approach to the interpretation of the Refugee Convention is possible and to look at how children's rights are dealt with in refugee law. This book looks at the most underdeveloped aspect of refugee law as it applies to children – their qualification as refugees. This book does not examine procedural aspects of seeking refuge. The focus surrounds the ways in which children are conceptualised within refugee law discourse, not how their applications are considered or how they are treated in the process of seeking asylum. Topics such as credibility, interview procedures, guardianship, participation or the voice of the child in the context of the asylum process are excluded from discussions. These subjects are not dealt with herein as they have already been dealt with, to a greater extent as compared with the topic at hand, in the refugee and children's rights discourses.[6] That said, while procedural[7] and care[8] aspects of child asylum are undoubtedly more developed in the literature, there is still work to do to ensure a fully CRC compliant asylum procedure. Though this is not the focus of the research, it is important to emphasise that without a children's rights approach to the substantive issues, child refugee claims are at risk of being wrongfully disallowed thus impacting upon children's access to other, including procedural, rights.

A dichotomy: children's rights and refugee law

There has traditionally been a dichotomy between refugee law and children's rights. There were concurrent developments in both areas of international law from the 1920s, which dealt with international protection. Children were not, however, referred to in the early development of refugee law.[9] Child refugees were dealt with instead in the context of either once-off administrative arrangements, such as the *Kindertransport* in the 1930s[10] or in the child-specific and non-binding 1924 Declaration of the Rights of the Child.[11] During this time, children were invisible within mainstream refugee discourse. This book looks to unpack the reasons for the dichotomy historically and to date. It looks to examine the reasons for the invisibility of children within early refugee discourse and the relative invisibility of children in contemporary refugee discourse. Today, there is evidence to show the interconnectedness between the two regimes. However, because the children's rights framework did not provide guidance as to the qualification of child refugees and because the Refugee Convention did not explicitly refer to children as potential beneficiaries of refugee protection, a series of bridges were required to narrow the gap between the two. These emerged in the form of guidance, but not until the 1990s.

Despite the indications that the gap is narrowing, the dichotomy persists. Contemporary literature on child refugees largely deals with procedural and social and economic needs unrelated to qualifying as a refugee. Child refugee research tends to view the child within refugee law holistically with qualification only forming a small part of the analysis. This area of research is heavily entrenched in welfare discourse.[12] Most of the available information on the qualification of child refugees comes from UN guidance materials produced by the Committee on the Rights of the Child (Committee) and the UNHCR. However, most references to 'child-specific forms of persecution' are only recent and somewhat limited.

The number and proportion of children seeking asylum is growing and alongside this is growing acceptance that children have agency and can exercise that agency in a variety of ways. The reasons for the dichotomy and the invisibility of children within refugee discourse are unpacked by examining the developmental path followed by children's rights law and refugee law. Points where they converge and diverge are analysed. The purpose of this exercise is to demonstrate the existing relationship between the two regimes and the potential for a children's rights approach. The extent to which the increase in the number of child asylum seekers and refugees, the expansion in children's rights and children's rights studies and the cross-pollination between the two regimes have impacted upon developments in child refugee law are analysed.

A children's rights approach

A wave of literature emerged, arising from the seventeenth and eighteenth centuries and later the Civil Rights movement in the US, which brought to light the important role children play in society. The conceptualisation of children emerging from a multitude of disciplines established that they had an evolving capacity to participate, make decisions and otherwise interact with the societies around them. Childhood was constructed as a period of growth and maturation where intervention was required to ensure protection from harm, which would interrupt or affect the child's development. The CRC codified the modern understanding of childhood developed outside the legal discipline. The CRC established children as rights holders with rights relating to their innate vulnerability, but also relating to their independent actions, behaviours, beliefs and decisions. The CRC and the discourses that preceded its adoption also established that adults have a role in ensuring children's access to many of their rights. Subsequent chapters develop on this conceptualisation and apply it in the context of refugee law with a view to ensuring that the analysis is cognisant of the wider children's rights framework and the childhood status quo that has developed over centuries and has been codified by the CRC.

Building upon the 'human rights approach'

Michelle Foster in her book, *International Refugee Law and Socio-Economic Rights: Refuge from Deprivation*, explored the challenges posed by migration caused by deprivation of social and economic rights where it engaged the Refugee Convention. She analysed the ability of the Refugee Convention to encompass refugee claims based on these violations. Foster suggested that the Refugee Convention can encompass violations of social and economic rights and highlighted a number of examples to support this. The main finding was that the Refugee Convention 'is capable of accommodating a more complex and nuanced analysis'.[13]

Foster attributed the change in tide to Hathaway who in 1991 in his book *The Law of Refugee Status* described persecution as the 'sustained or systemic violation of basic human rights demonstrative of a failure of state protection'. In this book, Hathaway suggested that the International Bill of Rights (IBR), comprising the Universal Declaration of Human Rights (UDHR), the International Covenant on Civil and Political Rights (ICCPR) and the International Covenant on Social, Economic and Cultural Rights (ICESCR), form the framework for the interpretation of persecution.[14] Foster and many others have contended that it is this interpretation that has opened the door to violations of rights that are related to gender, for example, and children.[15] One example of this expansion into children's rights is the recognition of children as refugees on the basis of female genital mutilation (FGM).[16] The assumption that a human rights approach to the interpretation of the Refugee Convention is possible forms the basis of this research. The hypothesis is that alongside a human rights approach, there should also be a children's rights approach.

Children as subjects of law and the Refugee Convention

Foster noted that the Refugee Convention was drafted with civil and political rights in mind (see Chapter 4) and as a result they are more prevalent in refugee case law. There is however reluctance across disciplines to attribute rights specifically to children, in particular those rights relating to agency. As a result, social and economic rights are more prevalent in child refugee case law than they are in the context of adult claims. The reluctance to view children as capable of exercising agency in respect of their civil and political rights points to an inherent difficulty in the application of the Refugee Convention in the case of children.

The primary challenge in dealing with child claims for protection is the dominant discourse on child agency, which places the child in a position secondary to adults – as an *object* of law. In other words, children are seen as objects of protection from harm by a third party (parent or other adult) rather than independent beings with a role to play in their own future outcomes.

Debates surrounding children as *subjects* of law, or children having agency, are not new. However, they have grown and developed significantly in the last 30 years. The modern origins of these debates are also evident as early as the seventeenth century (discussed in Chapter 2). It was not until the publication of the CRC, however, that the child-as-rights-holder and indeed the child as a participant in – or subject of – their own rights and futures emerged in the legal sphere (see Chapter 3). Child agency, and within that considering children as subjects of law, is a rapidly growing area of research and debate (see Chapters 2 and 3).

Sir Goodwin-Gill in 1995, reflecting on the CRC and its intersection with refugee law, concluded that children today are subjects of law.[17] However, in its application, human rights law including children's rights is still inconsistent as regards the treatment of children as either object or subject. Adult refugees are more often considered to have experienced a violation of civil or political rights whereas children are often seen as unable to exercise civil and political rights. This is discussed in Chapters 2 and 3 and looked at in the context of refugee law in Chapter 6.

The current definition of 'refugee' in international law requires some degree of agency and in many cases requires an individual to be the subject of persecution and thus the subject of protection (discussed in Chapter 5). Identifying in which instances children have been considered to be subjects of law is thus part of the analysis of the interpretation of the Refugee Convention considering children's rights. The theme of children being considered as objects and/or subjects of law, in particular in refugee law, is developed throughout.

Invisibility in refugee law

The understanding of children/childhood that developed in children's studies and children's rights does not exist in refugee law in the same way. In fact, children were not explicitly mentioned in the Refugee Convention despite having been a feature in international law since the 1920s. Historically, there was very little overlap between children's rights and refugee law. This is particularly evident in the context of children qualifying as refugees. It was the advent of the CRC and the debates and research that followed that influenced developments in other areas of law, including refugee law. Much of the research on this topic looks at refugee determinations relating to children within a refugee law bubble, with a seemingly obligatory and normative reference to children's rights,[18] in particular those contained within the CRC, without extensive analysis. As previously mentioned, comprehensive analysis of CRC-based rights and refugee law typically exist within the context of social and economic rights, unrelated to qualification. These studies tend to look at accessing the asylum procedure or accessing other fundamental rights or children's rights *while* seeking asylum. There is limited research on the definition of 'refugee' and how that relates to children. Furthermore, there is no research that looks at the CRC as a whole and the rights therein or examines instances where violations of those rights amount to persecution in refugee law.

Children's rights research tends to look at law from a children's rights perspective. Refugee research tends to look at law from a refugee law perspective. This is natural and to be expected. However, due to the fact the CRC emerged almost 40 years later than the Refugee Convention, it is perhaps time that refugee law was looked at from a children's rights perspective and specifically the definition of refugee and how children are conceptualised within it. This is the dominant subtheme of this research and part of the rationale for considering the potential for a children's rights approach. These discussions assist in buttressing the hypothesis that the Refugee Convention is sufficiently flexible to incorporate children's rights violations.

Part of examining the possibility of a children's rights approach is to analyse the conceptualisation of children in international law (discussed in Chapter 3), in the wider discourses on children and childhood (discussed in Chapter 2) and then in the context of refugee law (discussed in Chapters 5 and 6). There is, however, very little case law dealing with child refugees available through traditional and internationally or regionally recognised databases, such as Refworld[19] or the European Database of Asylum Law.[20] Firstly, this is perhaps due to the fact that the intersection of refugee law and children's rights law[21] is relatively recent. Secondly, the notion that children are secondary to adult applicants continues to pervade substantive refugee discourse and jurisprudence. Child refugee claims are often subsumed within head-of-household claims.[22] Thirdly, very few separated children[23] make their way to Global North countries to apply for asylum, despite the fact that they represent a significant proportion of refugees and displaced persons around the world.[24] Cases arising from separated children are important as they represent a single-named-applicant cohort within the child refugee demographic who are not subsumed within adult claims. However, the number of separated children seeking asylum is relatively low. This is discussed in Chapter 6.

The limited case law available poses a significant challenge. The fact that children are often subsumed within adult claims also means that sometimes the child-aspect of the claim is lost or considered secondary. There are nevertheless sufficient examples of child cases to draw some conclusions and assist in creating a picture of a potential children's rights approach.

Locating children's rights in refugee law: Article 6 and the 'Three Ps Approach'

Most literature on the interpretation of refugee law adopts a framework based on the five convention grounds: race, nationality, religion, membership of a particular social group and political opinion. This approach is well developed in refugee law. However, this research does not follow the five convention grounds approach for two reasons. Firstly, an approach that stems from the Refugee Convention itself is not child-focused or centred. An approach that stems from the CRC and other relevant rights provides a children's rights perspective to the analysis and perhaps mitigates the risk that the focus will remain on the well-established, yet somewhat limited, child-specific forms of persecution and indeed the existing refugee case law pertaining to children. Following the persecution criteria rather than the convention nexus facilitates a honing in on the children's rights violations rather than the convention nexus. Instead of structuring the research using the convention grounds, the traditional 'Three Ps approach' to interpreting the CRC is employed.

The Three Ps comprise provision, protection and participation rights. Provision rights include: right to life,[25] the highest attainable standard of health,[26] an adequate standard of living[27] and education.[28]

Protection rights include rights, which relate to protection from child abuse, neglect, exploitation, cruelty and special protection for children in precarious circumstances.[29]

Participation rights include the rights to freedom of expression,[30] thought, conscience, religion[31] and association.[32] In general, participation rights focus on the child's right to have their voice heard and their views considered including in respect of their social, economic, religious, cultural and political life.[33]

There is an argument against this relatively simplistic approach – it is that the CRC represented the status quo at the time of drafting and children's rights should be seen as something that is evolving, taking into account more recent developments in international law, guidance, literature from a variety of disciplines and case law. Critics argue that continuing to rely on the CRC equates to complacency. The argument is the same for utilising normative tools for the interpretation of the CRC.[34] This was kept in mind during the analysis of children's rights and their refugee nexuses and reflected upon in Chapter 3.

Development has been at the core of discussions outside children's rights law – in sociological and educational discourses. The focus of writings and theorising since the seventeenth century was on the need to provide for and educate children to ensure they were able to develop into active citizens. This view of childhood looks at children as 'adults-in-becoming'.[35] From the 1920s on, in children's rights law, after survival was ensured, development was to the fore. The CRC provides for survival and development in the same provision: '1. States Parties recognize that every child has the inherent right to life. 2. States Parties shall ensure to the maximum extent possible the survival and development of the child'.[36]

It could be easy to draw the conclusion that international refugee law deals only with rights that impact upon the right to survive. However, by including both survival and development in one provision in the CRC, Article 6, the drafters clarified that these rights go hand in hand and merely ensuring survival rights are not violated does not mean that the child is able to thrive, and as is argued throughout this book, it does not mean that the child is not at risk of persecution.

Including the two rights in the same provision indicates that development *en route* to adulthood is as important as merely surviving. The Committee clarified this point in 2003, stating that the development of the child in the context of Article 6 is 'a holistic concept, embracing the child's physical, mental, spiritual, moral, psychological and social development' and that 'implementation measures should be aimed at achieving the optimal development for all children'.[37] This is a close reflection of the work produced during the period of Enlightenment (see Chapter 2).[38] It is also a close reflection of the conceptualisation that arose from sociological discourses prior to and in light of the CRC.[39] The modern conceptualisation of children stems from the understanding of the 'period of childhood' – a period characterised by positive development.

Article 6 is relied upon as the benchmark for children's rights. Violations of rights that relate to the child's development whether short or long term are central to the refugee question. A violation of the child's right to develop, which goes to the core of children and childhood studies, should carry significant weight in the analysis of a refugee claim. Chapter 6 examines breaches in rights that impact upon positive development, in particular where the impact will be lasting and affect the person into adulthood, and the relationship those breaches may have with the convention grounds. In practice, however, Article 6 is not typically cited in case law. There are nevertheless instances where this right is traceable through other CRC rights or through the sociological understanding of children that has developed over the last number of centuries (as discussed in Chapter 2). The following two examples of child refugee cases illustrate this point.

The first example relates to FGM. UNHCR has referred to FGM as a child-specific form of persecution thereby linking it to refugee law.[40] There is a significant body of case law on FGM and children. In *RRT Case No. 1101038*, the Australian Refugee Review Tribunal found two girls to be refugees on the basis of FGM and the known health risks associated with the procedure, including excessive bleeding, death, illness and birth complications.[41] It is arguable that the Tribunal saw this procedure as something that would affect the applicants' physical and psychological well-being and would not be conducive to achieving optimal development. The Committee, as mentioned above, argued that these elements are part of a holistic interpretation of Article 6.

The second example is education. The right to education on the surface may not seem to have a direct link with refugee law, yet violations of this right have been considered to amount to persecution. UNHCR identified discriminatory measures that result in 'serious restrictions' on a person's right to 'normally available educational facilities' as a potential form of persecution.[42] In *D. [a minor] v Refugee Appeals Tribunal & Anor*, the Irish High

Court heard a case submitted on behalf of a child who would be denied access to education due to his ethnicity. Judge Hogan found that the breach of the right to education did amount to persecution, adding that the denial of education would mean that the applicant would 'effectively be excluded from any meaningful participation' in society.[43] The right to education goes to the core of sociological and historical theorising on children and the period of childhood (discussed in Chapter 2) and it is part of the holistic interpretation of Article 6, part of achieving optimal development, including the child's mental, moral and social development, as established by the Committee (see above). These cases are revisited in Chapter 6 and additional cases are discussed where there is a link with Article 6, including for example the right to a family environment in the case of separated children.[44]

Methodology of analysis

Due to the international nature of the scope of the study, experiences of the operation of law in a variety of jurisdictions, in particular those jurisdictions in the Global North with an established system for determining asylum applications are examined. The key elements of children's rights law, specifically around the experiences commonly associated with childhood and positive development, are examined to establish an understanding of the host of rights that require protection and, in instances where those rights are breached, may amount to persecution in refugee law. This analysis draws on corresponding developments in international human rights law and refugee law. This process aims to assess the parameters and the potential of the Refugee Convention definition of 'refugee' in its application in the case of children. The increase in the availability of case law from a variety of jurisdictions and courts online has made the adoption of this approach possible. In considering the interpretation of the Refugee Convention in respect of children, key jurisprudence from all over the world, primarily from higher courts, is considered.

Global trends are identified, allowing for contemplations around reform of the law in this case in reference to the full adoption and adherence to a children's rights approach to interpreting the Refugee Convention. Changing attitudes towards children and refugees over time are also considered in order to support the narrowing of the gap between the two legal regimes (children's rights and refugee law) and to support the potential for its continued narrowing.

Due to the limited case law that deals specifically with children's *qualification* as refugees, the analysis also draws on existing secondary research on children, childhood and children's rights law.

The primary focus of the present research is the CRC *and* the Refugee Convention as they are both primary sources of international law in the protection of child refugees and asylum seekers. There are 148 States Parties to both the Refugee Convention and 1967 Protocol relating to the Status of Refugees[45] and it remains the foundational source of refugee law internationally.[46] The CRC has been ratified by more countries than any other Convention,[47] and is seen as the cornerstone of the children's rights regime.[48] However, various other sources of law and guidance, including leading research in the area are also analysed. Furthermore, guidance from the Committee and UNHCR is also heavily relied upon as a significant source in bridging the gap between children's rights and refugee law.

In summary, this book identifies which violations of children's rights amount to persecution and examines whether or not the Refugee Convention provides a satisfactory framework for the determination of child refugee applications and whether or not a children's rights approach to the interpretation of the Refugee Convention is possible and, in this regard, what the main trends are. Above all, this research aims to conceptualise the child refugee by identifying characteristics associated with declarations of refugee protection. The scope is limited to discussions on children's rights violations in the context of refugee law. Some elements of the refugee decision-making process, such as internal relocation, are excluded from this analysis as this research looks at whether or not a violation of a children's rights is seen as amounting to persecution. Concepts such as internal relocation are excluded from the research due to the fact that they are neither core to the Refugee Convention nor are they universally applied in decision making procedures across the globe.

Notes

1 The total number of people of concern to UNHCR in 2015 was estimated to be 65.3 million. See: United Nations High Commission for Refugees, *Global Trends: Forced Displacement in 2015* (2015).

2 United Nations High Commission for Refugees *Statistical Yearbook* (2014). These statistics were not disaggregated by region.

3 See: United Nations High Commission for Refugees, *Global Trends: Forced Displacement in 2015* (2015).

4 Ann Quennerstedt, 'Children's Rights Research Moving into the Future – Challenges on the Way Forward' (2013) 21 *International Journal of Children's Rights* 233.

5 See United Nations High Commissioner for Refugees, 'Guidelines on International Protection: Child Asylum Claims under Articles 1(A)2 and 1(F) of the 1951 Convention and 1967 Protocol relating to the Status of Refugees' HCR/GIP/09/08 22 December 2009.

6 See, for example: UN High Commissioner for Refugees, *The Heart of the Matter – Assessing Credibility when Children Apply for Asylum in the European Union* (UNHCR 2014); Jacqueline Bhabha, 'Demography and rights: women, children and access to asylum' (2004) 16 *International Journal of Refugee Law* 227; Ciara Smyth, *European Asylum Law and the Rights of the Child* (Routledge 2014) 6; Separated Children in Europe Programme, *SCEP Statement of Good Practice* (4th edn, Save the Children 2010); Mark Evenhuis, 'Child-Proofing Asylum: Separated Children and Refugee Decision Making in Australia' (2013) 25 *International Journal of Refugee Law* 535.

7 See, for example: Mark Evenhuis, 'Child-Proofing Asylum: Separated Children and Refugee Decision Making in Australia' (2013) 25 (3) *International Journal*

of Refugee Law 535; UN High Commissioner for Refugees (UNHCR), 'The Heart of the Matter – Assessing Credibility when Children Apply for Asylum in the European Union', December 2014.

8 See, for example: Samantha Arnold, Martine Goeman and Katja Fournier, 'The Role of the Guardian in Determining the Best Interest of the Separated Child Seeking Asylum in Europe: A Comparative Analysis of Systems of Guardianship in Belgium, Ireland and the Netherlands' (2014) 16 *European Journal of Migration and Law* 467.

9 With some exceptions, such as the constitution of the International Refugee Organization. Discussed in Chapter 4.

10 See for example, Anthony Grenville, 'The Kindertransport: An Introduction' in Andrea Hammel and Bea Lewkowicz (eds), *The Kindertransport to Britain 1938/39: New Perspectives* (Brill 2012). Discussed in Chapter 4.

11 1924 Declaration of the Rights of the Child. Discussed in Chapter 3.

12 See, for example: Jacqueline Bhabha, 'Seeking Asylum Alone: Treatment of separated and trafficked children in need of refugee protection' (2004) *International Migration* 42 (1) 141; Hans Anderson et al. (eds), *The Asylum-Seeking Child in Europe* (Cente for European Research at Goteborg University 2005); Sandy Ruxton, *Separated children seeking asylum in Europe: a programme for action* (Save the Children Sweden 1999); Everett Ressler, Neil Boothby, and Daniel J. Steinbock, *Unaccompanied children: Care and protection in wars, natural disasters, and refugee movements* (OUP 1988); Ilse Derluyn and Eric Broekaert 'Unaccompanied refugee children and adolescents: The glaring contrast between a legal and a psychological perspective' (2008) 31 (4) *International Journal of Law and Psychiatry* 319; Israel Bronstein and Paul Montgomery, 'Psychological distress in refugee children: a systematic review' (2011) 14 (1) *Clinical Child and Family Psychology Review* 44; David Tolfree, *Community based care for separated children* (Save the Children Sweden 2003); Linda Piwowarczyk, 'Our responsibility to unaccompanied and separated children in the United States: A helping hand' (2005) 15 *Boston University Public Interest Law Journal* 263.

13 Michelle Foster, *International Refugee Law and Socio-Economic Rights: Refugee from Deprivation* (CUP 2007) 1.

14 James Hathaway, *The Law of Refugee Status* (Butterworths 1991) 104–5 in Michelle Foster, *International Refugee Law and Socio-Economic Rights: Refuge from Deprivation* (CUP 2007) 27.

15 Michelle Foster, *International Refugee Law and Socio-Economic Rights: Refuge from Deprivation* (CUP 2007) 16.

16 FGM is also considered in adult claims and is often considered as a development in the area of gender-based rights. Michelle Foster, *International Refugee Law and Socio-Economic Rights: Refuge from Deprivation* (CUP 2007).

17 Sir Guy Goodwin-Gill, 'Unaccompanied refugee minors: The role and place of international law in the pursuit of durable solutions' (1995) 3 *International Journal of Children's Rights* 405.

18 See, for example the analysis in Sir Guy Goodwin-Gill and Jane McAdam, *The Refugee in International Law* (3rd edn OUP 2011) 130; James Hathaway, *The Rights of Refugees under International Law* (CUP 2005).

19 UN High Commissioner for Refugees, 'Refworld' <www.refworld.org> accessed 12 July 2016.

20 European Council on Refugees and Exiles, 'European Database of Asylum Law' <www.asylumlawdatabase.eu> accessed 12 July 2016.

21 See Jane Fortin, *Children's Rights and the Developing Law* (n 1) 31–35. Discussed in Chapter 2.

22 Jacqueline Bhabha, *Child Migration and Human Rights in a Global Age* (PUP 2014) 221. Discussed in Chapter 6.

23 The Separated Children in Europe Programme define separated children as 'Separated children are under 18 years of age, outside their country of origin and separated from both parents, or their previous legal, or customary primary caregiver'. See: Separated Children in Europe Programme, *SCEP Statement of Good Practice* (4th edn, Save the Children 2010) 3.
24 Jacqueline Bhabha, 'Demography and rights: women, children and access to asylum' (2004) 16 *International Journal of Refugee Law* 227.
25 Convention on the Rights of the Child, Article 6.
26 *Ibid*, Article 24.
27 *Ibid*, Article 27.
28 *Ibid*, Article 28. UNICEF refers to these rights as 'Survival and Development Rights' in 'The Convention on the Rights of the Child Survival and development rights: the basic rights to life, survival and development of one's full potential' <www.unicef.org/crc/files/Survival_Development.pdf> accessed 12 July 2016.
29 UNICEF, 'The Convention on the Rights of the Child Protection rights: keeping safe from harm' <www.unicef.org/crc/files/Protection_list.pdf> accessed 12 July 2016.
30 Convention on the Rights of the Child, Article 40.
31 *Ibid*, Article 41.
32 *Ibid*, Article 15.
33 UNICEF, 'The Convention on the Rights of the Child Participation rights: having an active voice' <www.unicef.org/crc/files/Participation.pdf> accessed 12 July 2016.
34 Ann Quennerstedt, 'Children, But Not Really Humans? Critical Reflections on the Hampering Effect of the "3 p's"' (2010) 18 *International Journal of Children's Rights* 619.
35 See: Allison James and Adrian James, *Key Concepts in Childhood Studies* (2nd edn, Sage 2012) 58.
36 Convention on the Rights of the Child, Article 6.
37 General Comment No. 5 (2003) General measures of implementation of the Convention on the Rights of the Child (arts. 4, 42 and 44, para. 6) para 12.
38 See: John Locke, *Some Thoughts Concerning Education* (1693) <www.bartleby.com/37/1/> accessed 23 August 2014; Jean-Jacques Rousseau, *Emile, or on Education* in Leo Damrosch (ed.), *The Essential Writings of Jean-Jacques Rousseau* (Vintage 2013) 229–289. Discussed in Chapter 2.
39 See: Jane Fortin, *Children's Rights and the Developing Law* (3rd edn, CUP 2009); David Archard, *Children: Rights and childhood* (2nd edn, Routledge 2004). Discussed in Chapter 2.
40 United Nations High Commissioner for Refugees, 'Guidelines on International Protection: Child Asylum Claims under Articles 1(A)2 and 1(F) of the 1951 Convention and 1967 Protocol relating to the Status of Refugees' HCR/GIP/09/08 22 December 2009 31.
41 *RRT Case No. 1101038*, [2011] RRTA 307, Australia: Refugee Review Tribunal, 14 April 2011.
42 UN High Commissioner for Refugees, *Handbook and Guidelines on Procedures and Criteria for Determining Refugee Status under the 1951 Convention and the 1967 Protocol relating to the Status of Refugees* (UNHCR 2011) para 54.
43 *D. [a minor] v Refugee Appeals Tribunal & Anor* [2011] IECH 431 at 23. This case has since been overturned by Supreme Court decision *E.D. (Education) v The Refugee Appeals Tribunal, The Minister for Justice and Equality & Law Reform* [2016] IESC 77.
44 See for example, *AA (unattended children) Afghanistan CG [2012] UKUT 00016 (IAC)*. In this case the fact that the applicant minor did not have a safe

family environment to return to factored in to the final decision to grant refugee protection on appeal. Discussed in Chapter 6.

45 The 1967 Protocol relating to the Status of Refugees removed the temporal and geographical limitations to the original definition of refugee in the Refugee Convention. This is discussed in Chapter 4. UN High Commissioner for Refugees, 'States Parties to the 1951 Convention relating to the Status of Refugees and the 1967 Protocol' <www.unhcr.org/protect/PROTECTION/3b73b0d63.pdf> accessed 12 July 2016.

46 See James Hathaway, 'The Rights of Refugees under International Law' (CUP 2005) and Sir Guy Goodwin-Gill and Jane McAdam, 'The Refugee in International Law' (3rd edn OUP 2007).

47 All UN recognised countries ratified the Convention on the Rights of the Child except the United States of America <http://treaties.un.org/Pages/ViewDetails.aspx?src=IND&mtdsg_no=IV-11&chapter=4&lang=en> accessed 12 July 2016.

48 See Jane Fortin, *Children's Rights and the Developing Law* (3rd edn, CUP 2009).

2 Children, childhood and refugee law

Abstract

Chapter 2 looks at the characteristics associated with childhood in the context of child and childhood studies. Firstly, it defines the concepts 'child' and 'childhood' to be relied upon throughout. Secondly, it unpacks the meaning of development that emerged as prominent in childhood discourses from the seventeenth century on. Lastly, Chapter 2 seeks to show that the early developments in child and childhood studies, philosophy and rights-based discourses continue to be relevant and indicate that children's rights have perhaps evolved less than we might have expected. The purpose of this discussion is to not only show that the issues grappled with for centuries persist, but also that there is work to be done in general children and childhood studies, children's rights *and* refugee law. The focus of this book is child refugee law and therefore these discussions largely inform subsequent analyses of case law and modern legislation pertaining to child refuge.

Introduction

The two key concepts most relevant to discussions on the qualification of child refugees are 'child' and 'childhood'. Due in part to the late publication of the Convention on the Rights of the Child 1989 (CRC) (relative to other human rights instruments), the sociological constructions of 'child' and 'childhood' have had a significant impact on the development of international children's rights law. In fact, childhood studies and children's rights debates had become quite sophisticated prior to the publication of the CRC. Although the CRC has recently been criticised for representing the status quo of over 20 years ago, it nevertheless benefited from debates, research, law and policy concerning children up to the late 1980s. The impact of sociological and historical debates on children and childhood, including in the very specific discipline of 'childhood studies', can still be seen in the implementation and interpretation of children's rights law, human rights law *and* refugee law. Although it is not possible to say that societies' views of the role of children have not developed, it is possible to show that the debates, theories and constructions of childhood that existed from the *Ante Christum Natum*[1] era onwards are still relevant and observable in the application and interpretation of law, including refugee law.

A conceptualisation of childhood that builds upon historical theorising around children and their role in society is established in this chapter. The continued impact theorists, philosophers and academics from the period of Enlightenment have had on modern international law, including refugee law, is discussed. The origins and the deeply engrained perception of children as second class citizens in terms of civil and political rights and their position on a pedestal in terms of social and economic rights are also discussed. It is also demonstrated in this chapter that the right to survival and development[2] has formed the foundation of historical and modern conceptualisations of childhood. Development has been at the fore from the first major turning point in children's rights – when the child became not just the property of the parent. Ancient Roman law is often referred to as the epitome of the objectification of children in law as it provided for the right of the father to not only give life to his child but also to take it away.[3]

The understandings of child agency prior to the CRC are also discussed. Child agency in pre-CRC discourses was always visible, always important and always contentious. Child agency formed part of the discourse on childhood from the seventeenth century, yet it was regarded with trepidation. Children, in respect of agency, were seen as half-formed. Early theorists viewed children as unable to form views of their own or to reason with any degree of consistency, and that it was the 'process' of childhood that prepared them to exercise their citizenship rights *as adults*, but not before. The view that children were inconsistent in their ability to reason and the reluctance to view children as able to exercise their agency or form views of their own are observable in refugee case law. The same trepidation and conflict that permeated early childhood theorising and even contemporary sociological discourse also permeates modern refugee law. It is argued that the views of the writers, philosophers and academics included in this chapter are therefore not so far removed from the interpretation of modern refugee law in the case of children.

Firstly, the concepts 'child' and 'childhood' are defined in this chapter to be relied upon throughout this book in dealing with the analysis of refugee law in respect of child claimants. Secondly, this chapter demonstrates the importance and indeed the primacy of the right to survival and development (subsequently codified in Article 6 of the CRC). Lastly, this chapter seeks to show that early developments in child and childhood studies, philosophy and rights-based discourses continue to be relevant, indicating that children's rights have perhaps evolved less than we might have expected, in particular when it comes to agency. The purpose of this discussion is to not only show that the issues grappled with for centuries persist, but also that there is work to be done in general children and childhood studies, children's rights *and* refugee law. These discussions largely inform the subsequent analyses of case law and modern legislation pertaining to child refuge.

Indicators of childhood and being a child and refugee law

The refugee child in effect is a minority by two categorisations, namely: the child in relation to the majority adult group and the refugee in relation to the majority of the human race who are not classified as refugees.[4] Social theorist, Wirth, defined a minority as a group of people residing on the peripheries of others in society due to 'their physical or cultural characteristics'. Wirth noted that the minority group is discriminated against and is identified as different by the surrounding society.[5]

The perceived differences between adults and children define childhood in any given society at any given point in time. The concept of the period of childhood is equally as important as the concept 'child' itself. This is because the child can often be defined by the attributes or characteristics associated with childhood. And in contemporary society, or at least sections of society that engage in this debate, the period of childhood exists and is something to be protected.[6] For this reason, children are often conceived of in sociological discourse and the law, in particular refugee law, as forming a social group. This chapter looks both at how children are conceived of in society and what characteristics define or indicate childhood. It is precisely these characteristics that inform children's rights and thus rights that can be violated and in some cases amount to persecution. This section discusses the key characteristics and indicators of childhood.

Age, as emphasised by Archard and Ariès, is almost universally considered to be an indicator of childhood, at least within the western construct of childhood.[7] Children in these discussions and in this book are people under the age of 18, recognising the contribution of the CRC in Article 1: 'For the purposes of the present Convention, a child means every human being below the age of 18 years unless under the law applicable to the child, majority is attained earlier'.[8]

Age is an important aspect of refugee law and has been referred to in judgments as an indicator of childhood and as a characteristic associated with being a member of a particular social group (see Chapter 5).

In considering the need to provide for adequate education, Locke, Rousseau and others noted that children require certain protections in order to develop into adulthood. Locke in *Some Thoughts Concerning Education*, for example, remarked on the necessity of good nutrition to engage fully with education. Education has developed as a key indicator of childhood, perhaps the key indicator. Locke therefore expanded on the process of becoming an adult to include health,[9] which is now embedded as standard in childhood studies.[10] Health is also a provision right that derives from the CRC. The Committee on the Rights of the Child's (Committee) Comment No. 5 demonstrated that both rights (education and health) were encapsulated by Article 6, the right to survival and development: a holistic concept, embracing the child's physical, mental, spiritual, moral, psychological and social development (see Chapter 3).[11]

Rousseau, and later Postman and Archard,[12] commented that children also need protection from the corrupt outside world. Rousseau argued that it was their youth and innocence that required protection. Rousseau described youth and innocence as not only setting children apart from adults, but as something that should also be protected and thus considered part of childhood.[13] The CRC rights associated with the right to protection relate to *inter alia* economic exploitation,[14] abuse, harm and neglect.[15] The Committee in Comment No. 5 also drew out the link between protection rights and elements of development concerning physical, mental and even psychological needs. Rights relating to the protection of childhood are most often discussed in the context of refugee law compared with other rights groupings (ie provision and participation). In fact, as discussed in Chapter 6, the guidance, literature and the case law to date supports the view that protection rights are dominant in the refugee context.

The aforementioned authors and theorists also mentioned one other key aspect of childhood – agency. Most acknowledged that children had agency, but argued that they were unable to exercise it consistently. The view during the period of Enlightenment and into the twentieth century (and perhaps beyond), as discussed below, was that children required education to enable them to become active participants in society *as adults*. Despite the reluctance to attribute agency to children, even early philosophers recognised that children could formulate views or participate in society, at least sometimes. Although the Committee's elaboration on the right to develop, Article 6, did not specifically refer to the right to participation or the right to be heard, rights we typically attribute to child agency, it does refer to the child's mental, spiritual, moral and social development.[16] These needs can all be traced back to the seventeenth and eighteenth centuries. Locke, Rousseau and Kant, as discussed below, all believed education facilitated the mental, spiritual, moral and social development of children. Locke, for example, often referred to education as a pathway to becoming virtuous adults.

Despite not referring to child agency, the Committee showed that the objective of Article 6 was 'aimed at achieving the optimal development for all children' and the outcome often of providing education in this regard is children participating by expressing their views or behaving according to their own developing opinions and wishes. The Preamble of the CRC clarifies that the 'child should be fully prepared to live an individual life in society'.[17] It was these developments in the late-twentieth century that demonstrated that children could also participate *during* childhood, a period almost universally characterised as a process of development. Therefore, participation rights was the least-developed category of rights prior to the adoption of the CRC, but the 'child agency' seed was nevertheless planted from as early as the seventeenth century.

In summary, the most common indicators of childhood, or being a child, are age, innocence, vulnerability and the need for the provision of protection and assistance (eg nutrition and health) from a third party ***and*** their evolving capacity to reason, which must be cultivated through education. This chapter also establishes that childhood is mainly characterised by development. It is considered a process. However, what indicates childhood may simply be that it is not adulthood and that being a child is simply not being an adult.[18] It is established that children are different and therefore their rights are different. However, this does not seamlessly translate into refugee law.

The meaning of children's rights is well outlined in international guidance and literature. However, the way the child is conceptualised within asylum decisions and State legislation and policy is rarely defined. At times, children are considered the same as adults in the determination of the substance of their cases. It may also be said that States simply do not spend much time developing laws, guidance and an evidence base related to children seeking international protection.

At other times, children, in particular separated children, are deemed too vulnerable to even access asylum procedures.[19]

The former challenge may relate to a lack of visibility. The latter challenge relates to the perception of vulnerability.

There is also a tendency to view children as dependent, vulnerable, objects in need of protection. The view that children are secondary to adults and can be protected by their family permeates asylum procedures worldwide. This has resulted in child claims often being subsumed within adult claims. These challenges relate to matters of procedure, but they indicate inherent difficulties facing child refugee applicants and explain the low numbers of child asylum seekers in the Global North and the limited case law.

The conceptualisation of childhood, which has developed across a variety of disciplines, is only beginning to trickle into the area of refugee law. There is evidence to suggest that the gap between these two areas of study, and two areas of law, has begun to narrow.[20] This book aims to contribute to the narrowing of this gap. The following discussions take a step back to unpack the contributions made by theorists and researchers and their relationship with the origins of children's rights, examining the relevance of historical and contemporary perceptions or understandings of children and how that has also influenced refugee law.

A paradigm shift: the emergence of childhood

In considering the protection needs of children, including in the context of refugee law, one needs to reflect on those characteristics that belong or are attributed to children. Those characteristics have evolved, as stated above, but how much have they evolved and how far are they from the origins of children's rights and childhood studies? This section explores contributions from theorists and early literature on children and childhood to provide a baseline. The seventeenth century marked a turning point in conceptualising children – children were identified as persons worthy of investment, as the human capital of the future. Children needed to develop into productive adults. It was exactly this point, development, which underscored the works of the few theorists engaging in this debate in the seventeenth and eighteenth centuries. This section looks at theorising around development and how that has impacted upon contemporary discourse around children in the sociological sphere and indeed how that has influenced or is relevant to international law, including refugee law.

In 1962, Phillippe Ariès published *Centuries of Childhood*, a comprehensive and historical overview of theorising and developments relating to children. He traced the evolution of the child as a social construct. Ariès referred to the contributions made by Locke, Rousseau, Kant[21] and other early writers and theorists. These authors were responsible for contributing to, reinforcing and commenting on an early paradigm shift in childhood studies. Ariès argued that until the seventeenth century, or the Age of Enlightenment, children were not considered as anything other than the property of man.[22]

John Locke, a seventeenth-century English philosopher and physician, became a heavily influential writer on childhood and education.[23] Locke made a number of literary contributions revolving around understanding, thinking and education. Locke, in his first major work, *An Essay Concerning Human Understanding*, argued that the human mind began as a white slate,[24] building on Plato's *tabula rasa*.[25] Plato believed that the mind could be moulded and had few innate ideas, unlike his predecessors who had argued that humans were born with certain principles or ideas.[26] Based on this premise, Locke stated in *Some Thoughts Concerning Education* that the child had capacity to reason from a young age and that parents should treat their children as persons capable of such. He argued that children merely needed guidance and experience to achieve adult levels of reasoning. Despite the recognition of children's agency as early as the seventeenth century, we have only been engaging in this debate in policy and law, including child-specific law, in recent years.

In 1689 in *Two Treatise of Government*, Locke reiterated that the child was rational and capable of reason, but only inconsistently.[27] Locke contended that as children gained knowledge and experience, their views became more important and more reasoned. The crux of his argument was that children required education to become their future selves.[28] This conceptualisation of children is known today as the adult-in-becoming approach, a perspective that is well-established yet sometimes challenged as not being child-centred.[29] Locke contended that it was the parents' responsibility to ensure the child was led down the right path[30] arguing that children were the 'property' *or* 'temporary property' of their parents.[31] It is therefore noteworthy that Locke, although he began to create a picture of the child as an individual, viewed the child within the family more so than as a subject of rights in their own right. This is developed further in subsequent sections and chapters as it is the main conflict that exists in contemporary children's rights law. It also exists in refugee law in the context of the role of the parent as protector, persecutor or as a barrier to accessing rights.

Locke, writing in the seventeenth century, wrote about the role of the parents in teaching and guiding their children. Rousseau,[32] writing in the eighteenth century, wrote about the role of 'Tutors' in educating children, a step towards externalising the right to education. Rousseau is often associated with laying the foundations for thought on a more egalitarian approach to education,[33] unlike Locke who focused his writings on the role of the parents, with a particular lens on those belonging to the aristocracy.[34]

Religious reformations and the development of the public school system in the eighteenth century also supported this move. Religious orders as early as the seventeenth century applauded parents who sent their children to school and recognised them as moral superiors. The result of such reinforcement was increased interest in school enrolment and a devaluing of child labour.[35] It is perhaps for this reason that international labour laws were the first to articulate children's rights specifically and in dedicated legal instruments (discussed in Chapter 3). Ariès contended that this represented a further turning point in conceptualising the child – the point when education became the cornerstone of human development.[36]

Postman and Archard highlighted that Rousseau viewed the surrounding society as corrupt, but viewed the child as inherently good,[37] requiring education to reinforce their natural tendencies[38] through structure, rather than by guidance as Locke suggested. Stainton Rogers labelled this approach as the 'discourse of control',[39] which was characterised by the need to teach children right from wrong until they are able to reason for themselves. Adults within this discourse were responsible for ensuring that the child's long-term interests were taken into account.[40]

Rousseau's views on children and their capacity also differed from Locke's. Rousseau disagreed with Locke's theory of rationality, which as he argued, 'thought of the man in the child without thinking of what he is before being a man'.[41] He believed that children needed to learn to be rational rather than assumed to be rational from a young age. He contended that children could not understand or believe in religion, to use an example. Rousseau argued that children were capable of reciting what was taught to them, but they were unable to think critically, which would have enabled them to believe in religious doctrine.[42] Wall extrapolated that Rousseau's views meant that children could not access social rights associated with being a full member of society.[43] The view that children are unable to hold religious convictions or political opinions continues to pervade refugee case law concerning children. In a case involving children who claimed asylum on the basis of their political opinion, where the child applicant testified that they were caught handing out pamphlets, the Norwegian decision maker took the position that the children were not capable of forming political views (discussed in Chapter 6).[44]

This dichotomy existed from the seventeenth and eighteenth centuries. On the one hand, children were viewed as objects of law, persons in need of protection who were not necessarily capable of forming their own views – views linked with citizenship. On the other hand, children were increasingly viewed as subjects of law with the capacity to reason and develop political and other views or opinions. Despite the view of Locke, Rousseau and Kant that only adults could access their citizenship rights, children have since been shown to adopt views of their own and at times have found themselves at risk of, or experiencing, persecution as a result.

Rousseau's belief that children could not be socialised until they reached adolescence set Rousseau apart from Locke. However, Kant, to some degree, agreed. Immanuel Kant, a German philosopher, also wrote on the education of children during the eighteenth century.[45] He believed that education served to provide guidance on the path to rationality.[46] He also argued that children did not host innate wisdom, but that their actions were led by impulse and play. Kant suggested a more disciplinarian approach, falling under the umbrella of the 'discourse of control'. He argued that children needed to be taught to overcome their natural impulses[47] in order to prepare them to follow the laws of society.[48] Kant's view of children was therefore slightly more cynical than Locke and Rousseau. Locke believed children were inherently good and merely needed guidance. Rousseau viewed the surrounding society as bad and argued that children needed protection from the outside world. Kant, however, believed that children themselves needed discipline to learn to reason. All three conceptualisations of children can be seen in contemporary discourse, as discussed in the following sections.

Wall[49] and Dwyer noted that Kant nevertheless recognised that children were beings capable of acting with some autonomy.[50] However, Kant contended, like Locke and Rousseau, that only adults could be framed as subjects of rights within society.[51]

The above-mentioned theorists believed children had an evolving capacity to reason that needed to be cultivated through education with a view to earning full citizenship rights once they reached adulthood.[52] None of the authors discussed above suggested that children had rights of their own, but their discussions on their evolving capacity to reason provided a foundation for contemporary children's rights. However, it is important to note that Locke and Rousseau in particular discussed children and childhood merely in the context of their educational needs and not their wider capacity to engage with the rights regime. In fact, quite the opposite is true: the aforementioned theorists did not view children as rights holders. They viewed children as existing in a development limbo awaiting maturation. Their contributions are nevertheless useful in grounding discussions and highlighting the origins of the conflicts we still see today in law and sociology.

The following section looks at the development of the modern international children's rights movement beginning in the 1960s. The movement provides important contributions in respect of our understanding of children. The discussions below begin from the 1960s (following the publication of Ariès seminal work) and conclude with the adoption of the CRC (1989). Chapter 3 picks up from this point and discusses the developments in children's rights stemming from international law, while reflecting on the contributions discussed above.

The modern children's rights movement

Childhood studies and debates have grown and expanded since the period of Enlightenment, but did not hit their stride until the 1980s.[53] Prior to the 1980s, very little was written about children from a sociological perspective. Historical sociologists such as Durkheim, Comte, Marx and Parsons, for example, did not address childhood in their studies.[54] Quennerstedt remarked upon the limited published research and indeed interest in the area prior to this time.[55] Nevertheless, the children's rights movement was gaining momentum in the 1960s and 1970s and some child-focused literature in the sociology discipline emerged.[56] The principal focus of this discourse up until the 1980s, like in the literature of the seventeenth and eighteenth centuries, was to emphasise the socialisation of the child[57] – the adult-in-becoming.[58] The new discourses built upon early work, seeing children as requiring protection in the most basic sense, but also having agency. They began to be viewed as participants in society rather than an element of society left to adults to control.[59] Building on the views of Locke, Rousseau and others on capacity, children were starting to be seen as having a role in their own development and interactions with people around them, in particular their families, and were thus increasingly becoming studied.[60] The expansion is also attributed to debates surrounding the CRC and the publication and the global process of drafting and ratifying it.[61] This time was marked by a general consensus in research that children were considered to be independent members of society with rights to participate and with important roles to play.[62]

This shift did not come without its challenges, criticised by those who did not believe *any* rights should be attributed to children.[63] The changing perception of children in society brought about tensions between the role of children and the role of parents in accessing rights and protections,[64] based on the fear that children's rights would undermine the rights and the role of the family.[65] It is these tensions and the lack of inclusion in mainstream sociological research that have likely resulted in children's rights not featuring in mainstream human rights law and refugee law. The lack of child refugee case law is consistent with the general tendency to address their rights in a sphere siloed from mainstream discourses. These tensions are discussed below.

The beginning of the Children's Rights Movement

The Civil Rights Movement in the United States and developments across the industrialised world increased public sympathy around minority rights, including the rights of children.[66] Advocates in the United States during the Movement in the 1960s and 1970s began to campaign for constitutional rights to be applied to children as well as to adults – separate from the family unit.[67] The literature focuses on two main children's rights approaches: the liberationist and protectionist frameworks. Liberationists viewed children as rights holders to whom all constitutional rights, or adult rights, apply.[68] Protectionists viewed children as having rights 'in their own right', but also requiring third party protection from adult responsibilities and harm.[69] These two views are discussed below. These developments have informed international children's rights law (discussed in Chapter 3).

Liberationists argued that children had capacity for self-determination believing, as Holt[70] and Farson argued, that children had a fundamental right to participate in decisions affecting them.[71] Holt concluded in his 1974 book, *Escape from Childhood: The Needs and Rights of Children*, that children should be viewed as having rights to: work, own and sell property, travel, have a minimum salary, vote, have ownership over their education, use drugs and control their private and sexual lives[72] *should they choose to*.[73] He suggested that these rights were not absolute, but that if children had the capacity to take on the responsibilities typically attributed to adults, they should be able to do so.

Fortin argued that the liberationist paradigm may have impacted negatively upon the children's rights movement as a whole as it fed into fears relating to diminishing parental rights. However, she also noted that it led to a re-examining of children's capacities to make decisions and contribute to decision-making processes.[74] For example, in 1979, Hillary Rodham [Clinton] argued that children should be viewed by the courts as having rights and legal capacity in their own right.[75] Advocates during the 1960s and 1970s increasingly addressed the rights of children on a spectrum that correlated with children's individual capacities.[76]

The liberationist discourse also brought into focus the gap that exists between protection rights and participation rights and the fact that attempts at closing that gap remained contentious in the 1970s (and beyond). Fundamentally, the reactions to the floating of the liberationist approach indicated reluctance generally to attribute rights to children, which supports findings in subsequent chapters on the low numbers of child refugees compared with their adult counterparts, the limited child refugee case law and the low recognition rate associated with separated children seeking asylum.

The liberationist view emphasised agency, drawing out participation rights. Chapter 6 finds that exercising agency in the case of children is often either hard to substantiate or results in a low recognition rate compared with claims grounded in protection rights, for example.

Although the liberationists reflected some of the core principles relating to children and childhood developed by their predecessors, the liberationist framework did not withstand the test of time and was largely overtaken by more protection-minded writers and activists. The protectionist framework incorporated some liberationist philosophy into their understanding of children.[77] Henry Foster in his 'Bill of Rights' advocated for the child's right to equal treatment, while also emphasising the need to: protect children from hazardous work; ensure that children have access to necessary medical care, for example; and ensure administrative procedures take into account children's best interests.[78] Freeman, in 1983, put forward his argument for the protection of children on the basis of their vulnerability, but he also argued that children must be cared for in such a way that they are capable of becoming responsible for themselves.[79] Protectionists held that rights must be interpreted in relation to the child's age and capacity.[80] Their views were not far off from those developed during the period of Enlightenment.

Building on the inherent conflicts in attributing rights to children, Wendy Stainton Rogers provided a division of the protectionist framework into two separate discourses for conceiving of children's rights, or two 'discourses of childhood'.[81] She argued that the 'welfare discourse' viewed the child as pure and innocent and childhood as a time of growth and enjoyment (as children were described in Rousseau's *Emile*, for example). This discourse is reflected in the drive to improve, for example: services for children, access to courts, child participation in decisions that affect them and access to recourse when parents or other adults fail to provide adequate protection.[82]

Similar to Kant's views, the second discourse, the 'discourse of control', viewed the child as inherently bad and argued that education served to teach right from wrong. Parents within this discourse were considered to be responsible for ensuring that the child's long-term interests were taken into account. Stainton Rogers suggested that each discourse represented a different side of the agenda to protect the best interests of the child.[83]

The picture of childhood we have based on the liberationist and protectionist approaches, both competing and overlapping, is that children play an important role in society and that they also have the capacity to participate in that society, including in relation to their own lives and future outcomes. The debates during this time also recognised the innate vulnerability of children and recognised that children, required certain protections. Both 'protection from harm' and rights relating to self-determination serve to aid the child in becoming an active citizen and member of society. The protectionist approach therefore encapsulated aspects of childhood that corresponded with protection, provision *and* participation rights. It is therefore possible to see the link between the more sociological (and pre-CRC) discourses and the CRC itself. The children's rights movement and the contributions that preceded and followed shaped contemporary conceptualisations of childhood and children, including in the context of refugee law. The developments during this time closely reflect the contributions of the early theorists, discussed earlier in this chapter, supporting the view that development and agency were core themes in the development of the different children's rights approaches and thus should also be considered important in the context of refugee law.

The following section unpacks *understandings* of childhood. Childhoods exist differently – varying by culture, community, religion or country. However, international law and the discourse herein largely stem from concepts of children and childhood deriving from the Global North. The following section asks how the conceptualisation of childhood may differ in other parts of the world and to what extent those differences contribute to our understanding of childhood in the context of international law, including refugee law. The purpose of including this discussion relates to the global nature of refugee law – a regime that serves to provide surrogate protection in *one* country when *another* country fails to fulfil their protection obligations to their citizens. One question that arises in the context of global childhoods and refugee law is whether or not determination bodies define persecution relative to the receiving country, i.e. relative to the country to which the child would otherwise be returned, *or* relative to a global conceptualisation of children or childhood. This question arises again in Chapter 6 and while it is not possible to fully answer it based on the limited case law, it is addressed and is highlighted as an area for potential future research throughout.

Global childhood

Since the beginning of the children's rights movement, culminating in the publication of the CRC, there has been a push to establish a global standard for childhood or a 'global meaning of childhood'.[84] Political, economic and technological developments in the past thirty or forty years have resulted in increased movement of people and information across borders.[85] Exchanges and remittances[86] of information influence countries, cultures or peoples, thus affecting understandings of children and childhood worldwide. An increase in non-governmental organisations and the use of the media to highlight matters concerning children globally has also resulted in more information being made available about the deprivation of children.[87] In addition, the CRC and other regional frameworks such as the African Charter on the Rights and Welfare of the Child 1999[88] and initiatives such as the Millennium Development Goals[89] have progressed the establishment of a global conceptualisation of childhood.[90] James, Jenks and Prout argued that these developments have resulted in children being considered one global minority group.[91] Wyness described this phenomenon as a: 'dominant unitary model of childhood, a Western, affluent world view of childhood held up as a norm by international organizations and powerful nation-states'.[92]

More recently, there has been a push to discuss childhood in terms of childhoods, reflecting the diversity of the world's children and their circumstances.[93]

The global standard approach provides a baseline for other childhoods to be compared against. Childhoods that do not satisfy the standard are seen as deficit childhoods. Fleer, Hedegaard and Tudge described deficit childhoods as those located in less-affluent regions of the world that need to be brought up to meet the global standard.[94] The result of this approach may be seen to demonise a particular society based on the way it understands childhood and thus treats children. The best example of this is the case of child labour. In some countries it is an economic necessity to engage children in labour. Child labour may be demonised where it is in conflict with the rights that protect children from labour harmful to their development or where the child labourer has not reached a sufficient age.[95]

It is the threshold of harm that is of interest to these discussions and refugee law generally. The discussions in this book establish instances where a breach of the right of the child to develop and to be free from harmful labour practices, for example, amounts to persecution. Cases dealing with child labour, and other forms of harm constituting deficit childhood, are analysed in Chapter 6 and the question is asked whether or not the determination bodies consider the threshold relative to the Western construction of childhood, to the child's country of origin and/or to the global standard as established by the CRC. The answer to this question is informed by the wider divide between the 'Global North' and the 'Global South'.

It is also important to note that the literature on childhood does not deal with children in refugee situations. In fact, even within the literature that looks at global childhood(s), there is very infrequent reference to children who are refugees or children who are in need of refugee protection. There is research on the needs, mainly welfare, of children in refugee camp or reception settings,[96] however. There are countless studies on the experiences and needs of children who are in protracted circumstances of displacement, in camps[97] or living on the streets.[98]

The needs of children in global childhood studies are most commonly compared against the existing understanding of childhood as developed in the Global North despite the recognition that there exists different conceptualisations of childhood. This is also the case for international law, i.e. it was also drafted and developed in the Global North.[99] These studies tend to focus on the rights contained within the CRC. Studies that seek to define childhood do so in a general sense from the Global North perspective rather than from the developing context. Furthermore, the CRC experienced near-universal ratification and thus is seen to amount to a global standard. The idea of a 'global standard' and the term 'deficit childhood' are also useful in the context of refugee protection.

Locke through to Foster framed their contributions around the Global North (in the case of Locke and Rousseau, their contributions were framed exclusively around education in the Global North), where rapid industrialisation and growing wealth allowed space for discussions on fundamental and personal freedoms and protection. That is not to diminish their contributions, but to contextualise the approaches adopted by these writers and reiterate the limitations in applying their contributions in respect of children's rights law and refugee law. Although the aforementioned discourses are Western-centric, the same can be said about both the CRC and the Refugee Convention as mentioned above.

Regardless of the region or economic situation or birthplace of childhood studies and children's rights, some children globally are unable to avail of rights typically considered to belong to them. It is the violation of these rights that is of interest to this research. The lack of research on the qualification of refugees, or refugees in general, in the context of global childhood studies also reinforces the idea that a dichotomy exists between children's rights and refugee law and shows that this dichotomy goes beyond international law and is heavily engrained across disciplines. This is revisited throughout this book.

Conflicts within the paradigm shift: an externalisation of rights, romanticism and the role of the family

The shift towards public education influenced the children's rights movement. A push emerged to externalise children's rights. This shift meant that parents were no longer the sole educator of their children and it introduced the notion that the State was also responsible for elements of the care and upbringing of the children in their jurisdiction. This in turn has influenced international children's rights law in that education, a provision right, must be provided by the State (as discussed in Chapter 3).

The shift also brought about a formalised external element to the experience of childhood, namely, educators. Educators, who were either based in religious or educational institutions, had an external influence on the child. The public school system in particular mapped out a new family structure that, as Ariès noted, placed the child outside the adult world into a space of their own.[100] In response to this, however, Ariès noted that a new dynamic between the family and society was created. Ariès argued that the response was to introduce the notion of 'private life', with families raising 'a wall of private life between the family and society'.[101]

Ariès described this shift in the conceptualisation of children, arising from the period of Enlightenment, as the romanticisation of children. Children in the Global North were needed less and less for labour and were seen more and more as a source of entertainment and something to be nurtured.[102] The conceptualisation of childhood that we are accustomed reflects this shift. The family has the responsibility to ensure the child has a positive experience of childhood.[103] This is reflected in various examples of child protection legislation across the globe. The recent amendment to the Irish constitution addressed this point of law:

> In exceptional cases, where the parents, regardless of their marital status, fail in their duty towards their children to such extent that the safety or welfare of any of their children is likely to be prejudicially affected, the state as guardian of the common good shall, by proportionate means as provided by law, endeavour to supply the place of the parents, but always with due regard for the natural and imprescriptible rights of the child.[104]

'Protection' is at the fore in contemporary international discourse and 'family' is right behind it. Child agency is now a common and often competing aspect of the experience of childhood.

Current discourse asserts therefore that children, consistent with their capacity, should be facilitated in participating in aspects of their experience of childhood, including in making decisions around their future. Discourse around agency has therefore evolved considerably since the times of Locke and Rousseau. Self-determination forms part of this debate.[105] Children have rights to self-determination as decisions made in childhood impact upon their experiences of adulthood. Examples of children exercising their right to self-determination may include child stars (musicians, actors) or athletes (gymnasts, football players). A child may wish to enter into these industries or competitions based on an innate and/or cultivated talent that manifests at a young age. Another example relates simply to choices made in education, a process that, as Rousseau acknowledged, children should have a role in. Children in their teenage years may wish to enrol in certain classes or sit certain exams to improve their chances of realising their future career goals. The realisation of future goals (including having a family) and career objectives is part of the experience of adulthood, but it is something that also begins in childhood.

Agency and self-determination are therefore important aspects of childhood, considered in parallel with children's evolving capacities. Childhood was described by theorists in previous sections as a process and the process is completed by achieving reason and an ability to care for one's self *en route* to self-actualisation.[106] Health, education, protection, etc. must be provided to ensure the child's right to positive development is not impacted upon or breached.

Education in pursuit of adulthood, as addressed herein, is different from encouraging participation *during* childhood. Children's rights are moving more towards the promotion of participation rights during childhood, yet ambivalence persists.

By achieving reason through education it is foreseen that children may also then form opinions relating to religion and politics, for example, which may conflict with societal norms and thus place them in a position of risk – regardless of whether or not a given society views them as entitled to exercise civil and political rights traditionally associated with adulthood. This presents a challenge to interpreting the rights of the child, a challenge that permeates refugee case law on the topic of participation rights. Bhabha and

Crock described refugee determination bodies' approach to cases of children invoking violations of civil and political rights as one characterised by 'trepidation'.[107] This view and the approach of determination bodies runs contrary to the trends in refugee law – civil and political rights are dominant over social and economic rights in decision making concerning adults.[108] However, protection rights, most often of a social and economic nature are dominant in refugee case law concerning children, as discussed in Chapters 6 and 7.

Although agency is a dominant theme, second to protection, in the conceptualisation of childhood established herein, it remains contentious, including in the application of law.

The developments and conflicts discussed in this chapter are still present in today's discourses – both sociological and legal. From the seventeenth century, capacity, or child agency, the right to a protected childhood *and* the rights of the family unit dominated the discourse. The underlying conflict between attributing rights to the child and the rights of the parent was already apparent. The two pillars, protection from harm and childhood *and* autonomous rights, nevertheless remain two aspects of the one main objective: development. The sensitivities around the division of authority between the State and the parents and the perception of children as having capacity, as subjects of law, continue today and they may also account for, firstly, the late (in the context of international human rights law) drafting of the CRC and the lack of visibility of children in other areas of human rights law.

A conceptualisation of childhood

A conceptualisation of children is established here based on the contributions above. Children exist within the period of childhood. The parameters of childhood vary but include: health, access to adequate resources to ensure good health and participation in other aspects of childhood, family and the protection of the family, protection from economic exploitation, protection from harm, development including through education, and lastly participation and the ability to exercise agency. In this way we can see that these characteristics of childhood also correspond to the Three Ps. The right to protection from harm generally, from economic exploitation and protection deriving from family specifically fall within the protection rights category. Health, adequate standard of living, development deriving from the family and education rights all fall within the provision rights category. The ability to exercise agency falls within the participation rights category. As discussed in Chapter 1, this was reiterated by the Committee in 2003 in the context of Article 6 of the CRC:

> The Committee expects States to interpret 'development' in its broadest sense as a holistic concept, embracing the child's physical, mental, spiritual, moral, psychological and social development. Implementation

> measures should be aimed at achieving the optimal development for all children.[109]

By referring to the child's physical, mental, spiritual, moral, psychological and social development in the context of interpreting Article 6, the Committee established the wide scope of this right.

Physical development relates to health and freedom from harm, such as abuse and freedom from forced labour, for example. These are protection (and provision in the case of health) rights as contained within the CRC. Protection rights may also relate to mental and psychological development. Spiritual, moral and social development may relate to education and other provision rights, such as the right to play. In addition, these aspects of development also correspond with participation rights. For example, the right to religion as contained in the CRC is provided for as a child-specific right, a right that may involve the child exercising their agency by expressing beliefs or behaving consistent with, or in contravention of, behaviours associated with a given religion. Provision rights are in place to facilitate development (health, etc.) Protection rights serve to ensure no harm can impact upon the child's development. Participation rights are in some way the effect of positive development, but they are also increasingly recognised as part of the process. Developmental interventions, especially education, should serve to improve the child's ability to exercise their agency *en route* to adulthood. Adulthood is characterised by citizenship rights, rights involving agency and the ability to reason. All three categories of rights serve to facilitate development in line with Article 6 of the CRC, and all three categories overlap.

One of the aims of this chapter was to establish that Article 6, or the right to survival and development, is at the core of contemporary and indeed historical understandings of childhood. Chapter 3 further develops this principle, but it is this core understanding of childhood as a period of development that is presumed to also form the foundation for debates around refugee protection. In cases where rights specific to children are breached, they are also presumed to violate the child's right to survival and development. It is therefore suggested that a child-centred approach to the interpretation of the Refugee Convention should start from the understanding that the experience of positive development should not be interrupted. Chapters 3 and 6 examine interruptions to development where there is a link to a convention ground and asks in which instances these violations are considered, or should be considered, to amount to persecution.

Limitation to the modern conceptualisation of children's rights

Children within the rights discourse are now a visible social group and there is an acknowledgement that they have a role to play in society, as discussed throughout this chapter. However, both sociological and legal research points to one overarching challenge facing children who seek to access their rights and that is the perception and treatment of them by others.[111] In Chapter 3, this barrier is discussed in terms of accessing legal rights and exercising legal agency – reflecting on the necessity to have a third party involved in both the process of accessing their rights, but also the assessment of their interests. Considering, as Federle notes, 'the notion of best interests seldom, if ever, redounds to the child's advantage'.[112] Federle argues that the interest approach disadvantages children and further embeds notions of their incompetency.[113] It is thus those with power, as compared with the powerless children, who ultimately decide which rights children have and whether or not claims from children will indeed be recognised.[114] Freeman referred to this as 'liberal paternalism'.[115] It is argued that claims from children are so easily dismissed because they are not considered to have autonomy or agency by the elite, or those with decision-making powers. Therefore, the rights that children have remain incongruent with the rights children may access, in particular those associated with autonomy. To put it another way – children infrequently access their rights notwithstanding the fact that they indeed have rights to access. This perception likely contributes to the invisibility of children in refugee case law and literature and the inconsistency in decision making (discussed in Chapter 6).

Conclusions

This chapter is somewhat of a prelude to the discussions to come. Chapter 2 established the conceptualisation(s) of childhood that exist outside of the legal discipline. Chapter 3 demonstrates that it is this conceptualisation that has informed international law. This chapter also established that the concepts 'child' and 'childhood' have been evolving, albeit not free of conflict and tension, for centuries. The contributions from non-legal disciplines is an important part of analysing whether or not the legal responses to child refugees reflects other societal norms associated with, and understandings of, childhood. The analyses undertaken in this chapter set a baseline for gauging progress in the development of international law, including refugee law, in its application in the case of children. The baseline unearthed herein also reflects the main themes associated with modern conceptualisations of child and childhood as seen through the lens of international children's rights law (Chapter 3). The conflicts identified in this chapter can also be traced in the development, interpretation and application of children's rights law (Chapter 3), including refugee law (Chapters 4 and 6).

The principal purpose of Chapter 2 was to establish a conceptualisation to be relied upon in subsequent chapters. However, the principal finding was that in fact the main trends, themes and, most importantly, conflicts are still relevant today – including in the context of refugee law. Reluctance to attribute agency rights to children has always been a feature in child and childhood studies. The discussions indicate that the same trepidation associated with attributing agency to children, which still permeates the discourse has very early origins. The contribution this chapter makes to the field and to this research is primarily that modern conceptualisations of children has not significantly evolved. Perhaps children have access to more rights generally, but the difficulties they encounter accessing those rights reflect conflict and perceptions that date back to Enlightenment. Chapter 6 examines the inconsistent approaches relied upon to interpreting children's rights in the context of refugee law and it asks whether or not it is possible to suggest that the inconsistencies stem from ambivalence associated with child agency, with its origins in the seventeenth century.

Lastly, this chapter also reflects on the limited literature that bridges children's rights and refugee discourses. The lack of literature supports the hypothesis that a dichotomy between children's rights and refugee law persists. Children who may be in need of refugee protection did not form part of the discourse around conceptualising children and childhood outside the legal discipline. Even in the literature that looks at global childhood(s), there is very infrequent reference to children who are refugees or children who are in need of protection. There is some research on the needs, mainly welfare, of children in refugee camp settings or in the context of reception conditions, etc.

As mentioned, this chapter serves as a prelude to the rights-based discussions in subsequent chapters. The following chapters look at developments in international children's rights law with a particular focus on the CRC (Chapter 3), developments in refugee law where children were considered with a particular focus on the Refugee Convention (Chapter 4), the possibility of a children's rights approach to the interpretation of the Refugee Convention and making a case for its development (Chapter 5) and violations of children's rights amounting to persecution in the context of refugee law (Chapter 6). The conceptualisation of children and childhood, developed in this chapter, which revolves heavily around the right to survival and development, serves to provide a foundation from which we can examine the overarching question – which children's rights when violated amount to persecution. This exercise was undertaken to ensure the socio-legal analyses in Chapters 3 to 6 stem from child and childhood discourses. This research builds upon a multi-disciplinary conceptualisation of children and within that childhood. These points are revisited throughout this book and in particular Chapter 6.

Notes

1 I refer to Plato (BC) and his *Tabula rasa*.
2 Today this is represented by Article 6 of the CRC.
3 Twelve Tables (754–449 BC) in Michelle Wirth, 'Semiotics of Parenthood in Legal Perspective: Using Semiotic Tools to Deconstruct Legal Determinations of Who Holds Parenthood Obligations and Privileges' in Jan Broekman and Francis Mootz III (eds), *The Semiotics of Law in Legal Education* (Springer 2011) 174.

4 Jacqueline Bhabha and Wendy Young, 'Not Adults in Miniature: Unaccompanied Child Asylum Seekers and the New U.S. Guidelines' (1999) 11 (1) *International Journal of Refugee Law* 766.
5 Louis Wirth, 'The Problem of the Minority Groups' in Ralph Linton (ed.), *The Science of Man in the World Crisis* (Columbia University Press 1945) 347–372.
6 See Rosalind Ekman Ladd, *Children's Rights Re-Visioned: Philosophical Readings* (Wadsworth Publishing Co Inc 1995).
7 Phillippe Ariès, *Centuries of Childhood* (Pimlico 1996) (originally published in 1962) 13; David Archard, *Children: Rights and Childhood* (2nd edn, Routledge 2004) 19. See also: Jane Fortin, *Children's Rights and the Developing Law* (3rd edn, CUP 2009); Michael Wyness, *Childhood* (Polity 2015).
8 Convention on the Rights of the Child, Article 1.
9 John Locke, *Some Thoughts Concerning Education* (1693).
10 See, generally: Michael Wyness, *Childhood* (Polity 2015); David Archard, *Children: Rights and childhood* (2nd edn, Routledge 2004).
11 General Comment No. 5 (2003) General measures of implementation of the Convention on the Rights of the Child (arts. 4, 42 and 44, para 6) para 12. See Chapter 1.
12 Neil Postman, *The Disappearance of Childhood* (Dell Publishing Co 1982) 59; David Archard, *Children: Rights and Childhood* (2nd edn, Routledge 2004) 22.
13 Jean-Jacques Rousseau, Émile, or, On Education (originally published in 1762) in Jean-Jacques Rousseau, *The Essential Writings of Jean-Jacques Rousseau* (Vintage 2013) 229–290.
14 Convention on the Rights of the Child 1989, Article 32.
15 *Ibid*, Article 9.
16 General Comment No. 5 (2003) General measures of implementation of the Convention on the Rights of the Child (arts. 4, 42 and 44, para 6) para 12.
17 Convention on the Rights of the Child 1989, Preamble Recital 7.
18 Archard reflecting on Ariès' contention that childhood did not exist before the seventeenth century. Archard believed there has always been a distinction between adults and children and thus childhood existed at least to some degree. David Archard, *Children: Rights and childhood* (2nd edn, Routledge 2004).
19 See, for example: Samantha Arnold et al., *Durable Solutions for Separated Children in Europe, National Report: Ireland* (Irish Refugee Council 2015) 51.
20 See Jacqueline Bhabha, *Child Migration and Human Rights in a Global Age* (PUP 2014) 205 and Chapter 6.
21 Howard Ozmon and Samuel Craver (eds), *Philosophical Foundations of Education* (6th edn, Pearson 1999) 45–46.
22 In fact he argued that childhood did not exist prior to the seventeenth century. However, that has since been challenged by Archard and others. See: Phillippe Ariès, *Centuries of Childhood* (Pimlico 1996) (originally published in 1962); David Archard, *Children: Rights and childhood* (2nd edn, Routledge 2004).
23 John Wall, 'Human Rights in Light of Childhood' *International Journal of Children's Rights* (2008) 16 530.
24 As interpreted by John Wall, 'Human Rights in Light of Childhood' *International Journal of Children's Rights* (2008) 16 528.
25 Neil Postman, *The Disappearance of Childhood* (Dell Publishing Co 1982) 59. John Locke, *An Essay Concerning Human Understanding* (1690); Plato (circa 369 BC) Theaetetus line 191a–196c.
26 See, generally: Peter Carruthers, *Human Knowledge and Human Nature. A New Introduction to an Ancient Debate* (OUP 1992) Chapter 1.
27 Preface in John Locke, *Some Thoughts Concerning Education* (1693).
28 John Locke, *Some Thoughts Concerning Education* (1693).

29 Allison James and Adrian James, *Key Concepts in Childhood Studies* (2nd edn, Sage 2012) 58.
30 John Locke, *Some Thoughts Concerning Education* (1693).
31 John Wall, 'Human Rights in Light of Childhood' *International Journal of Children's Rights* (2008) 16 529; John Locke, *Some Thoughts Concerning Education* (1693) <www.bartleby.com/37/1/> accessed 23 August 2014.
32 A Genevan philosopher noted to have 'captured the imagination of Europe'. See: Harry Hendrick, 'Constructions and Reconstructions of British Childhood: An Interpretative Survey, 1800 to the Present' in Allison James and Alan Prout, *Constructing and reconstructing childhood: Contemporary issues in the sociological study of childhood* (Routledge 2015) 36.
33 See: Paul Heywood Hirst and Patricia White, *Philosophy of Education Major Themes in the Analytic Tradition Volume III Society and education* (Routledge 1998) 16.
34 John Locke, *Some Thoughts Concerning Education* (1693).
35 Phillippe Ariès, *Centuries of Childhood* (Pimlico 1996) (originally published in 1962) 125–130.
36 *Ibid.*
37 Neil Postman, *The Disappearance of Childhood* (Dell Publishing Co 1982) 59; David Archard, *Children: Rights and childhood* (2nd edn, Routledge 2004) 22.
38 Leo Damrosch (ed.), *The Essential Writings of Jean-Jacques Rousseau* (Vintage 2013) 229–230.
39 Wendy Stainton Rogers, 'Constructing Childhood, Constructing Child Concern' in Pam Foley et al. (eds), *Children in Society: Contemporary Theory, Policy and Practice* (Palgrave 2001) 29.
40 *Ibid* 29–30.
41 Jean-Jacques Rousseau, *Emile, or on Education* in Leo Damrosch (ed.), *The Essential Writings of Jean-Jacques Rousseau* (Vintage 2013) 229–289.
42 *Ibid.*
43 John Wall, 'Human Rights in Light of Childhood' *International Journal of Children's Rights* (2008) 16 529.
44 See Kate Halvorsen, 'Asylum Decisions on Child Applicants Report on 4-Country Pilot Project' (Ministry of Local Government and Modernisation 2004). Discussed in further detail in Chapter 6.
45 See, for example: Susan Turner, 'Justifying Corporal Punishment of Children Loses its Appeal' *International Journal of Children's Rights* (2003) 11 219.
46 Susan Turner, 'Justifying Corporal Punishment of Children Loses its Appeal' *International Journal of Children's Rights* (2003) 11 219.
47 *Ibid.*
48 Howard Ozmon and Samuel Craver (eds), *Philosophical Foundations of Education* (6th edn, Up Saddle River, NJ: Merrill 1999) 45–46.
49 John Wall, 'Human Rights in Light of Childhood' *International Journal of Children's Rights* (2008) 16 529.
50 James Dwyer, *Religious Schools v. Children's Rights* (Cornell University Press 1998) 67.
51 Susan Turner, 'Justifying Corporal Punishment of Children Loses its Appeal' *International Journal of Children's Rights* (2003) 11 219.
52 The discourse herein relates to education. It does not sit easily with the rights discourse. It nevertheless contributes to our understanding of childhood and the trajectory of the conceptualisation that ultimately influenced the children's rights regime.
53 See: Ann Quennerstedt, 'Children's Rights Research Moving into Future –

Challenges on the Way Forward' (2013) 21 *International Journal of Children's Rights* 233.

54 Anne Marie Ambert, 'Sociology of sociology: The place of children in North American sociology' in Patricia Adler and Peter Adler, *Sociological Studies of Child Development* (Vol 1, JAI Press 1986) 11–31.

55 Ann Quennerstedt, 'Children's Rights Research Moving into the Future – Challenges on the Way Forward' (2013) 21 *International Journal of Children's Rights* 233.

56 See: Jane Fortin, *Children's Rights and the Developing Law* (3rd edn, CUP 2009); David Archard *Children: Rights and Childhood* (2nd edn, Routledge 2004); Lucinda Ferguson, 'Not merely rights for children but children's rights: The theory gap and the assumption of the importance of children's rights' (2013) 21 *International Journal of Children's Rights* 177; Ann Quennerstedt, 'Children's Rights Research Moving into Future – Challenges on the Way Forward' (2013) 21 *International Journal of Children's Rights* 233; Christine Alice Corcos, 'The Child in International Law: A Pathfinder and Selected Bibliography' (1991) 23 *Case Western Reserve Journal of International Law* 23:2 171; Mark Ensalaco, 'The Right of the Child to Development' in Mark Ensalaco and Linda Majka, *Children's Human Rights: Progress and Challenges for Children Worldwide* (Rowman & Littlefield Publishers, INC 2005); Michael Freeman, 'The Future of Children's Rights' (2000) 14:4 *Children & Society* 277; Jill Marie Gerschutz and Margaret Karns 'Transforming Visions into Reality: The Convention on the Rights of the Child' in Mark Ensalaco and Linda Majka, *Children's Human Rights: Progress and Challenges for Children Worldwide* (Rowman & Littlefield Publishers, INC 2005).

57 Anne Marie Ambert, 'Sociology of sociology: The place of children in North American sociology' in Patricia Adler and Peter Adler, *Sociological Studies of Child Development* (Vol 1, JAI Press 1986) 11–31.

58 Anne Marie Ambert, 'Sociology of sociology: The place of children in North American sociology' in Patricia Adler and Peter Adler, *Sociological Studies of Child Development* (Vol 1, JAI Press 1986) 11–31.

59 See, for example: Martha Minow, 'What Ever Happened to Children's Rights?' (1995–1996) *Minnesota Law Review* 80 268.

60 See, for example: Edwin Kirkpatrick, *Fundamentals of Child Study: A Discussion of Instinct Trends and Other Factors in Human Development with Practical Applications* (4th edn, Macmillan 1929); Ruth Andrus, *A Tentative Inventory of the Habits of Children from Two Years to Four Years of Age* (Teacher's College, Columbia University 1924); Ada Arlitt, *Psychology of Infancy and Early Childhood* (McGraw-Hill 1928); Sara Josephine Baker, *The Growing Child* (Brown 1923); Josephine Foster and John Anderson, *The Young Child and His Parents: A Study of One Hundred Cases* (University of Minnesota Press 1927).

61 See: Ann Quennerstedt, 'Children's Rights Research Moving into Future – Challenges on the Way Forward' (2013) 21 *International Journal of Children's Rights* 233.

62 Jens Qvortrup, Marjatta Bardy, Giovanni Sgritta and Helmut Wintersberger (eds) *Childhood Matters. Social Theory, Practice and Politics* (Avenbury 1994); Allison James and Adrian James, *Constructing Childhood. Theory, Policy and Social Practice* (Palgrave Macmillan 2004); Allison James, Chris Jenks and Alan Prout, *Theorising Childhood* (Polity Press 1998) 235; Pamela Reynolds, Olga Niewenhuys and Karl Hanson, 'A view from anthropology – Introduction' (2006) 13(3) *Childhood*: 291; Nick Lee, *Childhood and Human Value. Development, Separation and Separability* (Open University 2005).

63 Jane Fortin, *Children's Rights and the Developing Law* (3rd edn, CUP 2009) 30.

64 Ann Quennerstedt, 'Balancing the rights of the child and the rights of the parents in the Convention on the rights of the child' (2009) 8 (2) *Journal of Human Rights* 162–176.

65 Jane Fortin, *Children's Rights and the Developing Law* (3rd edn, CUP 2009) 4.

66 *Ibid.*

67 See, for example: Richard Farson, *Birthrights* (Macmillan 1974); John Holt, *Escape from Childhood: The Needs and Rights of Childhood* (Dutton 1974); Beatrice Gross and Ronald Gross, *The Children's Rights Movement: Overcoming the Oppression of Young People* (Anchor 1977).

68 See, generally: John Holt, *Escape from Childhood: The Needs and Rights of Childhood* (Dutton 1974); Jane Fortin, *Children's Rights and the Developing Law* (3rd edn, CUP 2009).

69 See, generally: Richard Farson, *Birthrights* (Macmillan 1974); Jane Fortin, *Children's Rights and the Developing Law* (3rd edn, CUP 2009).

70 In John Holt, *Escape from Childhood: The Needs and Rights of Childhood* (Dutton 1974), Holt concluded that children should be viewed as having rights to: work, own and sell property, travel, have a minimum salary, vote, have ownership over their education and educational choices, use drugs and control their private and sexual lives *should they choose to* (emphasis added).

71 John Holt, *Escape from Childhood: The Needs and Rights of Children* (no 45) 18–19; Richard Farson *Birthrights* (Macmillan 1974) 3.

72 John Holt, *Escape from Childhood: The Needs and Rights of Childhood* (Dutton 1974); also in Jane Fortin, *Children's Rights and the Developing Law* (3rd edn, CUP 2009) 5.

73 Jane Fortin, *Children's Rights and the Developing Law* (3rd edn, CUP 2009).

74 In Jane Fortin, *Children's Rights and the Developing Law* (3rd edn, CUP 2009) 5, Fortin notes that 'There is now a fairly widespread view that it is wrong to underestimate children's abilities and moreover that they should be encouraged to develop their independence. A general interest in this notion continues to underlie much of what is written about children's rights today'.

75 Hillary Rodham, 'Children's Rights: A Legal Perspective' in Patricia Vardin and Ilene Brody, *Children's Rights: Contemporary Perspectives* (Teachers College Press 1979); Martha Minow, 'What Ever Happened to Children's Rights?' (1995–1996) 80 *Minnesota Law Review* 269.

76 See: Martha Minow, 'What Ever Happened to Children's Rights?' (1995–1996) 80 *Minnesota Law Review* 273.

77 See, generally: Richard Farson, *Birthrights* (Macmillan 1974); Jane Fortin, *Children's Rights and the Developing Law* (3rd edn, CUP 2009); John Holt, *Escape from Childhood: The Needs and Rights of Childhood* (Dutton 1974); Helen Baker, *Growing up Unheard* in Beatrice Gross and Ronald Gross, *The Children's Rights Movement: Overcoming the Oppression of Young People* (Anchor 1977) 187.

78 Henry Foster, *A 'Bill of Rights' for Children* (Thomas 1974).

79 Michael Freeman, *The Rights and Wrongs of Children* (F. Pinter 1983).

80 Henry Foster, *A 'Bill of Rights' for Children* (Thomas 1974) xv and 6–7.

81 Wendy Stainton Rogers 'Constructing Childhood, Constructing Child Concern' in Pam Foley et al. (eds), *Children in Society: Contemporary Theory, Policy and Practice* (Palgrave 2001) 29.

82 *Ibid.*

83 *Ibid*, 29–30.

84 See, generally: Michael Wyness, *Childhood* (Polity 2015); A. Bame Nsamenang 'Cultures in early childhood care and education' in Marilyn Fleer, Marianne Hedegaard and Jonathan Tudge (eds), *Childhood Studies and the Impact of*

Globalisation: Practices at Global and Local Levels (Routledge 2009); Pam Foley et al. (eds), *Children in Society: Contemporary Theory, Policy and Practice* (Palgrave 2001); Madeleine Leaonard, *The Sociology of Children, Childhood and Generation* (Sage 2016).

85 James Mittleman, 'Restructuring the global division of labour: old theories and new realities' in Stephen Gill (ed.) *Globalisation, Democratisation and Multilateralism* (Macmillan 1997).

86 See, for overview: Paolo Boccagni and Francesca Decimo, 'Mapping social remittances' (2013) 10 (1) *Migration Letters* 1–10.

87 Malcolm Langford et al. (eds), *The Millennium Development Goals and Human Rights: Past, Present and Future* (CUP 2015).

88 African Charter on the Rights and Welfare of the Child 1999.

89 See, generally: Malcolm Langford et al. (eds), *The Millennium Development Goals and Human Rights: Past, Present and Future* (CUP 2015).

90 Michael Wyness, *Childhood* (Polity 2015) 69.

91 Allison James, Chris Jenks and Alan Prout, *Theorizing Childhood* (Polity 1998).

92 Michael Wyness, *Childhood* (Polity 2015) 61.

93 See: Nick Lee and Johanna Motzkau, 'Navigating the Bio-politics of Childhood' (2011) 18 *Childhood* 7–19.

94 Marilyn Fleer, Marianne Hedegaard and Jonathan Tudge, 'Constructing childhood: global-local politics and practices' in Marilyn Fleer, Marianne Hedegaard and Jonathan Tudge (eds), *Childhood Studies and the Impact of Globalisation: Practices at Global and Local Levels* (Routledge 2009).

95 Michael Wyness, *Childhood* (Polity 2015) 61.

96 See, for example: Daniel Steinbock, 'Unaccompanied Refugee Children in Host Country Foster Families' (1996) 8 *International Journal of Refugee Law* 6; Muireann Ni Raghallaigh, 'The negotiation of culture in foster care placements for separated refugee and asylum seeking young people in Ireland and England' (2015) 22 (2) *Childhood* 263.

97 See, for example: Brechtje Paardekooper et al., 'The Psychological Impact of War and the Refugee Situation on South Sudanese Children in Refugee Camps in Northern Uganda: An Exploratory Study' (1999) 40(4) *Journal of Child Psychology and Psychiatry*; 'Recommendations of the Seminar on the Psychological Well-Being of Refugee Children organized by Catholic Child Bureau (September 23–27, 1991 Geneva Switzerland)' (1992) (2) *International Journal of Refugee Law* 285.

98 See, for example: Benno Glauser, 'Street children' in Allison James and Alan Prout, *Constructing and reconstructing childhood: Contemporary issues in the sociological study of childhood* (2015) 128; Lorraine Young and Hazel Barrett, 'Adapting visual methods: action research with Kampala street children (2001) *Area* 33 (2) 141; Tobias Hecht, *At home in the street: Street children of Northeast Brazil* (CUP 1998).

99 See, generally: Brian-Vincent Ikejiaku, 'International Law is Western Made Global Law: The Perception of Third-World Category' (2013) 6 *African Journal of Legal Studies* 337.

100 Phillippe Ariès, *Centuries of Childhood* (Pimlico 1996) (originally published in 1962) 125–130.

101 *Ibid*, 397.

102 *Ibid*.

103 Universal Declaration of Human Rights, Article 16.3. See Chapter 3.

104 Constitution of Ireland, Article 42a(1)(2)(1°).

105 See, generally: Allison James and Alan Prout, 'Hierarchy, boundary and agency: Toward a theoretical perspective on childhood' (1995) 1 *Sociological Studies of*

Childhood 77–101; Richard Farson, *Birthrights* (Macmillan 1974); John Holt, *Escape from Childhood: The Needs and Rights of Childhood* (Dutton 1974); Beatrice Gross and Ronald Gross, *Introduction to the Children's Rights Movement: Overcoming the Oppression of Young People* (Anchor Books 1977).

106 Self-actualisation is achieved when a person experiences positive development throughout childhood and beyond and eventually attains the skills and knowledge needed to achieve their individual potential. See, generally: Abraham Maslow, *Toward a psychology of being* (3rd edn, Wiley 1999).

107 Jacqueline Bhaba and Mary Crock, *Seeking Asylum Alone – a Comparative Study: Unaccompanied and Separated Children and Refugee Protection in Australia, the UK and the US* (Themis Press 2007) 106.

108 See: Michelle Foster, *International Refugee Law and Socio-Economic Rights: Refugee from Deprivation* (CUP 2007).

109 General Comment No. 5 (2003) General measures of implementation of the Convention on the Rights of the Child (arts. 4, 42 and 44, para 6) para 12.

110 General Principles are commonly used to interpret the CRC. The General Principles contextualise the Convention, all four are understood to encompass all other CRC rights. Jane Fortin, *Children's Rights and the Developing Law* (3rd edn, CUP 2009) 37.

111 Jens Qvortrup, William Corsaro and Michael-Sebastion Honig, *The Palgrave Handbook of Childhood Studies* (Palgrave 2009) 387.

112 Katherine Hunt Federle 'Children's Rights and the Need for Protection' (2000) 34(3) *Family Law Quarterly* 423.

113 *Ibid* 422–424.

114 Katherine Hunt Federle 'Rights Flow Downhill' (1994) 2(4) *International Journal of Childhood Studies* 344; Michael Freeman, *The Rights and Wrongs of Children* (F. Pinter 1983) 54–60.

115 Michael Freeman, *The Rights and Wrongs of Children* (F. Pinter 1983) 54–60.

3 International Children's Rights Law

Abstract

This chapter expands upon the contemporary conceptualisation of childhood discussed in Chapter 2 and identifies additional characteristics that derive from the Convention on the Rights of the Child and other sources of international law. The purpose of these two chapters is to establish a conceptualisation of childhood to be used as a framework for subsequent chapters. The purpose of this is to carry these discussions over to the context of refugee law to analyse to what extent breaches in children's rights intersect with refugee law and when those breaches may amount to persecution. The structure follows the 'Three Ps Approach'.

Introduction

The Convention on the Rights of the Child (CRC) represents the culmination of the international children's rights movement and a solidification of the conceptualisation of children arrived at in Chapter 2. The CRC is now the foundation of modern children's rights law. The rights contained within the CRC are rights that are directly attributed to children 'irrespective of the child's or their parent's or legal guardian's race, colour, sex, language, religion, political or other opinion, national, ethnic or social origin, property, disability, birth of other status'.[1] In addition to the CRC, children have rights as set out in the Universal Declaration of Human Rights (UDHR),[2] the International Covenant on Civil and Political Rights (ICCPR),[3] the International Covenant on Economic and Social Rights (ICESR)[4] and international labour laws, including the Worst Forms of Child Labour Convention (WFCLC).[5] The existence of children's rights is therefore not disputed. This chapter rather looks at how children are conceptualised within international law and the way these provisions may interact with refugee law.

Origins of children's rights in international law

The Covenant of the League of Nations (1919)[6] referred specifically to children in Article 23(a)(b):

> Subject to and in accordance with the provisions of international conventions existing or hereafter to be agreed upon, the Members of the League:
> (a) will endeavour to secure and maintain fair and humane conditions of labour for men, women, and children, both in their own countries and in all countries to which their commercial and industrial relations extend,[7]

Additionally, Article 23(c) required members to 'entrust the League with the general supervision over the execution of agreements with regard to trafficking[8] in women and children...'[9] Both paragraphs (a) and (c) of the Covenant recognised the vulnerability of children while also placing the responsibility to prevent harm on the State,[10] reminiscent of the protectionist approach.

The International Labour Organization (ILO) published 13 Conventions between 1919[11] and 1973,[12] which addressed children's rights and protections, specifically in relation to minimum age,[13] the hours children could work[14] and health.[15] The most recent iteration of children's rights in the context of labour was the WFCLC, adopted in 1999. It is viewed alongside the Minimum Age Convention 1973 (No. 138) as fundamental to the rights regime under the aegis of the ILO. The main objective of the WFCLC[16] was to oblige ratifying States to prohibit and eliminate the worst forms of child labour for all persons under age 18.[17] Uniquely for mainstream international law, children were visible within these developments.[18] Developments in early international labour law reflected the increased value placed on education and the devaluing of child labour as highlighted by Ariés (discussed in Chapter 2).[19] Chapter 2 identified the clear link between development and labour, establishing that harmful labour practices can affect the right to develop. Looking ahead, exploitative and harmful labour practices feature prominently in child refugee case law. Protecting children from harmful labour that impacts upon the child's development therefore has both early origins and continued relevance in international law, including refugee law (discussed further throughout this chapter).

The 1924 Declaration recognised and outlined the responsibility of 'mankind' to ensure certain rights were afforded children regardless of their 'race, nationality or creed':[20]

> The child must be given the means requisite for its normal development, both materially and spiritually;
> The child that is hungry must be fed; the child that is sick must be nursed; the child that is backward must be helped; the delinquent child

> must be reclaimed; and the orphan and the waif must be sheltered and succoured;
> The child must be the first to receive relief in times of distress;
> The child must be put in a position to earn a livelihood, and must be protected against every form of exploitation;
> The child must be brought up in the consciousness that its talents must be devoted to the service of fellow men.[21]

As early as 1924, this international document, written in the Global North, referred to the protection needs of those who were experiencing deficit childhoods.[22]

Not only were the needs of children during times of distress prioritised, but requisite conditions for childhood were also outlined. The 1924 Declaration therefore painted a picture of a childhood that entailed: (1) protection from harm and illness, (2) education so that children acquired the necessary skills to earn a living and serve others and (3) protection from exploitation. This conceptualisation implied that children: (1) were vulnerable to harm and exploitation, (2) required intervention or protection from others to prevent harm and (3) had a right to childhood, a period of growth. This reflects the conceptualisation put forward by early theorists in the seventeenth and eighteenth centuries and the main contributions in modern childhood studies reflecting the general 'baseline' of positive development for the conceptualisation of children.

In 1959, the United Nations (UN) General Assembly adopted the second Declaration of the Rights of the Child,[23] which expanded on the rights contained within the 1924 Declaration and also included principles deriving from the UDHR. The preamble stated that the child 'by reason of his physical and mental immaturity, needs special safeguards and care, including appropriate legal protection, before as well as after birth'.[24] The provisions referred to the responsibility of parents, governments and the international community to protect the child from: harm, including in the workplace, and exploitation, including trafficking and neglect.[25] The 1959 Declaration, like its predecessor, nevertheless presented a romanticised, or Rousseauian, conceptualisation of the child, which placed the child firmly at the centre of society.

The Declarations represented a period in the children's rights movement characterised by the notion that the international community had a responsibility to intervene or protect children experiencing deficit childhoods. The 1924 and 1959 Declarations grounded accepted notions of children's rights in international guidance, as declarations are non-binding,[26] and provided a framework for the development and expansion of the international children's rights movement. Both documents, and the burgeoning human rights framework (see below), contributed to the successful drafting and near-universal ratification of the CRC.

In the years between the 1924 and 1959 Declarations, the UDHR and the Convention relating to the Status of Refugees (Refugee Convention) were adopted by the General Assembly of the UN in 1948 and 1951, respectively. Neither document attributed rights to children with the exception of the right to education,[27] but neither excluded them from rights that were attributed to 'all members of the human family'[28] or refugees,[29] respectively. This may be emblematic of the drafters' ambivalence towards attributing rights to children. Throughout history, commentators and authors have remarked upon the fear that articulating the rights of children would result in the destabilisation of the family unit.[30]

In the years following the UDHR's entry into force, the International Bill of Rights (IBR) emerged, comprising the ICCPR[31] and the International Covenant on Economic, Social and Cultural Rights (ICESCR).[32] The ICCPR and the ICESCR were adopted almost 20 years after the 1959 Declaration. The ICESCR and the ICCPR were the first examples of mainstream international human rights law that codified rights explicitly referring to children.

These documents made clear that the international community and individual States had a duty to protect people from abuses of their fundamental rights. Children were among those who were considered to require protection from human rights abuses and who had rights, albeit largely in the context of their families. The provisions arising from the IBR are discussed under the provision, protection and participation rights headings.

Convention on the Rights of the Child 1989 and *life, survival and development*

The main aim of the CRC was to establish an exhaustive and legally binding instrument that established standards and guidance for the entitlements and freedoms of children.[33] The CRC contains 54 articles of which 41 relate to the rights of children, specifically.[34] The Preamble refers to earlier treaties, including the UDHR and the 1924 and 1959 Declarations. It emphasised the need to extend particular care to children. The rights contained in the Convention cover both civil and political rights as well as economic, social and cultural rights.[35] A children's rights approach to the interpretation of the Refugee Convention would thus encompass both sets of rights (discussed in Chapters 5 and 6).

The General Principles contextualise the Convention, all four are understood to encompass all other CRC rights[36] and govern the implementation and interpretation of the rights within the CRC.[37] The four[38] General Principles are: the right to life, survival and development; the right to non-discrimination; the best interests principle; and the right to have one's views heard.[39] The principles serve to guide our understanding of children's rights in the modern age. Indeed, the present research shows that the only General Principle that comprehensively covers all the rights of the child and reflects the conceptualisation of children established in Chapter 2 is Article 6.

Article 6, as already discussed, refers to the child's right to survival and development: '1. States Parties recognize that every child has the inherent right to life. 2. States Parties shall ensure to the maximum extent possible the survival and development of the child'.[40]

'Development' is referenced a number of times throughout the Convention in respect of children's health,[41] family,[42] culture,[43] spiritual needs,[44] social integration,[45] economic support,[46] education,[47] moral education[48] and language.[49] Thus this right does not only serve to emphasise the children's right to life alone as already elucidated in the UDHR,[50] for example, but also to emphasise the children's right to develop into healthy, productive adults, as confirmed by the Committee (see below).[51] This principle reinforces the view, as established in Chapter 2, that childhood is a period of development and preparation for adulthood. Agency is an outcome of positive development, it accompanies spiritual, social, moral and mental development, all considered aspects of Article 6 by the Committee (see below).

This principle is defined by the content in the rest of the CRC, like the other General Principles. The right to life and development is therefore interpreted to mean a period of growth that takes into account the many different facets of childhood, including education, religion, culture, health and integration. The Committee captures this in General Comment No. 5 (2003) *General measures of implementation of the Convention on the Rights of the Child (arts. 4, 42 and 44, para. 6)* (Comment No. 5) in the interpretation of Article 6:

> Article 6: the child's inherent right to life and States parties' obligation to ensure to the maximum extent possible the survival and development of the child. The Committee expects States to interpret "development" in its broadest sense as a holistic concept, embracing the child's physical, mental, spiritual, moral, psychological and social development. Implementation measures should be aimed at achieving the optimal development for all children.[52]

As detailed in Chapter 1, this interpretation encompasses rights contained in all three categories of the Three Ps Approach.

It is arguable that the period of childhood, one characterised by development and positive growth, is encapsulated by Article 6. All other rights contained within the CRC provide for protection, provision and participation rights that aim to ensure the child is able to survive, live, thrive and have the chance to self-actualise. This provision and how it is developed throughout the CRC highlights the multi-faceted nature of childhood and the different areas that require protection.

It is argued that development must form part of the analysis of the threshold for persecution. In the case of child refugees the test that is applied in this analysis should stem from Article 6. However, it is not possible to suggest that any violation of a children's right will amount to persecution. The child applicant must show that their experience is different from the status quo in their country of origin. It is the differential impact stemming from discrimination that bridges the gap between a violation of a children's right as a standalone concept and the Refugee Convention. Chapter 6 examines Article 6 in the context of refugee law and instances where a children's rights violation *may* amount to persecution.

The sections below look at the provisions contained within the CRC under three headings, corresponding with the Three Ps rights groupings: provision rights, protection rights and participation rights.

Provision rights

As discussed throughout, children have rights of their own, but they often need adults to facilitate access to those rights, including provision rights. Provision rights are those which adults, in particular the State, provide to children. These rights include health, adequate standard of living, family unity and education, all of which have been referred to in child refugee case law. The role of the family and the rights that derive from family life and unity are discussed in a separate section below as family crosses over into all three rights categories. Stainton Rogers categorised this area of rights as forming part of the 'welfare discourse' that refers to childhood as a time of growth.[53] These rights are therefore underscored by the right to develop, ie Article 6 of the CRC. Provision rights are visible within child refugee case law. This breaks from the norm somewhat as provision rights largely relate to social and economic rights – an area that is less developed and more contentious in adult cases.[54] This section introduces these rights in international children's rights law and indicates how they may be relevant in the context of refugee law.

Health

The United Nation Children's Fund (UNICEF) classified the right to health as one associated with 'survival and development'.[55] Article 24 of the CRC and Article 12.2(a) of the ICESCR[56] embeds the children's right to health in law. Article 24.1 of the CRC states that children have the right:

> to the enjoyment of the highest attainable standard of health and to facilities for the treatment of illness and rehabilitation of health. States party shall strive to ensure that no child is deprived of his or her right of access to such health care services.

Article 24 also requires States to implement measures to prevent infant and child mortality,[57] combat disease and malnutrition[58] and work towards 'abolishing traditional practices prejudicial to the health of children'.[59]

In Article 23, the CRC provides that children require special care and that States should support children and families in ensuring children with disabilities 'enjoy a full and decent life, in conditions that ensure dignity'.[60] Article 25 provided that all persons have a right to the highest attainable standard of health, also highlighting the importance of family, but specifically the mother and child. It provided that '[m]otherhood and childhood are entitled to special care and assistance'.[61]

In refugee law, the right to health has been cited in a variety of child cases. Examples include instances where children due to their particular background (corresponding with convention grounds: race, nationality, membership of a particular social group, etc.) may have been prohibited from accessing medical treatments[62] or subjected to female genital mutilation.[63] Health has nevertheless been applied in child (and adult) cases inconsistently, as discussed in Chapter 6.

Standard of living

The CRC also mentions economic needs, referring to the obligation to ensure children have access to adequate economic support. Article 26 requires States to take necessary steps to ensure children benefit from social security and social insurance.[64] This is followed by Article 27, which states that children have the right to 'a standard of living adequate for the child's physical, mental, spiritual, moral and social development'.[65] This paragraph, Paragraph 1, requires the State to recognise this right. Paragraph 2, however, provides, mirroring early theorising by Locke, that it is the parents' responsibility to 'secure, within their abilities and financial capacities, the conditions of living necessary for the child's development'.[66]

Locke, who wrote about the aristocracy in the West, contended that children's rights were limited by their parents' circumstances, ie the child's right to subsistence only extended as far as the parent's means to provide such subsistence.[67] The CRC requires the State to ensure parents are equipped to provide a standard adequate for development, while still recognising that the child's standard of living may be relative to the parents' resources. Noguchi contended that adult wages/employment conditions should nevertheless be adequate to ensure children do not *need* to/are not *required* to access the labour market.[68]

This right raises questions not only about the divide in responsibilities between the State and the parents, but it also raises questions around the universality of the CRC and the different standards that might apply depending upon the country in which the child was born, or into which economic circumstances the child was born.

The CRC nevertheless includes protection from poverty at least to some degree as part of protecting childhood. Poverty overlaps with and is underscored by many other rights, including health and education, and also the General Principles, including Article 6. The right to an adequate standard of living to promote positive development is grounded in the protectionist approach, discussed in Chapter 2. Social and economic deprivation or disadvantage is an indicator of risk of other rights violations and interruptions to development.

On its own, the right to an adequate standard of living relates primarily to cases where children, due to discrimination (with a link to a convention ground), are unable to access basic services and who would otherwise, without a grant of protection, be unable to obtain national identity, access the labour force in the future or be eligible for social welfare support. The right to an adequate standard of living does not often feature in child refugee case law as *the* primary reason of persecution, but it is, as stated herewith, often an indicator of risk of violations of other rights. For example, the right to an adequate standard of living may be referred to in the context of human trafficking – child applicants who experience social and economic deprivation are more likely to be subjected to human trafficking or re-trafficking.[69]

Another example is children born in contravention of China's one-child rule, who have been recognised as refugees as they would be deprived of education or healthcare or economically disadvantaged.

These cases emphasise the link between an adequate standard of living and becoming productive citizen adults, with a link therefore with development.[70] Instances where the right to an adequate standard of living arise are discussed in detail in Chapter 6.

Education

Education has long been seen as a fundamental right of children and as part of the experience of childhood, as established in Chapter 2.[71] It has also been described as a way to break cycles of poverty and exploitation.[72] The UDHR in Article 26, and Article 13 of the ICESRC,[73] provides the right to education to 'everyone', noting that elementary education should also be compulsory, attributing the obligation to provide this right to the State. Although the provision in the UDHR did not explicitly mention children, it is clear by the reference to elementary education that children were the intended subjects. Article 26.2 of the UDHR, reflecting the intention of the 1924 Declaration, defines education as something that:

> shall be directed to the full development of the human personality and to the strengthening of respect for human rights and fundamental freedoms. It shall promote understanding, tolerance and friendship among all nations, racial or religious groups, and shall further the activities of the United Nations for the maintenance of peace.[74]

The ICESCR, in Article 13,[75] stipulates that education is a right that belongs to children, specifically:

> The States Parties to the present Covenant recognize the right of everyone to education. They agree that education shall be directed to the full

> development of the human personality and the sense of its dignity, and shall strengthen the respect for human rights and fundamental freedoms. They further agree that education shall enable all persons to participate effectively in a free society, promote understanding, tolerance and friendship among all nations and all racial, ethnic or religious groups, and further the activities of the United Nations for the maintenance of peace.[76]

Firstly, Article 13 recognises that all persons have the right to education. Secondly, the ICESCR, like the UDHR, describes education as part of the process of developing into productive members of society in the same way as Locke saw education as a path to earning citizenship; preparing children for adulthood in the spirit of tolerance, understanding, equality, respect for the natural environment and responsibility.[77]

In Article 29, the CRC elaborates on the State's obligations to ensure education is aimed at the development of the child to their 'fullest potential'. This provision also refers to education as playing a role in teaching children to respect their parents, their cultural identity, language and the national values of the country in which the child is resident.[78] Also in this same vein, the CRC, in Article 31, articulates the child's rights to rest, leisure, play, and recreational, artistic and cultural activities reflecting a move towards a more romanticised conceptualisation of children (often considered to have originated with Rousseau).[79] Access to leisure, play and recreational activities are not dealt with in Chapter 6 as it has not arisen in the context of qualifying as a refugee in case law. It has however arisen in relation to the treatment of children seeking asylum.[80] The rights discussed herein, including the rights to leisure and play, support the view that childhood is a period marked by growth.

Education is a significant part of law and theorising around childhood. The CRC reiterates this position and it placed the obligation to provide this right on the State. All treaties also refers to non-discrimination in education based on religion, race, etc. The CRC refers specifically to non-discrimination in the context of the socio-economic circumstances of children and families. The CRC links the right to education to a number of other children's rights, including the right to an adequate standard of living, acknowledging that social and economic disadvantage may increase the risk of a violation of the right to education.

The CRC and the Refugee Convention establishes that refugee parents also share the responsibility to ensure their children receive primary education, while maintaining the right to align their children's education with their culture and religious beliefs.[81] The right is therefore limited by the role of the parents. However, read in conjunction with the child's right to be heard and also the best interests principle, it may be argued that children have a say in the direction of their education in accordance with their age and maturity. However, this illustrates the conflict that exists in the application of any children's right – children and their views and interests *and* those that belong to parents or other adults.

Education has arisen in refugee case law. In one example, *D. [a minor] v Refugee Appeals Tribunal*, the court noted that the child, as a result of being denied education, would not be able to meaningfully participate in Serbian society.[82] The High Court also referred to the infamous case in the United States, *Brown v. Board of Education*, highlighting the link between education and development.[83] Participation in society is the goal of development, thus this right also breaches the child's overarching Article 6 right. This case is expanded upon in Chapter 6.

Non-discrimination

As discussed throughout, violations of provision rights may be considered to fall within the scope of the Refugee Convention. The General Principle of non-discrimination, Article 2 of the CRC, deriving from the UDHR[84] and as included in the ICCPR,[85] is a useful tool to determine whether or not a violation of a provision right (and indeed other rights) amounts to persecution within the Refugee Convention. Article 2 requires 'States to ensure all children on a given State's territory have access to the rights in the Convention regardless of their background or their parents'.[86] The principle of non-discrimination is useful in establishing, at least theoretically, the universality, including within a given society, of the rights in the CRC. Although this does not assist in defining or conceptualising childhood, other than to say that all childhoods should be equal within a society or legal system, it impacts upon other rights and, generally, the experience of a positive childhood. In the context of refugee law, non-discrimination has featured in a number of cases that fall within each of the Three Ps rights categories. Discrimination, in particular when it is State sanctioned or condoned, has often been a key reasoning behind a grant of protection on the basis of a violation of a children's right – it often serves to establish the causal link with a convention ground, ie a violation of a right linked to discrimination on the basis of one's race, nationality, religion, membership of a particular social group or political opinion (the convention grounds). Chapter 6 analyses case law where there is an overlap between the Refugee Convention and the principle of non-discrimination.

Protection rights

International law began from the perspective that children are vulnerable to exploitation. Protection rights aim to prevent abuse, harm, neglect and anything that may have an adverse effect on the standard of childhood established by the CRC – impacting upon their right to develop as established in Chapters 1 and 2. Protection-based rights in terms of development can be considered as rights relating to 'physical, mental, spiritual, moral, psychological and social development' with the overall objective of 'optimal development' in mind.[87] Protection rights arising from the CRC and other treaties are discussed below where links with refugee law were also identified (discussed in Chapter 6). This section discusses the following protection themes: labour and other forms of exploitation, including prostitution, pornography and trafficking; military conscription and gang recruitment; and child marriage.

Labour exploitation

Child labour is often regarded as a consequence of poverty,[88] or something that perpetuates a cycle of poverty.[89] In the global context some families may view child labour as essential to survival. We still see this today. The majority of child labourers can be found in developing countries, where a family's livelihood might depend on income from some or all of their children.[90] The right to education in the case of poor and rural families as part of the conceptualisation of childhood therefore does not necessarily reflect the demands of a particular society.[91] Nevertheless, and as discussed in the previous chapter, education was a key marker in the evolution of the children's rights movement. Concerns around labour exploitation led to the inclusion of interventions in the CRC, ICESCR, ICCPR and ILO Conventions that aimed to ensure that work did not interfere with education and health.[92]

Article 8 of the ICCPR prohibits slavery, servitude and compulsory labour.[93] The ICCPR does not, however, specifically mention children. The ICESCR, on the other hand, in Article 10 provides that

> Children and young persons should be protected from economic and social exploitation. Their employment in work harmful to their morals or health or dangerous to life or likely to hamper their normal development should be punishable by law. States should also set age limits below which the paid employment of child labour should be prohibited and punishable by law.[94]

Building upon the early ILO treaties, the CRC provides for protections for children engaged in labour. Article 32.1 of the CRC provides:

> States Parties recognize the right of the child to be protected from economic exploitation and from performing any work that is likely to be hazardous or to interfere with the child's education, or to be harmful to the child's health or physical, mental, spiritual, moral or social development.

The CRC makes clear that labour exploitation affects development. Article 32 of the CRC requires States to ensure work performed by children is not hazardous or harmful to the child's mental or physical health or moral, spiritual or social development. States are required to implement measures to provide: a minimum age for employment, regulation of hours and conditions of employment and penalties or sanctions to ensure the provision's effective enforcement.[95] The reference to minimum age requirements for children engaging in work requires States to consider other international instruments, like the ILO Conventions. The Implementation Handbook of the CRC also heavily references the ILO Conventions.[96]

Increased attention on child labour followed the CRC's entry into force.[97] The WFCLC (adopted some 10 years after the CRC) is viewed alongside the Minimum Age Convention 1973 (No. 138) as fundamental to the rights regime under the aegis of the ILO. The main objective of the WFCLC[98] was to oblige ratifying States to prohibit and eliminate the worst forms of child labour for all persons under age 18,[99] which included slavery, debt bondage, sale, trafficking, forced military conscription, prostitution, pornography, use of children to produce or traffic harmful or illegal substances, and work, which by its nature, 'is likely to harm the health, safety or morals of children'.[100] This convention was drafted from the perspective that children are in a position of vulnerability and are at risk of exploitation – a protectionist approach.[101] The WFCLC experienced the fastest ratification of any other ILO convention.

Labour in the context of the WFCLC, as argued by Noguchi, encompassed self-employment, unpaid work and working for/with family.[102] Under the WFCLC, parental consent cannot override the provisions therein nor the ILO standards in respect of labour.[103] Article 19 of the WFCLC, for example, requires States to

> take all appropriate legislative, administrative, social and educational measures to protect the child from all forms of physical or mental violence, injury or abuse, neglect or negligent treatment, maltreatment or exploitation, including sexual abuse, while in the care of parent(s), legal guardian(s) or any other person who has the care of the child.[104]

This raises important questions regarding the role of parents – in particular when parents are perpetrators of forced labour, sexual exploitation and trafficking (discussed in Chapter 6). The role of family has arisen in the context of refugee law in respect of labour exploitation, including when unattached, or separated, children cannot avail of family-based protection from economic exploitation.

Provisions relating to education occur most frequently across a variety of treaties thus education is the most represented right in children's rights law. However, the most comprehensive area of law in relation to children is international labour law (and other forms of economic exploitation). The link between economic exploitation and refugee protection is difficult to make with any degree of certainty as labour practices involving children vary greatly internationally. However, where the WFCLC and the CRC make reference to labour practices amounting to violence against children, it is perhaps easier to make a link. As mentioned above, exploitative and harmful labour practices feature in child refugee case law, particularly in the context of forced labour and trafficking (discussed in Chapter 6).

Other forms of economic exploitation

Alongside growth in awareness and interest in regulating child labour was a growing awareness of children being trafficked and sexually exploited and used in conflict.[105] Article 36 of the CRC requires States to prohibit 'all other' forms of exploitation, which negatively affects the child's welfare. Article 35 reiterates States' obligations to implement bilateral and multilateral measures to prevent trafficking of children for any purpose.[106] These provisions are especially relevant in cases of child exploitation that occur across borders – an area that has the potential to interact with refugee law. Importantly, the WFCLC allocates the responsibility to ensure adequate safeguards were in place not just to the State, but to the international community.[107]

Article 3(b) of the WFCLC[108] and Article 34 of the CRC state that the use, procurement or offering of a child under 18 in prostitution must be prohibited and eliminated[109] by implementing measures to prevent exploitation and abuse, in particular in relation to: the coercion of children to engage in unlawful sexual activities and the exploitation of children in prostitution and unlawful sexual practices and pornographic performances and materials.[110] The WFCLC states that prostitution, child pornography and the sale and trafficking of children are crimes of violence against children in addition to being crimes of labour exploitation. One of the Optional Protocols to the CRC, on the the Sale of Children, Child Prostitution and Child Pornography,[111] provides additional guidance in this regard,[112] referring to the WFCLC in the preamble.[113] In the area of refugee law, cases have arisen relating to the rights listed herein. In *Bian v. Canada* for example, the Federal Court of Canada held that the child applicant was unable to consent to being trafficked and was a refugee on that basis.[114]

Involvement in other illicit trades

The CRC also outlines States' responsibilities to protect children from involvement in the drugs trade and also to prevent children from being exposed to drugs culture. Article 11 requires States to 'take measures to combat the illicit transfer and non-return of children abroad'.[115] Article 33 of the Convention requires States to implement measures to prevent children from using, and children's involvement in producing and trafficking, illicit drugs.[116] This provision is relevant in the context of refugee law as it relates to child involvement in gangs, an emerging and prominent area, in particular where it intersects with exclusion, discussed in Chapter 6.[117]

Military conscription

Article 38 establishes States parties' obligations to ensure children are not exploited during times of conflict. Article 38.1 reiterates the obligation to respect international humanitarian law.[118] Article 38.2 requires States to take all feasible measures to ensure children under the age of 15 do not have an active role in conflicts, this includes the recruitment of children under the age of 15 into national armed forces. Recruits must be 17 in the United States (however, those under 18 must have consent from guardians)[119] and 16 in the United Kingdom (however, those under 17 must have consent from guardians).[120] Countries where participation in military is mandatory like Israel and South Korea, the minimum age is 18 (however, Israel reserves the right to call 17 year olds for service dependent on a health assessment).[121] The Optional Protocol on Children in Armed Conflict, which was adopted by the United Nations General Assembly in 2000 and entered into force in 2002, requires States to 'take all feasible measures to ensure that members of their armed forces who have not attained the age of 18 years do not take a direct part in hostilities'– both forced and voluntary.[122]

Child soldiers have been a visible group of refugees within the discourse over the years.[123] It is a prominent area of research in humanitarian law[124] and in the area of refugee law.[125] Cases involving underage military recruitment were not hard to find in the main asylum law databases used for this research. Underage military recruitment is discussed in detail in Chapter 6 and its relationship with exclusion is also developed in light of the current literature and available case law.

Child marriage

There is a significant body of research on the experience of forced child marriage.[126] In addition, it is listed as a 'child-specific form of persecution' in the Guidelines.[127] In 1979, the Convention on the Elimination of all Forms of Discrimination Against Women (CEDAW) was adopted and contained a provision relating to child marriage. Article 16.2 notes that:

> The betrothal and the marriage of a child shall have no legal effect, and all necessary action, including legislation, shall be taken to specify a minimum age for marriage and to make the registration of marriages in an official registry compulsory.[128]

There was no mention of this protection in the CRC, but Article 24 of the CRC, as discussed above, requires States to work towards 'abolishing traditional practices prejudicial to the health of children',[129] which may be relevant.

Although protection from child marriage was not mentioned in the CRC, due to its inclusion in the refugee discourse and also other UN treaties and guidelines (see Chapter 5), it is nevertheless a relevant aspect of the protection of childhood. Child marriage is also discussed in Chapter 6 as it features in child refugee case law and literature.

Other non-economic forms of harm

Indiscriminate violence

Article 38.4 of the CRC reiterates State's obligations to ensure protection for the civilian population, including the protection and care of children who are affected by armed conflict. Despite the origins of the international children's rights movement as discussed in the previous chapter, this is the only explicit reference to protecting children during times of war or conflict in the CRC. It is only dealt with briefly in Chapter 6 as indiscriminate violence is not mentioned in the UNHCR Guidelines. However the effects of war often form part of claims involving children and are discussed throughout Chapter 6.

Torture, inhuman or degrading treatment or punishment

Article 37 of the CRC requires States to ensure the child is not 'subjected to torture or other cruel, inhuman or degrading treatment or punishment' or imprisoned indefinitely for crimes committed when under the age of 18. In the context of prison or detention, Article 37 reiterates the child's right to liberty, noting prison or detention should only be used as a last resort. Article 37 provides that where a child is imprisoned, they should be treated with humanity, respect and dignity with access to legal advice and other assistance.[130] Article 37 reflects the purpose of, and provisions contained within, the Convention against Torture and other Cruel, Inhuman or Degrading Treatment or Punishment (Convention against Torture), which was adopted by the General Assembly in 1984.[131] This Convention builds upon Article 5 of the UDHR[132] and Article 7 of the ICCPR.[133] Both Articles 5 and 7 of the respective treaties state that no one shall be subjected to torture or to cruel, inhuman or degrading treatment or punishment. However, neither Article mentions children. Additionally, the Convention against Torture does not mention children or minors at any point. Therefore, the CRC plays an important role in explicitly including children within this right.

Torture, inhuman or degrading treatment and punishment may be used to interpret the threshold of persecution in the context of mainstream refugee law.[134] In the context of children, the Guidelines refers to the potential for harm arising from domestic abuse, which may amount to torture.[135] Torture or other cruel, inhuman or degrading treatment or punishment has arisen in refugee law. For example, in *Juan Carlos Martinez-Mejia*, the child applicant was granted protection on the basis of abuse at the hands of his stepfather; the abuse was determined to amount to torture (discussed in Chapter 6).[136]

'Protection rights' is the most prominent of the rights groupings in the refugee literature and case law (discussed in Chapter 6), which is likely reflective of the prioritisation of the protection of the child and the tendency to view children as vulnerable and in need of protection as established in Chapter 2.

Participation rights

As discussed in Chapter 2, the CRC introduced self-determination and capacity rights into international children's rights law. The CRC was influenced by the general consensus that children were considered to be independent members of society with rights to participate and with important roles to play.[137] The changing perception of children in society nevertheless brought about tensions. The literature highlighted resistance to attributing rights, in particular participation rights, to children from all sections of society,[138] including in political discourse.[139]

The basis for contemporary debate on agency is children's evolving capacities and their ability or inability to make decisions or participate in decision-making. In mainstream children's rights debates, there has been growing interest in understanding what is meant by 'agency' concerning children.[140] Firstly, the literature has explored the relationship between agency and children's ability to participate in the realisation of their rights.[141] Secondly, it has explored how capacity relates to the nature of rights made available to children, for example, whether they are provision, protection or participation rights.[142] In large part, the literature recognises that the roots of 'child agency' have very early origins.[143]

In considering approaches to children seeking international protection, the legal capacity of child applicants has been a topic of recent debate. The present debates surround the content of children's rights. The main divide rests between protection and provision rights considered to be within the purview of the parents, guardians and/or the State[144] *and* participation rights, which may be civil and political in nature. Participation rights encompass instances where children assert views and invoke rights historically considered to belong to adults.[145] The extent to which this conflict is present in international protection decision-making, law, and policy is consistent with the imbalance between the literature and practice. On the one hand, there is extensive literature and guidance supporting the view that children have capacity and rights in their own right and are considered subjects of law. On the other hand, there is very little case law or guidance on children qualifying as refugees in their own right. This is in part due to the fact that the intersection of refugee law and children's rights law is relatively new (discussed in Chapter 5).

Agency in the Convention on the Rights of the Child

Article 12, a General Principle, explicitly references the child's right to participate in the realisation of, or access to, their CRC rights. Article 17 of the CRC recognises the importance of providing information to children that supports children's 'social, spiritual and moral well-being and physical and mental health'.[146] Accordingly, this information should not only educate, but also empower children to access their rights.

The child, pursuant to Article 8, has the right to preserve their identity 'including nationality, name and family relations' 'without lawful interference'.[147] This provision, read in conjunction with Article 12, allocates the right to have and maintain an identity regardless of family or parental relationships or circumstances. In fact, family ties, or origins based on family background, is not mentioned in this provision. It is however referred to in Article 2, which deals with non-discrimination, as discussed above. Articles 13, 14, 15 and 30 also address the child's individual and autonomous rights to freedom of expression,[148] thought, conscience and religion,[149] freedom of association and peaceful assembly[150] and the protection of the right to practise their religion and speak their language (respectively).[151] These rights signal an acceptance that children are individuals, with important roles to play in society. They indicate that children have their own identities and have rights to express their identity.

Article 16.1 provides a fundamental and autonomous right to unlawful interference of the child's privacy, family life and correspondence: 'No child shall be subjected to arbitrary or unlawful interference with his or her privacy, family, or correspondence, nor to unlawful attacks on his or her honour and reputation'.[152] This right is attributed to adults in all human rights treaties mentioned in this chapter. Article 16.1 is thus important in acknowledging that this most basic human right also applies to children *in their own right*. These articles in particular support the notion that children are rights holders with the potential capacity to participate in society in a way that is consistent with their identity.

Despite the historical reluctance to attribute agency to children, even early philosophers recognised that children could formulate views or participate in society, at least sometimes. Article 12 provides that their views should not only be heard but also 'given due weight in accordance with the age and maturity of the child'.[153] An additional tenet of being able to form views, as discussed above, is having access to information. The CRC provides that

> The child shall have the right to freedom of expression; this right shall include freedom to seek, receive and impart information and ideas of all kinds, regardless of frontiers, either orally, in writing or in print, in the form of art, or through any other media of the child's choice.[154]

The CRC provides the right to the child to receive information as part of the right to freedom of expression. Therefore, the CRC confirms that agency and participation rights are closely linked with education and the process of development. This link was illustrated by Locke, Rousseau and many others and, as we can see, it is still relevant today.

A children's rights approach would in the least require recognition that children, in line with their evolving capacities, have legal agency in the context of refugee law.

In the context of refugee law, agency or participation, rights are often linked with the religion and political opinion convention grounds. There are a number of examples in refugee case law where children have exercised their agency and have invoked these two grounds. However, the category of participation rights is the newest area of children's rights law and refugee law and it continues to be the most contentious of the Three Ps (discussed in Chapter 6).

Determining agency

All provisions in the CRC have one main limitation in respect of child 'agency': this relates to the best interests principle. The best interests principle, Article 3 of the CRC, is thought to inform all rights as its scope covers 'all actions concerning children': 'In all actions concerning children, whether undertaken by public or private social welfare institutions, courts of law, administrative authorities or legislative bodies, the best interests of the child shall be a primary consideration'.[155]

In 2003, the Committee explained that the best interests must be deduced from the wider rights of the child as contained within the convention, rather than through a subjective assessment of welfare needs.[156] Fortin noted that the principle requires that decision-makers consider the child's best interests only as *a* primary consideration, reflecting the drafters' acknowledgement that sometimes other considerations must be taken into account; for example, the protection of society or the wishes of the family unit. Fortin gave the example of a child offender. The best interests of the child may come second in balancing children's rights with the need to protect society from the child concerned.[157]

Paragraph 2 of Article 3 reiterates the primacy of the parents by noting that in all measures taken by the State in an effort to protect and care for children in their jurisdiction, the State must take into account both the child's individual rights *and* the responsibilities of the parents (or legal guardians):

> States Parties undertake to ensure the child such protection and care as is necessary for his or her well-being, taking into account the rights and duties of his or her parents, legal guardians, or other individuals legally responsible for him or her, and, to this end, shall take all appropriate legislative and administrative measures.[158]

The concept of the best interests is unique to children in international law, reinforcing the assumption that children have different and special needs in comparison to adults and that the experiences of childhood need to be tailored to ensure children's best interests are taken into account. The principle however also provides that adults play a role in assessing those interests. It is therefore subject to third party interpretation. In the case of refuge, the third party is likely the family or nominated guardian,[159] the determination body or the court or a combination of these parties. In decision-making procedures in the case of refugee protection, parents, governmental agencies or officials or adjudicators may weigh the views of children not only in relation to the child's capacity, but, as Bhabha argued, also their opinions, perhaps coupled with their own prejudices (discussed in Chapter 6).[160]

The best interests principle in the context of refugee law is largely reflected in case law as procedural. States are reluctant to include this principle in refugee legislation due to the fear that the definition of persecution could be influenced by a best interests assessment. From the literature[161] and case law[162] it is clear that a best interests assessment may be *a* consideration and even *a primary* consideration, but it does not impact upon the interpretation of persecution *per se*. The best interests principle is most widely referred to in relation to aspects of the child's claim unrelated to the refugee qualification process, such as care arrangements, age determinations and safeguards in the determination of a child's claim.[163] These procedural elements impact upon the child's ability to access asylum and participate in the asylum procedures. However they fall outside of the scope of this research. These insights nevertheless in part explain the inconsistencies associated with child refugee claims (see Chapter 6).

Right to be heard

The Committee stated in the *travaux préparatoires* that there was no incompatibility between the best interests principle and the right to be heard. In the drafting stage of the CRC the right of the child to be heard formed part of Article 3.[164] The provision was moved and became a General Provision in its own right. It therefore applies across all other rights contained within the CRC in its own right.[165] This move was significant as it served as recognition of the right and ability of children to exercise their agency. The contention is that one cannot determine the best interests of the child without consulting the child. The principle, as written in Article 12, articulates the child's right to have their voice heard in all matters that affect them if they are capable of forming their own views:

> 1. States Parties shall assure to the child who is capable of forming his or her own views the right to express those views freely in all matters affecting the child, the views of the child being given due weight in accordance with the age and maturity of the child.
> 2. For this purpose, the child shall in particular be provided the opportunity to be heard in any judicial and administrative proceedings affecting the child, either directly, or through a representative or an appropriate body, in a manner consistent with the procedural rules of national law.[166]

Article 12 provides that the views of the child should not only be heard but 'given due weight in accordance with the age and maturity of the child'. This principle is most relevant for discussions around participation rights. Article 12 not only recognises the established view that children's capacities are evolving, but that they also have the right to contribute to decision making around their interests and future. Child agency has therefore been a growing concept with very early origins. Attributing agency to children, however, has been wrought with conflict. Locke, Rousseau, Kant and the protectionists and others that followed recognised the child's ever-evolving ability to reason and thus interact with the world around them (see Chapter 2), but also argued that this right had a ceiling. The protectionists reinforced the view that children could participate and indeed had agency, but that others, namely adults or family, had a role in determining their best interests as well including as regards their futures.[167]

Article 12, perhaps more than any other provision, places children in the centre of the rights regime and recognised children as important actors in the realisation of their rights, including those considered to be protection based. However, refugee law, like all other areas of international human rights law, has not interpreted or applied this right consistently. Chapter 6 asks why participation rights are the least developed in child refugee jurisprudence. Chapter 6 asks if it is to do with society's long-held view that children are not-yet-fully-formed, not-yet capable of reason or developing religious or political views (see Chapter 2).

The role of the family in the Convention on the Rights of the Child and provision, protection and participation rights

The right to a family environment and the role of family are relevant to each category of rights. The international children's movement brought with it a paternalistic view of family and State responsibilities. In the UDHR, child-specific provisions relating to children were mainly constructed within the family unit. Article 16 recognises the family as the natural unit,[168] requiring States Parties to ensure that the family was protected, and by extension, ensure children were protected within the unit. Even today, post-CRC, there is an assumption in law that the child receives protection and access to rights through the family unit. This is of course not absolute as, in some instances, the State may be required to intervene to protect children. It is nevertheless clear that the objective of provisions relating to children in the IBR revolves around protection – the outcome of sufficient protection being access to developmental rights, namely health and education. Overtime, this began to change. International guidance and law following 1989 created a universal code-of-conduct for childhood,[169] removing the exclusive responsibility to protect and promote children from the family unit.[170]

The CRC addresses two of the most pronounced and competing children's rights paradigms in the developed world[171] the role of the parents in protecting and promoting children's rights *versus* the rights of children. The

CRC was often, and continues to be, criticised by some as placing children's rights in contrast to adults' rights.[172] The CRC took 10 years to draft, which is an indication of the challenges (or the lack of will) encountered marrying the two strands of children's rights and the articulation of children's rights, generally. The CRC exists somewhere between the two: the rights of the child in respect of familial protection and nurturing *and* the child's individual rights.

All international human rights treaties discussed throughout this chapter emphasise the importance of the family unit. The CRC also reiterates this point. In its preamble, the CRC states that the best place for a child to be raised is in a family environment:

> Convinced that the family, as the fundamental group of society and the natural environment for the growth and well-being of all its members and particularly children, should be afforded the necessary protection and assistance so that it can fully assume its responsibilities within the community.[173]

This area of rights is important in defining children and childhood for the purposes of both provision and protection rights. International human rights law, and indeed domestic law, has long prioritised the family unit as a unit in need of protection for the benefit of society. Parents have a distinct and prominent role in raising, educating, providing for economically and emotionally, and protecting children during the period of childhood. The CRC clarifies therefore that it is both the parent's right and responsibility to raise and protect their children.

Article 5 in the CRC states that parents have the overarching right and responsibility to provide their children with guidance to exercise their rights.[174] Article 9 reinforces this by outlining the State's responsibility to ensure family unity is preserved.[175] The right to family unity also plays an important role in refugee law as introduced below and discussed in Chapter 6.

Article 9, Paragraph 1 makes clear that the responsibility to care for the child lies with the parents and only in circumstances where a competent body (competent authority subject to judicial review) determines that it is in the best interests of the child is it possible to proceed with separating the child from family members. Paragraph 1 emphasises that this may be necessary in instances of abuse or neglect. Paragraph 2 provides for all parties to have their voices heard. Although children were not specifically mentioned in this paragraph, we can assume they were included in reference to 'all interested parties' if read in line with Article 12.[176] Article 9 therefore not only introduced the notion that parents are one of the many 'enforcers' of children's rights as set out in the CRC, but equally, the State has a role in ensuring the parents are carrying out, and able to carry out, their responsibilities. Although this provision does not frame the child as a subject of law, it does establish a limit to the omnipotence of the parent and the institution of family, where the best interests is concerned *and* it provides an avenue through which the child can be heard.

Paragraph 3 of Article 9 also articulates the child's right to access and maintain relationships with parents in the case of separation.[177] This paragraph frames the child as a subject of this law in that it is *their* right to access their parents (except when it is not in their best interests). It is arguable that Article 9 is both objective and subjective in nature as it recognises the children's right to access their parents, but this right may be limited by an external assessment of the child's best interests, as discussed previously.

The role of the family is also important in the context of refugee law as discussed in Chapter 1 as it relates to the family-as-protector, and the family-as-persecutor, or the potential for the family to either provide access to rights or act as a barrier to accessing rights. The significance of the link between Article 6, the right to family, and child refugees is emphasised by the case of separated children. The right to survival and development is considered to be within the purview of the parents as stated above. In the case of separated children, this relationship is missing and thus the primary protector of rights relating to survival and development is missing. The link between Article 6 and the role of the parent as protector and indeed persecutor is looked at in Chapter 6.

The following section looks at the only CRC provision that refers specifically to refugee law, which establishes a formal link between the CRC and the Refugee Convention. This section shows to what degree the two conventions are aligned before moving on to the examination of children in the development of refugee law (see Chapter 4) and the examination of the possible scope for the application of the CRC in the interpretation of the Refugee Convention (see Chapter 5).

Children's rights and refugee law – an indirect link?

The mainstream international treaties and declarations referred to in this chapter span nearly six decades (from the ILO Minimum Age (Industry) Convention, 1919 (No.5) to the entry into force of the ICCPR and the ICESCR in 1976). The invisibility of children in refugee law prior to the CRC (discussed in Chapter 4) and the invisibility of children in human rights law prior to the CRC illustrates the dichotomy between children's rights and refugee law. Of all the treaties and declarations mentioned in this chapter, only the UDHR provides for 'the right to seek and to enjoy in other countries asylum from persecution'.[178]

While the CRC mentions child refugees, it deals with refugee protection in only one provision, Article 22:

> 1. States Parties shall take appropriate measures to ensure that a child who is seeking refugee status or who is considered a refugee in accordance with applicable international or domestic law and

procedures shall, whether unaccompanied or accompanied by his or her parents or by any other person, receive appropriate protection and humanitarian assistance in the enjoyment of applicable rights set forth in the present Convention and in other international human rights or humanitarian instruments to which the said States are Parties.

2. For this purpose, States Parties shall provide, as they consider appropriate, co-operation in any efforts by the United Nations and other competent intergovernmental organizations or non-governmental organizations co-operating with the United Nations to protect and assist such a child and to trace the parents or other members of the family of any refugee child in order to obtain information necessary for reunification with his or her family. In cases where no parents or other members of the family can be found, the child shall be accorded the same protection as any other child permanently or temporarily deprived of his or her family environment for any reason, as set forth in the present Convention.[179]

This provision deals with a number of points of law. It does not explicitly provide a right to seek refugee protection, however. It nevertheless refers to other 'applicable international or domestic law...' that may provide that right (such as the UDHR). This Article articulates rights pertaining to the family and other protection and social and economic rights for children who are seeking refugee status or who are recognised as refugees. It can be assumed that within this right children have the right to seek asylum, but again it is not provided for explicitly.

The CRC in this provision, like the Refugee Convention (to be discussed in Chapters 4 and 5), focuses more on the social and economic rights of the beneficiary rather than the process or the criteria associated with qualifying for refugee protection. This provision requires States Parties to provide appropriate protection and assistance 'in the enjoyment of' rights set out in the CRC and other relevant instruments. This is provided for in Paragraph 1. Paragraph 2 focuses specifically on reunification with family and the provision of a family environment in the case of children deprived of one. In balancing the rights set out in Article 22 it is evident that the right to family (specifically a family environment) is the most prominent.

The dichotomy between the two regimes even in light of the CRC and Article 22 therefore persists in modern international children's rights law. In Summary, Article 22 states that those rights which normally apply generally to children *also* apply to refugee children or children seeking refuge. It does not provide a right to seek refuge, an avenue through which a child might do so or criteria for the qualification of children as refugees. It does not suggest that a violation of any right may amount to persecution. This is revisited in Chapter 4 in the context of Refugee Law.

Conclusions

Childhood as constructed in this chapter, based on international law and in particular the CRC, paints a picture of both vulnerability and autonomy. Children require the State and their families to provide certain supports and services to enable them to develop. The provision rights discussed included family, health, education and an adequate standard of living. Children also require protection from exploitation and harm that might interrupt their development including: deprivation of a family environment, labour and sexual exploitation, involvement in illicit trades, military conscription, child marriage and protection from harm such as harmful religious practices (e.g. female genital mutilation). Lastly, today, children are seen in law as rights holders in their own right with rights to participate in decisions affecting them. The participation rights discussed herein focussed on identity and the expression of identity. Childhood within the CRC and within this book is underscored by the right to develop. Childhood requires protection and the provision of services to ensure the child is able to exercise their agency in accordance with their growing capacity. The process of childhood, as portrayed in international law, is a process of development *en route* to adulthood. This conceptualisation is a close reflection of that which exists in other disciplines and it is evident that the themes, divergences and conflicts have very early origins both in sociology and in international law.

As discussed in Chapter 1, a dichotomy exists between children's rights and refugee law. The picture of childhood as discussed in Chapter 2 has become in some ways universal due to the CRC and its wide ratification. The question asked throughout this book on the whole relates to how this conceptualisation of children and childhood has influenced, or indeed should influence, refugee law.

The following chapter, Chapter 4, discusses the development of refugee law. It looks in particular at the extent to which children were considered in refugee law and other protection initiatives leading up to the adoption of the Refugee Convention. This analysis informs discussions on the scope for a children's rights approach in Chapter 5.

Notes

1 Convention on the Rights of the Child 1989, Article 2.
2 Universal Declaration of Human Rights 1948.
3 International Covenant on Civil and Political Rights 1976.
4 International Covenant on Economic and Social Rights 1976.
5 Worst Forms of Child Labour Convention (no. 182) 1999.
6 Frederick Samuel Northedge, *The League of Nations: its life and times, 1920–1946* (Leicester University Press 1998).
7 The Covenant of the League of Nations 1919, Article 23(a)(b).
8 The United Nations Office on Drugs and Crime, in their 2004 *Protocol to Prevent, Suppress and Punish Trafficking in Persons, Especially Women and Children, supplementing the United Nations Convention against Transnational*

Organized Crime, define trafficking in persons as: 'the recruitment, transportation, transfer, harbouring or receipt of persons, by means of the threat or use of force or other forms of coercion, of abduction, of fraud, of deception, of the abuse of power or of a position of vulnerability or of the giving or receiving of payments or benefits to achieve the consent of a person having control over another person, for the purpose of exploitation'. The United Nations goes on to define exploitation as: 'at a minimum, the exploitation of the prostitution of others or other forms of sexual exploitation, forced labour or services, slavery or practices similar to slavery, servitude or the removal of organs'.

9 The Covenant of the League of Nations 1919, Article 23(c).

10 *Ibid*, Article 23(a) & (c).

11 ILO Minimum Age (Industry) Convention, 1919 (No.5).

12 International Labour Organization, Minimum Age Convention 1973 (No. 138).

13 International Labour Organization, Minimum Age (Sea) Convention 1920 (No. 7), International Labour Organization, Minimum Age (Agriculture) Convention 1921 (No. 10), International Labour Organization, Minimum Age (Trimmers and Stokers) Convention 1921 (No. 15), International Labour Organization, Minimum Age (Non-Industrial Employment) Convention 1932 (No. 33) revised in 1937 (No. 60), International Labour Organization, Minimum Age (Fisherman) Convention 1959 (No. 112), International Labour Organization and Minimum Age (Underground Work) Convention 1965 (No. 123) and *ibid.*

14 International Labour Organization, Minimum Age (Industry) Convention 1919 (No. 5). Revised 1948 (No. 90). It provides that no person under 18 years of age should be employed during the night with some exceptions for those aged 16 and over. This convention was ratified by 72 States. For more information on ratifications, see: <www.ilo.org/dyn/normlex/en/f?p=1000:11300:0::NO:11300:P11300_INSTRUMENT_ID:312150> accessed 28 January 2014.

15 *Ibid.*

16 Entered into force November 2000. International Labour Organization, Worst Forms of Child Labour Convention 1999 (No. 182).

17 International Labour Organization, Worst Forms of Child Labour Convention 1999 (No. 182), Article 1.

18 See: Yoshie Noguchi, '20 years of the Convention on the Rights of the Child and International Action against Child Labour' (2010) 18 *The International Journal of Children's Rights* 515.

19 The laws and policies around child labour had already been emerging at national levels, in particular in Britain. See: Education Act of 1918; International Labour Office, *Child Labour: A textbook for university students* (International Labour Organization 2004) 40; Children and Young Person's Act of 1933.

20 *Ibid.*

21 Declaration of the Rights of the Child 1924.

22 Marilyn Fleer, Marianne Hedegaard and Jonathan Tudge, 'Constructing childhood: global-local politics and practices' in Marilyn Fleer, Marianne Hedegaard and Jonathan Tudge (eds) *Childhood Studies and the Impact of Globalisation: Practices at Global and Local Levels* (Routledge 2009).

23 Declaration of the Rights of the Child 1959.

24 *Ibid.*

25 *Ibid.*

26 Antonio Cassese, *International Law* (2nd edn, OUP 2005) 321.

27 Universal Declaration of Human Rights 1948, Preamble, Article 26; Convention relating to the Status of Refugees 1951, Article 4.

28 Universal Declaration of Human Rights 1948, Preamble, Recital 1.
29 Convention relating to the Status of Refugees 1951, Article 1A(2).
30 See: Ann Quennerstedt, 'Balancing the rights of the child and the rights of the parents in the Convention on the rights of the child' (2009) 8 (2) *Journal of Human Rights* 162–176.
31 International Covenant on Civil and Political Rights, Adopted and opened for signature, ratification and accession by General Assembly resolution 2200A (XXI) of 16 December 1966 entry into force 23 March 1976.
32 International Covenant on Economic, Social and Cultural Rights, Adopted and opened for signature, ratification and accession by General Assembly resolution 2200A (XXI) of 16 December 1966 entry into force 3 January 1976.
33 Douglas Hodgson, 'The Historical Development and "Internationalisation" of the Children's Rights Movement' (1992) 6 *Australian Journal of Family Law* 25.
34 The remaining 13, largely, address enforcement measures.
35 UNICEF, 'Rights under the Convention on the Rights of the Child' (2014) <www.unicef.org/crc/index_30177.html> accessed 7 September 2016.
36 Jane Fortin, *Children's Rights and the Developing Law* (3rd edn, CUP 2009) 37.
37 UNICEF contended that these principles inform all rights generally in the CRC where applicable and relevant. UNICEF, 'Rights under the Convention on the Rights of the Child' <www.unicef.org/crc/index_30177.html> accessed 23 July 2016.
38 UNICEF considers Article 1 to be a general principle. <www.unicef.org/crc/files/Guiding_Principles.pdf> accessed 23 July 2016.
39 General Comment No. 5 (2003) General measures of implementation of the Convention on the Rights of the Child (arts 4, 42 and 44, para 6) para 12.
40 *Ibid*, Article 6.
41 *Ibid*, Article 24.
42 *Ibid*, Preamble, Recital 6.
43 *Ibid*, Article 30.
44 *Ibid*, Article 30.
45 *Ibid*, Article 27.
46 *Ibid*, Article 27.
47 *Ibid*, Article 28.
48 *Ibid*, Article 27.
49 *Ibid*, Article 30.
50 Universal Declaration of Human Rights 1948, Article 3.
51 General Comment No. 5 (2003) General measures of implementation of the Convention on the Rights of the Child (arts 4, 42 and 44, para 6) CRC/GC/2003/5 27 November 2003 para 12.
52 *Ibid*.
53 Wendy Stainton Rogers, 'Constructing Childhood, Constructing Child Concern' in Pam Foley et al. (eds), *Children in Society: Contemporary Theory, Policy and Practice* (Palgrave 2001). See Chapter 2.
54 See Michelle Foster, *International Refugee Law and Socio-Economic Rights: Refugee from Deprivation* (CUP 2007) and Chapter 6.
55 UNICEF, 'The Convention on the Rights of the Child: Survival and development rights: the basic rights to life, survival and development of one's full potential' <www.unicef.org/crc/files/Survival_Development.pdf> accessed 23 July 2016.
56 International Covenant on Economic, Social and Cultural Rights, Article 12.2(a) 2.
57 Convention on the Rights of the Child 1989, Article 24.2(a).
58 *Ibid*, Article 24.2(c).

59 *Ibid*, Article 24.3. Article 24 also requires States to work towards ensuring that parents and others have access to education to empower families to implement this Article.
60 *Ibid*, Article 23.1.
61 *Ibid*, Article 25.
62 United Nations High Commissioner for Refugees, *Guidelines on International Protection: Child Asylum Claims under Articles 1(A)2 and 1(F) of the 1951 Convention and 1967 Protocol relating to the Status of Refugees* HCR/GIP/09/08 22 December 2009 para 15.
63 *Ibid*, para 31.
64 Convention on the Rights of the Child 1989, Article 26.
65 *Ibid*, Article 27.
66 *Ibid*, Article 27.2.
67 John Locke, *First Treatises* (1689) <www.nlnrac.org/earlymodern/locke/documents/first-treatise-of-government> accessed 2 May 2014.
68 Yoshie Noguchi, 'ILO Convention No.182 on the worst forms of child labour and the Convention on the Rights of the Child' (2002) 10 *The International Journal of Children's Rights* 362.
69 United Nations High Commissioner for Refugees, 'Guidelines on International Protection: Child Asylum Claims under Articles 1(A)2 and 1(F) of the 1951 Convention and 1967 Protocol relating to the Status of Refugees' HCR/GIP/09/08 22 December 2009 11.
70 See: *Cheung v. Canada (Minister of Employment and Immigration)*, [1993] 2 F.C. 314, Canada: Federal Court of Appeal, 1 April 1993; *Chen Shi Hai* 201 C.L.R. 297.
71 See Chapter 2.
72 See, generally: United Nations, *The Millennium Development Goals Report, 2015* (United Nations 2015).
73 International Covenant on the Economic, Social and Cultural Rights 1966, Article 13.2.
74 Universal Declaration of Human Rights, Article 26.2.
75 International Covenant on the Economic, Social and Cultural Rights 1966, Article 13.3.
76 *Ibid*, Article 13.1.
77 Charter of the United Nations 1945; Universal Declaration of the Human Rights 1948; 1924 Declaration of the Rights of the Child; 1959 Declaration of the Rights of the Child; John Locke, *Some Thoughts Concerning Education* (1693) <www.bartleby.com/37/1/> accessed 23 August 2014; Jean-Jacques Rousseau, Émile, or, On Education (originally published in 1762) in Jean-Jacques Rousseau, *The Essential Writings of Jean-Jacques Rousseau* (Vintage 2013) 229–290. See Chapter 2.
78 Convention on the Rights of the Child 1989, Article 29.1.
79 *Ibid*, Article 31.
80 General Comment No. 17 *on the right of the child to rest, leisure, play, recreational activities, cultural life and the arts (art. 31);* See generally: Samantha Arnold, 'A Childhood Lost: Exploring the Right to Play in Direct Provision' (2013) 31 (10) *Irish Law Times.*
81 Convention on the Rights of the Child 1989, Article 4.
82 *D. [a minor] v Refugee Appeals Tribunal & Anor* [2011] IECH 431 at 24, since overturned by Supreme Court.
83 Brown v. Board of Education of Topeka 347 US 483 (1954) in *Ibid* at 18.
84 Universal Declaration of Human Rights 1948, Article 7; Convention on the Rights of the Child 1989, Preamble.

85 International Covenant on Civil and Political Rights 1966, Article 24; Convention on the Rights of the Child 1989, Preamble.
86 Convention on the Rights of the Child 1989, Article 2.
87 General Comment No. 5 (2003) General measures of implementation of the Convention on the Rights of the Child (arts 4, 42 and 44, para 6) CRC/GC/2003/5 27 November 2003 para 12.
88 Yoshie Noguchi, '20 years of the Convention on the Rights of the Child and International Action against Child Labour' (2010) 18 *The International Journal of Children's Rights* 517.
89 *Ibid*, 518–519.
90 See: International Labour Office, *Child Labour: A textbook for university students* (International Labour Organization 2004).
91 Clark Nardinelli, *Child Labor and the Industrial Revolution* (Bloomington 1990).
92 Yoshie Noguchi, '20 years of the Convention on the Rights of the Child and International Action against Child Labour' (2010) 18 *The International Journal of Children's Rights* 518–519.
93 International Covenant on Civil and Political Rights 1966, Article 8.
94 International Covenant on the Economic, Social and Cultural Rights 1966, Article 10.
95 Convention on the Rights of the Child 1989, Article 32.
96 UNICEF, *Implementation Handbook for the Convention on the Rights of the Child* (3rd edn, UNICEF 2007).
97 Yoshie Noguchi, '20 years of the Convention on the Rights of the Child and International Action against Child Labour' (2010) 18 *The International Journal of Children's Rights* 518–519.
98 Entered into force November 2000. International Labour Organization, Worst Forms of Child Labour Convention 1999 (No. 182).
99 International Labour Organization, Worst Forms of Child Labour Convention 1999 (No. 182), Article 1.
100 *Ibid*, Article 3.
101 For more information: Yoshie Noguchi, '20 years of the Convention on the Rights of the Child and International Action against Child Labour' (2010) 18 *The International Journal of Children's Rights* 520.
102 *Ibid*.
103 *Ibid* 533.
104 International Labour Organization, Worst Forms of Child Labour Convention 1999 (No. 182), Article 19.
105 Yoshie Noguchi, '20 years of the Convention on the Rights of the Child and International Action against Child Labour' (2010) 18 *The International Journal of Children's Rights* 518–519.
106 Convention on the Rights of the Child 1989, Article 36.
107 International Labour Organization, Worst Forms of Child Labour Convention 1999 (No. 182), Preamble.
108 *Ibid*, Article 3(b).
109 Convention on the Rights of the Child 1989, Article 34.
110 *Ibid*, Article 34.
111 Optional Protocol to the Convention on the Rights of the Child on the sale of children, child prostitution and child pornography adopted and opened for signature, ratification and accession by General Assembly resolution A/RES/54/263 of 25 May 2000 entered into force on 18 January 2002.
112 Optional protocols are treaties themselves. They are open to signature, accession or ratification. See: UNICEF, 'Advancing the CRC' <www.unicef.org/crc/

index_protocols.html> accessed 24 July 2016.
113 Optional Protocol to the Convention on the Rights of the Child on the sale of children, child prostitution and child pornography 2000, Preamble, Recital 9.
114 *Bian v. Canada (Minister for Citizenship and Immigration)*, IMM-1640-00, 11 Dec. 2000, para 46. See Chapter 6.
115 Convention on the Rights of the Child 1989, Article 11.
116 Convention on the Rights of the Child 1989, Article 33.
117 See: Michele Voss, 'Young and Marked for Death: Expanding the Definition of 'Particular Social Group' in 'Asylum Law to Include Youth Victims of Gang Persecution' (2005) *Rutgers Law Journal* 37 325; Jacqueline Bhabha, *Child Migration and Human Rights in a Global Age* (PUP 2014) 233; Jacqueline Bhabha and Wendy Young, 'Not Adults in Miniature: Unaccompanied Child Asylum Seekers and the New U.S. Guidelines' (1999) 11 (1) *International Journal of Refugee Law*.
118 Convention on the Rights of the Child 1989, Article 38.
119 10 U.S. Code § 505 – Regular components: qualifications, term, grade (a).
120 ForcesWatch, 'The recruitment of under 18s into the UK armed forces' <www.parliament.uk/documents/joint-committees/human-rights/Briefing_from_Forces_Watch_age_of_recruitment.pdf> accessed 24 July 2016.
121 CIA World Factbook, 'South Korea Military service age and obligation' (CIA 2015) <www.cia.gov/library/publications/the-world-factbook/fields/2024.html> accessed 24 July 2016; Canada: Immigration and Refugee Board of Canada, *Israel: Military service, including age of recruitment, length of service, grounds for exemption, and availability of alternative service (March 2009–January 2013)*, 13 February 2013 <www.refworld.org/docid/5152beb62.ht> accessed 24 July 2016.
122 Optional Protocol to the Convention on the Rights of the Child on Children in Armed Conflict Adopted and opened for signature, ratification and accession by General Assembly resolution A/RES/54/263 of 25 May 2000 entered into force on 18 January 2002.
123 See: Mathew Happold, 'Excluding Children from Refugee Status Child Soldiers and Article 1F of the Refugee Convention' (2002) *American University International Law Review* 17 (6) 1131.
124 See: David Rosen, 'Child Soldiers, International Humanitarian Law, and the Globalization of Childhood' (2007) *American Anthropologist* 109 (2) 296.
125 See: Mathew Happold, 'Excluding Children from Refugee Status: Child Soldiers and Article 1F of the Refugee Convention' (2002) *American University International Law Review* 17 (6) 1131; United Nations High Commissioner for Refugees on Child-Soldiers, reprinted in Refugee Law in Context: the Exclusion Clause 43, 44 (stating that "[t]he exclusion clauses do not distinguish between adults and minors").
126 UNICEF, *Child Marriage and the Law: Legislative Reform Initiative Paper Series* (UNICEF 2008).
127 United Nations High Commissioner for Refugees, 'Guidelines on International Protection: Child Asylum Claims under Articles 1(A)2 and 1(F) of the 1951 Convention and 1967 Protocol relating to the Status of Refugees' HCR/GIP/09/08 22 December 2009.
128 Convention on the Elimination of all Forms of Discrimination Against Women 1979, Article 16.2.
129 Convention on the Rights of the Child 1989, Article 24.
130 *Ibid*, Article 37.
131 Convention against Torture and Other Cruel, Inhuman or Degrading Treatment or Punishment Adopted and opened for signature, ratification and

accession by General Assembly resolution 39/46 of 10 December 1984 entry into force 26 June 1987, in accordance with article 27 (1).

132 Universal Declaration of Human Rights 1948, Article 5 No one shall be subjected to torture or to cruel, inhuman or degrading treatment or punishment.

133 International Covenant on Civil and Political Rights 1966, Article 7 No one shall be subjected to torture or to cruel, inhuman or degrading treatment or punishment. In particular, no one shall be subjected without his free consent to medical or scientific experimentation.

134 See, for example the analysis in James Hathaway, *The Rights of Refugees under International Law* (CUP 2005) 305–306.

135 United Nations High Commissioner for Refugees, 'Guidelines on International Protection: Child Asylum Claims under Articles 1(A)2 and 1(F) of the 1951 Convention and 1967 Protocol relating to the Status of Refugees' HCR/GIP/09/08 22 December 2009 para 33.

136 *Matter of Juan Carlos Martinez-Mejia* A 76 312 250, 5–6 (BIA 20 January 1999).

137 Jens Qvortrup, Marjatta Bardy, Giovanni Sgritta and Helmut Wintersberger (eds) *Childhood Matters. Social Theory, Practice and Politics* (Avenbury 1994); Allison James and Adrian James, *Constructing Childhood. Theory, Policy and Social Practice* (Palgrave Macmillan, 2004); Allison James, Chris Jenks and Alan Prout, *Theorising Childhood* (Polity Press 1998) 235.

138 See, for example: Richard Farson, *Birthrights* (Macmillan 1974); John Holt, *Escape from Childhood: The Needs and Rights of Childhood* (Dutton 1974); Ann Quennerstedt, 'Balancing the rights of the child and the rights of the parents in the Convention on the rights of the child' (2009) 8 (2) *Journal of Human Rights* 162–176.

139 The Comprehensive Child Development Bill of 1971, which outlined children's basic rights to health care, education, nutrition and development, cleared the Senate, but was vetoed by President Nixon as he suggested that the bill would weaken the family structure. See: H.R. 6748, 92d Cong., 1st Sess. (1971) in Rosalind Rosenberg, *Divided Lives: American Women in the Twentieth Century* (Hill and Wang 1992); Cynthia Lightfoot et al., *The Development of Children* (7th edn, Macmillan 2005).

140 See, for example: Kate Bacon and Sam Frankel, 'Rethinking Children's Citizenship: Negotiating Structure, Shaping Meanings' (2014) 22 *IJCR* 22; David Archard, *Children: Rights and Childhood* (2nd edn, Routledge 2004); Allison James and Adrian James, *Key Concepts in Childhood Studies* (Sage 2008).

141 *Ibid.*

142 Jane Fortin, *Children's Rights and the Developing Law* (3rd edn, CUP 2009).

143 Nessa Lynch, 'Restorative Justice through a Children's Rights Lens' (2010) 18 *IJCR* 161; Kingsley Davis, 'The Child and the Social Structure' (1940) 14 (4) *The Journal of Educational Psychology* 217: 'an individual's most important functions for society are performed when he is fully adult, not when he is immature'.

144 Geraldine van Bueren, *The International Law on the Rights of the Child* (Martinus Nijhoff Publishers 1998) 21; Michael Freeman, *A Commentary on the United Nations Convention on the Rights of the Child* (Martinus Nijhoff Publishers 2007) 16.

145 See: Sarah Joseph and Melissa Castan, *The International Covenant on Civil and Political Rights – Cases, Materials and Commentary* (3rd edn, OUP 2013) 35. See also: Chapter 2.

146 Convention on the Rights of the Child 1989, Articles 17.

147 *Ibid*, Article 8.

148 *Ibid*, Article 13.

149 *Ibid*, Article 14.
150 *Ibid*, Article 15.
151 *Ibid*, Article 30
152 *Ibid*, Article 16.1.
153 *Ibid*, Article 12.
154 *Ibid*, Article 13.
155 Convention on the Rights of the Child 1989, Article 3.1.
156 General Comment No. 5 (2003) General measures of implementation of the Convention on the Rights of the Child (arts. 4, 42 and 44, para. 6) para 12. See also: General Comment No. 14 (2013) on the right of the child to have his or her best interests taken as a primary consideration (art. 3, para. 1) CRC/C/GC/14.
157 Jane Fortin, *Children's Rights and the Developing Law* (3rd edn, CUP 2009) 38.
158 Convention on the Rights of the Child 1989, Article 3.2.
159 See: Samantha Arnold, Martine Goeman and Katja Fournier, *Durable Solutions for Separated Children in Europe, National Report: Ireland* (Irish Refugee Council 2015) 51.
160 Jacqueline Bhabha, *Child Migration and Human Rights in a Global Age* (PUP 2014) 207.
161 See, for example: Ciara Smyth, *European Asylum Law and the Rights of the Child* (Routledge 2014).
162 UNICEF and United Nations High Commissioner for Human Rights Regional Office for Europe, *Judicial Implementation of Article 3 of the Convention on the Rights of the Child in Europe: The case of migrant children including unaccompanied children* (UNICEF and United Nations Human Rights Office of the High Commissioner 2012).
163 See, for example: UNICEF and United Nations High Commissioner for Human Rights Regional Office for Europe, *Judicial Implementation of Article 3 of the Convention on the Rights of the Child in Europe: The case of migrant children including unaccompanied children* (UNICEF and United Nations Human Rights Office of the High Commissioner 2012); Ciara Smyth, *European Asylum Law and the Rights of the Child* (Routledge 2014).
164 Sharon Detrick, *A Commentary on the United Nations Convention on the Rights of the Child* (Martinus Nijhoff 1999) 89.
165 General Comment No. 5 (2003) General measures of implementation of the Convention on the Rights of the Child (arts. 4, 42 and 44, para. 6) para 12.
166 Convention on the Rights of the Child 1989, Article 12.
167 See Chapter 2.
168 *Ibid*, Article 16.3.
169 Ann Quennerstedt, 'Children's Rights Research Moving into the Future – Challenges on the Way Forward' (2013) 21 *International Journal of Children's Rights* 233.
170 Henry Foster, *A 'Bill of Rights' for Children* (Thomas 1974); Beatrice Gross and Ronald Gross, *Introduction to the Children's Rights Movement: Overcoming the Oppression of Young People* (Anchor Books 1977).
171 John Bennet, 'Supporting Family Responsibility for the Rights of the Child: An education viewpoint' (1996) 4 (1) *International Journal of Children's Rights* 45–56.
172 John Bennet, 'Supporting Family Responsibility for the Rights of the Child: An education viewpoint' (1996) 4 (1) *International Journal of Children's Rights* 45–56; Martha Minow, 'What Ever Happened to Children's Rights' (1995–1996) 80 *Minnesota Law Review* 267.
173 Convention on the Rights of the Child 1989, Preamble, Recital 5.

174 *Ibid*, Article 5.
175 *Ibid*, Article 91.
176 *Ibid*, Article 12.1.
177 *Ibid*, Article 9.
178 Universal Declaration of Human Rights 1948, Article 14.
179 *Ibid*, Article 22.

4 Children in the development of refugee law

Abstract

This chapter moves on to discussions on the development of refugee law and examines its historical evolution. It looks in particular at the extent children were considered during the drafting and in the publication of refugee arrangements/treaties and initiatives over the years. This analysis informs discussions on the children's rights approach in Chapter 5. The purpose of this chapter is to also provide background information on general refugee law and its development to inform subsequent and more detailed discussions on its relationship with children's rights law. This chapter draws out where children were considered in the historical development of refugee law.

Introduction

A children's rights approach to refugee law is not a modern innovation it is rooted in early international human rights law. Efforts to protect children at a global level were on the human rights agenda from the 1920s. Reflecting human rights efforts, rights regimes emerged in the areas of fundamental rights and freedoms[1] including social and economic rights,[2] and children's rights[3] during and following World War I. At the same time, various initiatives to deal with displacement, as a result of various conflicts, in particular in Europe, and fallen empires,[4] also emerged. Three distinct areas of international law emerged during this time: children's rights, human rights (fundamental rights, including social and economic rights) and migrant rights, reflected in bilateral and multilateral initiatives and agreements.

There is evidence that indicates that the areas mentioned here influenced each other. However, there is also evidence to suggest that pre-Convention on the Rights of the Child (CRC) children's rights did not influence human rights and refugee law in the same way that human rights law and refugee law, for example, influenced each other. This becomes most apparent when examining contemporary law. For example, the Convention relating to the Status of Refugees (Refugee Convention),[5] which was adopted by the United Nations (UN) General Assembly in 1951, includes contributions from human rights law. In addition to being the foremost treaty in respect of refugee law, it also provides for numerous human rights including social and economic rights applicable to those recognised as refugees, indicating that the Refugee Convention was influenced by the Universal Declaration of Human Rights (UDHR). Children's rights during this time, however, remained siloed.

The children's rights movement discussed in Chapter 2, made important contributions and heavily influenced the CRC. As Chapter 3 showed, the first drafting of an international treaty on the rights of the child began in 1924. There were very few initiatives targeting children and no international legal provisions specifically targeting children in relation to refugee situations between the 1920s and the 1950s, when refugee law was developing and when Europe was at war. The initiatives that did target children were *ad hoc*, limited and infrequent. Not much changed between 1951, when the Refugee Convention was adopted, and 1989, when the CRC was adopted. The CRC, which inspired development and expansion in children's rights law all over the world, including in international law, did impact upon children in refugee situations. However, aside from soft law guidance and case law, very little changed by way of a targeted approach to child refugee law. This chapter looks at the historical trajectory of children in refugee law, identifying where children's rights were considered in refugee discourse and law. It also discusses where the potential need of international protection was considered in the children's rights discourse and law up until the adoption of the Refugee Convention. Analysing the historical and contemporary debates and dialogues occurring in the space between children's rights law and refugee law provides a foundation for the promotion of a children's rights approach.

Children and the beginnings of international human rights law (pre-1951)

International laws have grown and expanded to meet new challenges in maintaining global peace and security. One of the ways it expanded was to seek to ensure all human beings have access to fundamental rights and freedoms wherever they might live.[6] The overarching regime of international law and the object and purpose of individual treaties, provide useful insights into the interpretation of the refugee paradigm as well as the children's rights paradigm. In order to understand the development of the children's rights and refugee regimes, it is necessary to look back at the relevant developments in international law, generally and in brief, and how those developments influence the way we interpret modern refugee law. This section therefore looks at the early developments of international refugee law, which looks specifically at the possibility of a children's rights approach to the interpretation of refugee law.

The creation of a system of international laws was built upon notions of cooperation and peace among States, while respecting the principle of statehood.[7] Nineteenth century international law, for example, the Hague Conventions, referred only to rules of warfare and not to the fundamental rights and everyday freedoms of people.[8] Although people were in some ways the beneficiaries of the rules of war, they were not the focus of the law. The focus was peace and cooperation among States.[9]

The State is the principal actor in the protection and promotion of all rights, including those considered 'human rights' in modern notions of statehood.[10] Equally, prior to the twentieth century, human rights or fundamental freedoms were largely considered within national frameworks, such as, the Magna Carta[11] and the constitutions that followed in common law countries.[12]

The shift to internationalise human rights occurred in response to the significant number of casualties in World War I.[13] The cost suffered by the human race during the nearly 4.5-year war encouraged world leaders to act to ensure this loss of life, which reached over 16 million, including 7 million civilians, never happened again.[14] World War I and later World War II left regions of the world and individual States in disarray. It was this and the discovery of actions during the wars and between the two wars that sparked widespread debate on the responsibility of the world to respond to situations of crisis, including in respect of children.

The League of Nations was established during the 1919 Paris Peace Conference, which ended World War I.[15] The remit of the League of Nations surrounded maintaining peace through negotiations and arbitration at the international level (in addition to disarmament and developing an approach to collective security).[16] The Covenant of the League of Nations represented a turning point in international law. The Covenant established an agreement among nations to not only work towards peace and security between countries,[17] but to also work towards maintaining a certain standard of living for citizens within each country participating in the League of Nations.[18] This was the first example in modern international law where individuals were acknowledged as having certain fundamental rights, including children (discussed in Chapter 3). The responsibility to ensure access to those rights was attributed to the State.

The Charter of the UN, published in 1945, the year World War II came to an end, set the scene for an elaboration of human rights, in general terms.[19] The UN replaced the dissolved League of Nations.[20] The Charter introduced human rights themes to serve as part of the foundation of UN membership.[21] With this in mind, in 1945, the UN began working towards drafting a 'Bill of Rights'.[22] The UDHR[23] was the first instrument produced by the Commission and was adopted on 10 December 1948.[24] The publication of the UDHR was the first step in setting a global standard for human rights.[25] The UN drafted this document in the hopes that the suffering experienced by the human race during (and prior to) World War II was never repeated.[26] The UDHR specifically mentioned the right to seek refuge.[27] Article 14.1 states that 'Everyone has the right to seek and to enjoy in other countries asylum from persecution'.[28] Children were not mentioned in this provision. Children were, in fact, not extensively referred to in the treaty. We may assume, however, that Article 14 applies to children as the rights in the UDHR apply to 'all members of the human family'.[29] Children were nevertheless relatively invisible in mainstream human rights discourse, including with respect to refuge, up to this point. This was not out of kilter with the wider societal perceptions of children up to the 1980s – invisibility was a key feature in society as well.

However, also during this time, the children's rights regime was developing in response to growing dialogue on the lived experiences of children worldwide. The first articulation of children's rights was published in 1924, the (non-binding) Declaration of the Rights of the Child. In 1946, the UN International Children's Emergency Fund (UNICEF) was established. This Fund became a permanent part of the UN during World War II. It provided food, healthcare and clothing to children experiencing starvation and suffering from disease.[30] UNICEF began working at the outset to eradicate disease in children while beginning to look towards introducing global laws to further protect children.[31] During this period, one can surmise that UNICEF took a strict protectionist and paternalistic approach to children's rights, focused almost exclusively on survival. The evidence during this period suggests that these developments did not significantly impact upon developments in mainstream human rights and refugee law, as discussed above.

Beginnings of refugee law

The expansion in international law to focus on human rights and freedoms helped pave the way for a singular convention on refugee protection as the developments during and in the aftermath of the world wars were responding not only to rights violations, but also to mass displacement in the context of the Cold War.[32] Both human rights and refugee law developed in response to both the harm experienced by people in their home countries and those forced to flee and left displaced. The topic of children and their protection was also at the fore, albeit in a separate sphere to mainstream human rights, during this time; a time marked by the establishment of Save the Children[33] and UNICEF.[34]

Even prior to World Wars I and II the global community suffered large displacement as a result of land demarcation following the fall of vast empires that governed Europe and Asia; for example, the Roman Empire or, more recently, the Ottoman Empire.[35] During periods where States changed hands or where land borders were renegotiated, people were displaced or re-homed based on race, ethnicity and geography and some were left stateless.[36] During and in the aftermath of World War I, peoples were already displaced *en masse* as a result of the formation of new States emerging out of the Caucasus and the Balkans.[37] In the years after the Great War it was estimated that there were more than 9 million refugees and 20 million internally displaced persons in Europe.[38] National responses were reactive and inconsistent in responding to large numbers of displaced persons. Among those, persons were left stateless and without access to rights afforded citizens in the countries in which they found themselves or the countries that had been established around them – making them foreigners in their own home. This time was characterised by States differentiating between the rights of citizens and the rights of non-citizens and the creation of systematic barriers to immigration. States were reasserting the importance of borders.[39] The beginning of refugee law therefore corresponded with the development of the modern State.

Hathaway's analysis of the early development of refugee law identified areas of rights that influenced the modern refugee regime. The first area of rights related to the development of aliens' rights. Aliens' rights initiatives, typically characterised by bilateral agreements, sought to establish a balance between the maintenance of borders and allowing movement of tradesmen.[40] Hathaway argued that, despite not relating to refugees specifically,[41] this rights regime introduced a number of themes relevant to the development of refugee law. Firstly, persons outside their country of origin had certain vulnerabilities. Secondly, States were subject to scrutiny from other States. Thirdly, States could provide rights in surrogate. These developments provided ways in which States could work together through bilateral agreements in an effort to ensure access to rights to individuals crossing borders.[42]

The second area of rights, identified by Hathaway, which related to the development of refugee law were those that developed around minority rights contained within the Minority Treaties introduced by the League of Nations after World War I.[43] The Treaties placed obligations on 'defeated' States to respect ethnic and religious minorities.[44] Hathaway described the subjects of the treaties as 'foreign citizens'.[45] In the aftermath of World War I, the Council of the League of Nations was set up to oversee adherence to the Minority Treaties. This was the first example of a collective response and oversight towards the protection of minorities.[46] The principal aim of this regime, and that relating to aliens, remained to avoid disturbing the peace and security of the international community.[47] However, individuals were also the beneficiaries of the treaties. The Minority Treaties also brought ethnic and religious themes to the fore, which still form part of the modern refugee framework.

During this time, progress was also made specific to refugees. In 1921, the League of Nations appointed the first High Commissioner for [Russian] Refugees, Dr Fridtjof Nansen.[48] The first example of a multilateral agreement towards protecting refugees was created in 1922 by Dr Nansen, the 'Nansen Passports'. These passports served as identity documents for categories of stateless persons, aimed at those forced to leave Russia,[49] to enable them to travel and avail of some of the rights they were unable to access when they were 'undocumented'.[50] This system did not define refugees in any concrete way, but it was the first global initiative with characteristics of international refugee law. Hathaway argued that this phase represented a period where States wanted to address the 'legal anomaly' that this situation presented.[51] This was in response to the concern that the presence of 'unauthorised' persons could potentially have a destabilising effect both socially and legally within their borders.[52]

The League of Nations subsequently introduced the Agreements of 31 May 1924, 12 May 1926 and 30 June 1928. All of which also dealt with 'categories' of refugees.[53] The 1926 Arrangement provided a definition of refugees with Russian and Armenian[54] origins based on their lack of recognition and protection from the Russian or Turkish Republic governments, respectively.[55] New categories or groups were added as crises arose.[56] The category or group approach provided a definition, which sought to protect people from a 'recognised' group who were outside of their country of origin without the protection of the government of their country of origin.[57] The Arrangements did not address the matter of children substantively.[58] However, that may not be surprising as the Agreements did not provide definitions beyond identifying categories of persons needing protection, rather than attempting to provide a definition that would allow for a more individualised approach. It is possible to assume that the Arrangements included children in the same way that they included adults, but that they were not referred to specifically and were perhaps assumed to form part of the family unit rather than a separate category of persons needing special protection.

In response to growing instability in Europe and the realisation that the refugee problem was not going to correct itself (coupled with frustrations arising from the *ad hoc* and piecemeal Nansen Arrangements),[59] the League of Nations produced the Convention relating to the International Status of Refugees, of 28 October 1933.[60] The 1933 Convention still referred to categories of peoples fearing persecution. The definition also provided that the refugee must have been outside of their country of origin and without the protection of that State.[61] The 1933 Convention was the first attempt to codify refugee law as binding international law, though only nine countries signed it.[62] The 1933 Convention built on the 1928 Arrangement and also introduced the idea of *non-refoulement*, or the principle of protecting victims, or potential victims of persecution, from forced return to face persecution.[63] The 1933 Convention aimed to combat States' failure to adequately respond to refugee crises during the lifetimes of the previous arrangements.[64] In addition, the 1933 Convention, like its predecessor, provided some social and economic rights associated with being recognised as a refugee.

Also during this period, a time marked by uncertainty within the League of Nations as to the future of the refugee mandate, the Nansen International Office was established to facilitate 'agreements that have been made for the benefit of refugees'. This work was to continue for a period of 10 years.[65]

The large number of persons fleeing Germany led to additional and revised treaties, including the Provisional Arrangement concerning the Status of Refugees coming from Germany of 4 June 1936[66] and the 1938 Convention concerning the Status of Refugees[67] coming from Germany. The 1938 Convention provided the following definition:

> (a) Persons possessing or having possessed German nationality and not possessing any other nationality who are proved not to enjoy, in law or in fact, the protection of the German Government. (b) Stateless persons not covered by previous conventions or agreements who have left German territory after being established therein and who are proved not to enjoy, in law or in fact, the protection of the German Government.[68]

It was reviewed and expanded in 1943, in the midst of World War II. The definition was expanded to include:

> all persons, wherever they may be, who, as a result of events in Europe, have had to leave, or may have to leave, their country of residence because of the danger to their lives or liberties on account of their race, religion or political beliefs.[69]

After World War II, this definition continued to evolve. Sir Guy Goodwin-Gill and Jane McAdam described this shift as a move from the group approach to a perspective that was 'apparently more closed and legalistic'.[70] Evidence of this can be found in the Constitution that governed the new International Refugee Organization (IRO) (the predecessor of the UN Refugee Agency) during its period of operation between 1946 and 1952,[71] and also within the Refugee Convention itself. The IRO relied upon pre-existing definitions of refugees while adding to the categories those affected by Nazi and Fascist movements and persons of Jewish origin, for example. Additionally, the IRO continued to recognise those considered refugees prior to World War II for reasons of race, religion, nationality or political opinion. The IRO specified that a refugee was someone who was unable or unwilling to avail themselves of the protection of the government of their country of origin.[72]

The work of the IRO also included displaced persons, including those forcibly moved from their country to enter into forced labour.[73] International labour law had at this point already produced treaties that targeted children as labourers requiring protection, as discussed in the previous chapter. It is therefore conceivable that children could have at least in theory benefited from the IRO's approach, if they were moved to another country for the purposes of labour exploitation. The constitution of the IRO was the first legal instrument to mention children (discussed below).

The IRO relocated 1 million Europeans in the aftermath of World War II. At the same time, states began to realise that refugees could not be repatriated. States responded by pushing for greater control over their own systems of providing refuge.[74] Additionally, the realisation that those who had been resettled would not be returning brought renewed focus to the social and economic rights of refugees.[75] This phase in the development of refugee law was 'characterised by the fact that the refugees would need to lead an independent life in the long-term in the countries that gave them shelter'.[76] The gap between human rights law and refugee law thus began to narrow.

Refugee law has evolved since the 1920s in a number of ways. There was a move away from the category approach to a more individualised approached to those considered refugees. The category approach was focused on short-term and reactive responses to emerging conflicts and mass displacement. In addition, and as a result of displacement, States began to re-assert introduce more border interventions, leading to legal separations between citizens and non-citizens. Two other significant developments occurred. Firstly, the Minority Treaties drew attention to the difficulties faced by ethnic and religious minorities and provided a framework for States to adhere to in order to ensure those minorities had access to basic social and economic rights. Secondly, the international community began to recognise that refugees were not always able to return to their countries of origin or residence and thus needed access to some social and economic rights afforded to the citizens of the host country. No legal developments in the area of refuge up to this point or the tangential areas of law that impacted upon the development of refugee law dealt with children specifically, with the exception of one reference in the constitution of the IRO, discussed below.

The historical trajectory of children in the refugee paradigm

Although the drafters of the Refugee Convention did not include any provisions relating to children's rights or the qualification of children as refugees specifically, this was not a reflection of the times. As outlined in the previous chapter, children's rights were and had been developing internationally before and during the drafting of the Refugee Convention. In fact, the international children's rights movement[77] had its origins in conflicts occurring before World War I. It continued to gain momentum during World War I, in the interwar period, into World War II and beyond.[78] The movement depicted children during this period as disproportionately affected by war and requiring protection from indiscriminate violence, starvation and disease.[79] The first output of the movement in international law was the 1924 Declaration of the Rights of the Child published under the auspices of the League of Nations, followed by a revised and expanded version in 1959 published under the auspices of the UN.[80] Neither document referred to the child's right to refuge, but acknowledged that children, internationally, needed protection from the hardships of war, conflict and also poverty, more generally. The 1924 Declaration asserted that 'mankind owes to the Child the best that it has to give', implying that the world community had a collective, or shared, responsibility to ensure children received adequate protection.

These developments and the assertion that children needed special protection and assistance did not, however, appear to influence the Refugee Convention. There remained a dichotomy in international law. Leading up to the drafting of the Refugee Convention there were nevertheless examples of children specifically benefitting from international protection through initiatives such as the *Kindertransport* (Children's Transport) (discussed below).[81] The *transport* and the 1924 Declaration indicated that governments and inter-governmental organisations recognised that children required international protection decades before the drafting of the Refugee Convention.

In the area of international children's rights law, one underlying trend emerged: children were seen as persons requiring protection. Goodwin-Gill highlighted the fact that the 1924 Declaration was drafted and submitted to the League of Nations in response to the problems faced by refugee children.[82] In 1919, five years prior to the publication of the Declaration, the International Labour Organization (ILO) drafted legislation establishing minimum standards to protect children in the labour force, including establishing a minimum age. Additionally, children and their specific protection needs were referred to in the Covenant of the League of Nations. There was therefore, an awareness around the need to protect children. It would stand to reason that this would have impacted upon the early development of modern refugee law, which began in earnest in 1921. However, as discussed above, this was not the case.

Earlier discussions showed that no refugee treaty or administrative arrangement mentioned the right of the child to seek refugee protection. Nevertheless, other child-specific initiatives emerged. Prior to 1939, for example, the UK had allowed entry for 471 German children between 1936 and 1938[83] and 3,800 children from the Basque region in Spain.[84] During World War I, the UK also allowed entry for several thousand Belgian children.[85]

The most prominent and well-known development in refugee law emerged in 1938, which highlighted the international community's concern for child refugees – the *Kindertransport*. It took place between 1938 and 1940.[86] This initiative was undertaken by private refugee organisations with approval from the government of the UK who waived the requirement to present passports and visas.[87] The *Kindertransport* was a name given to the British government's initiative to allow children to enter Great Britain from Germany (and annexed territories) on temporary travel visas. This initiative followed *Kristallnacht* (Night of the Broken Glass) on 9–10 November 1938.[88] The aim of the *Kindertransport* was to provide temporary safe haven to children under the age of 17 until such time as it was safe to return to their home to be cared for by their parents and families. The children travelled alone to Great Britain. The last transport left Germany 1 September 1939 just as World War II began. The last transport left the Netherlands 14 May 1940 when the Dutch surrendered to the German invasion. The *Kindertransport* brought 9,000–10,000 children to Great Britain, 7,500 of whom were Jewish.[89]

The 1946 Constitution of the IRO also included orphans less than 16 years of age as a category of refugee:[90] 'children who were war orphans or whose parents had disappeared'.[91] This conceptualisation was based on concern for child survivors of World War II.[92] This stream of refugee beneficiaries did not continue into the modern framework, at least as articulated in law. Although this category was never included in any of the multilateral treaties, including the Refugee Convention, it was nevertheless an indication of the recognition that children may require refugee protection.

These examples indicate that child refugees were persons of concern to the world community during and after World War II. However, they were not considered in mainstream refugee law discourse, beyond the singular mention in the IRO Constitution. However, due to the categorical nature of refugee law prior to 1951, one could suppose that drafters merely identified the group of persecuted persons, rather than specifying that the law applied to individuals, such as men, woman and/or children. It is also possible that children were seen as dependents in applications from the head-of-household protection-seekers and that this was perhaps why the only mention of children in the IRO Constitution provided for the protection of orphaned children.

Modern refugee law under the United Nations

The Office of the United Nations High Commissioner for Refugees (UNHCR) succeeded the IRO in December 1950 after the dissolution of the League of Nations.[93] The Refugee Convention undertook to incorporate past League of Nations arrangements and expanded upon them to reflect lessons learned from World War II as set out in the Statute of the UNHCR.[94] The Statute was informed by Article 14 of the UDHR, which provided the right to all persons to 'seek and enjoy asylum in countries other than their own'.[95] The Refugee Convention, which entered into force in 1954, was thus meant to serve as a full-length treaty to give effect to Article 14. It also established the agency as a non-political entity with the principal aim of providing international protection and to find 'permanent solutions for the problem of refugees'.[96] The original remit included working on behalf of those identified as refugees by previous treaties and arrangements and those who were determined refugees due to events occurring before 1 January 1951 and outside of their country of origin 'owing to a well-founded fear of being persecuted'[97] or, in accordance with the 1938 Convention, 'for reasons other than personal convenience'.[98]

In 1967, the Refugee Convention was revised in accordance with the 1967 New York Protocol relating to the Status of Refugees in order to remove the temporal and geographical limitations relating to the qualification of refugees. The shorthand 'Refugee Convention' is used to mean the Refugee Convention as amended by the 1967 Protocol throughout. The revised definition encompassed the original and expanded it to define the refugee as a person:

> who is outside the country of his nationality, or if he has no nationality, the country of his former habitual residence, because he has or had a well-founded fear of persecution by reasons of his race, religion, nationality or political opinion and is unable or, because of such fear, is unwilling to avail himself of the protection of the government of the country of his nationality, or, if he has no nationality, to return to the country of his former habitual residence.[99]

Refugee protection, whether for adults, or children (though not explicitly referred to in the definition) is provided to persons who: (1) are outside of their country of origin, (2) can not or are unwilling to seek the protection of their country or place of residence and (3) have a well-founded fear of persecution with a link to one of the five convention grounds. This definition does not contain any temporal, geographical or categorical limitations. This expansion was the key feature of the new agency.[100] Refugee determination became individualised, meaning the refugee applicant must show that they are individually at risk of persecution. This requirement presumably also applies to children. In this case, children must be conceived of as subjects of rights in the context of refuge to be able to avail of protection. Yet, the Refugee Convention does not articulate the right of the child to seek, or qualify for, protection.

The Refugee Convention was drafted during the Cold War and civil and political rights were to the fore. The invisibility of children within the Refugee Convention may therefore be consistent with the views of Locke and others and the findings in more recent literature on children's rights as discussed in Chapter 2 in that children were not (and often are still not) considered to be able to or eligible to access civil and political rights. This is revisited in Chapter 6 in the context of children and the intersection between civil and political rights and refugee law.

Children's rights were developing during this same time. The first draft of the 1959 Declaration on the Rights of the Child, which was submitted to the League of Nations in 1942, referred specifically to refugee children (although this did not make it into the final declaration).[101] Yet, these developments did not trickle into the early developments in international refugee law.

The Refugee Convention does not specifically refer to children as potential recipients of international protection. The Convention heavily references human rights principles and logic would suggest that children's rights, which were published decades later, also form part of a contemporary interpretation of the treaty based on the existing relationship between refugee law and human rights law. However, this applies mostly in the context of rights that flow from a grant of refugee protection. This is revisited in Chapter 5.

In July 1951, when the draft convention was finalised, the ILO, IRO, the Council of Europe and a number of non-governmental organisations, including two children's charities, were represented.[102] However, none of the above had voting rights; they were invited as observers. During the drafting of the Refugee Convention, the U.S. delegation proposed the inclusion of an 'unaccompanied children' category. The category would apply to the unaccompanied child who is

> sixteen years or under who is a war orphan, or whose parents have disappeared, who is unable or unwilling to avail himself of the protection of the government of his country of nationality, or former nationality, and who has not acquired another nationality.[103]

This category was not included as its continued relevance post World War II came into question. There were also concerns raised around undermining the role of the guardian in respect of war orphans.[104]

The Refugee Convention, which remains the cornerstone of international law relating to refuge, does not specifically mention children as potential persons requiring protection or any children's rights as emphasised throughout this section. This book asks, however, whether the convention is nevertheless capable of including children within the scope of the definition of refugee. Every indication points to the continued relevance and capacity of the Refugee Convention to encompass a wide variety of human rights and children's rights violations as potential acts of persecution. This is discussed in the next two chapters.

Considering these insights, it is possible to suggest that the protection of children was important in the development of international laws. However, these insights also indicate a reluctance to include children's rights in any primary international legal document – children's rights remained siloed. Chapter 2 discussed the sociological development of children, drawing further conclusions as to why mainstream international law did not undertake to significantly include child-specific provisions prior to 1989. The likely explanations in the case of refugee law, reflecting the discussions in Chapter 3, are that governments involved in the drafting of international legal instruments did not want to assign rights to children for fear of undermining the rights of the family unit and/or children were merely not considered as significant by the drafters.

Conclusions

The primary literature on the development of refugee law, such as that produced by Goodwin-Gill and Hathaway, did not address children in reference to the early development of this area of international law. The reason children were not discussed is likely due to the limited reference to children in early treaties and arrangements dealing with refugees. Furthermore, the Refugee Convention does not include any specific provisions for children. This is an indication of the lack of significance placed on children in earlier documents and during the drafting of the Refugee Convention. It is striking that children, although championed by the League of Nations and the UN as reflected in the 1924 and 1959 Declarations, were not considered important beneficiaries of protection in their own right at least in refugee law. This is perhaps a reflection of the ways in which society, including the international community and those responsible for drafting international treaties, viewed children. The indication is that children were not considered to be rights holders in their own right and perhaps the assumption was, in the context of refugee law, that the child had the same rights as the parents and that the child would be 'attached' to the family in these circumstances, with the exception of those orphaned by conflict and war. What is clear is that there has historically been a dichotomy in international law concerning child refugees, with children's rights on one side and refugee law on the other. The dichotomy continues and is observable in contemporary law. However, it is the interpretation of each area of law and the guidance on child refugees produced by the UN and the Committee on the Rights of the Child which has narrowed this gap somewhat. This is discussed in the following chapter.

The literature and the developments in refugee law up to the drafting of the Refugee Convention, which remains the cornerstone of international refugee law, fail to comprehensively analyse the applicability or relevance of the legal framework in the case of children. There is very little in the discourse that discusses child refugees prior to the CRC. The CRC has since had an impact upon international refugee law. The CRC did not come about until 1989, nearly 40 years after the Refugee Convention. It is arguable, therefore, that child refugee law is in its infancy.

There is some recent literature on children and refugee law that touches on the early development of international children's rights law and its connections with the modern refugee framework. However, there is very little discussion of the impact the movement had on the development of the Refugee Convention. Rather, the focus has been on the influence the CRC has had on the interpretation of the Refugee Convention. As highlighted in this chapter, this may be due to the seemingly inconsequential impact the early international children's rights movement had on the Refugee Convention.

Despite the lack of consideration for children, the developments in refugee law leading up to the Refugee Convention created greater possibilities for children fleeing a wider variety of circumstances to qualify as refugees. Despite refugee law becoming more exacting, the shift to focus on the individual expanded the applicability of the law to more people, not just groups identified by the international community. The evolution of refugee law therefore holds relevance in that children, in particular in the years following the drafting of the CRC, have been the subject of refugee law.

Chapter 5 seeks to establish whether or not a children's rights approach to the interpretation of the Refugee Convention is possible.

Notes

1 Universal Declaration of Human Rights 1948.
2 For example: Hours of Work (Industry) Convention, 1919 (No. 1).
3 Minimum Age (Industry) Convention, 1919 (No. 5) and Declaration of the Rights of the Child 1924.
4 See generally: Peter Fitzmaurice, 'Between the wars – the Refugee Convention of 1933: A contemporary analysis' in David Keane and Yvonne McDermott (eds) *The Challenge of Human Rights: Past, Present and Future* (Edward Elgar 2012) 236.
5 Convention relating to the Status of Refugees 1951.
6 Universal Declaration of Human Rights 1948.
7 Robert Jennings and Arthur Watts, *Oppenheim's International Law* (9th edn, Longman 2008).
8 Deitrich Schindler and Jiri Toman, *The Laws of Armed Conflicts* (Martinus Nihjoff 1988) 50–51. See also, Convention (IV) respecting the Laws and Customs of War on Land and its annex: Regulations concerning the Laws and Customs of War on Land 1907.
9 Antonio Cassese, *International Law* (2nd edn, Oxford University Press 2005).
10 See, Antonio Cassese, *Human Rights in a Changing World* (Temple University Press 1990).
11 Magna Carta 1215.
12 *Ibid*; English Bill of Rights 1689; French Declaration on the Rights of Man and Citizen 1789 and US Constitution and Bill of Rights 1791.
13 See, for example: Covenant of the League of Nations 1919, Article 8. See also, generally: Leo Grebler, *The Cost of the World War to Germany and Austria-Hungary* (Yale University Press 1940).
14 Frederick Samuel Northedge, *The League of Nations: its life and times, 1920–1946* (Leicester University Press 1998).
15 *Ibid.*
16 Covenant of the League of Nations, Preamble; Antonio Cassese, *International Law* (2nd edn, OUP 2005) 34–38.
17 The Covenant of the League of Nations 1919, Preamble.
18 The Treaty of Versailles 1919, the treaty that outlined the terms of the end of the war between Germany and the Allied forces, comprised 30 articles of the Covenant of the League of Nations 1919. Frederick Samuel Northedge, *The League of Nations: its life and times, 1920–1946* (Leicester University Press 1998).
19 Charter of the United Nations 1945, Preamble.
20 Antonio Cassese, *International Law* (2nd edn, OUP 2005).
21 Charter of the United Nations 1945.
22 Javaid Rehman, *International Human Rights Law: A Practical Approach* (Longman 2003) 54.

23 Universal Declaration of Human Rights 1948.
24 Forty-eight Members voted in favour of adopting the Declaration and eight abstained (Byelorussia Soviet Socialist Republic, Czechoslovakia, Poland, Ukraine, USSR, Yugoslavia, Saudi Arabia and South Africa). See: William Schabas (ed), *The Universal Declaration of Human Rights: The Travaux Préparatoires* (CUP 2013).
25 Javaid Rehman, *International Human Rights Law: A Practical Approach* (Longman 2003) 377.
26 United Nations, 'The Universal Declaration of Human Rights: History of the Document' <www.un.org/en/sections/universal-declaration/history-document/> accessed 13 July 2016.
27 Universal Declaration of Human Rights 1948, Article 14.
28 *Ibid*, Article 14.
29 *Ibid*, Preamble.
30 Douglas Hodgson, 'The Historical Development and "Internationalisation" of the Children's Rights Movement' (1992) 6 *Australian Journal of Family Law* 25.
31 UNICEF, 'About UNICEF: Who We Are' <www.unicef.org/about/who/index_introduction.html> accessed 22 March 2015.
32 See: James Hathaway, *The Rights of Refugees under International Law* (CUP 2005); James Hathaway, 'A Reconsideration of the Underlying Premise of Refugee Law' (1990) 31 *Harvard International Law Journal* 129; James Hathaway, *The Law of Refugee Status* (Butterworths 1991); Sir Guy Goodwin-Gill and Jane McAdam, *The Refugee in International Law* (3rd edn, OUP 2007).
33 Save the Children International comprises 30 member organisations in over 120 countries where they work to 'deliver change for children'. Save the Children International, 'About Us' <www.savethechildren.net/about-us> accessed 13 July 2016. It was established in 1920 (formerly called the International Save the Children Union).
34 UNICEF was established in 1946. UNICEF, 'Our History' <www.unicef.org/about/who/index_history.html> accessed 7 September 2016.
35 James Hathaway, 'The Evolution of Refugee Status in International Law: 1920–1950' (1984) 33 *International Comparative Law Quarterly* 348, 352, Stefanie Schmahl, 'Article 1 A para 1 (Definition of the Term 'Refugee')' in Andreas Zimmermann (ed.), *The 1951 Convention Relating to the Status of Refugees and its 1967 Protocol: A Commentary* (OUP 2011).
36 See, generally: James Hathaway, 'The Evolution of Refugee Status in International Law: 1920–1950' (1984) 33 *International Comparative Law Quarterly* 348.
37 Claudena Skran, *Refugees in Inter-war Europe The Emergence of a Regime* (Clarendon Press 1995) 13–64.
38 Peter Fitzmaurice, 'Anniversary of the forgotten Convention: The 1933 Refugee Convention and the search for protection between the world wars' (2013) 8(1) *The Researcher* 3.
39 James Hathaway, *The Rights of Refugees under International Law* (CUP 2005) 83.
40 Herman Walker, 'Modern Treaties of Friendship, Commerce and Navigation' (1958) 42 *Minnesota Law Review* 823 in James Hathaway, *The Rights of Refugees under International Law* (CUP 2005) 76–77.
41 James Hathaway, *The Rights of Refugees under International Law* (CUP 2005) 79.
42 *Ibid*, 79–81.

43 Gershon Bacon, 'Polish Jews and the Minorities Treaties Obligations, 1925: The View from Geneva' (2002) 18 *Gal-Ed* 145.
44 Peter Hilpold, 'The League of Nations and the Protection of Minorities – Rediscovering a Great Experiment' (2013) 17 *Max Planck Institute for Comparative Public Law and International Law* 87.
45 James Hathaway, *The Rights of Refugees under International Law* (CUP 2005) 81.
46 See: Peter Hilpold, 'The League of Nations and the Protection of Minorities Rediscovering a Great Experiment' (2013) 17 *Max Planck Institute for Comparative Public Law and International Law* 87 in James Hathaway, *The Rights of Refugees under International Law* (CUP 2005) 82.
47 James Hathaway, *The Rights of Refugees under International Law* (CUP 2005) 82.
48 Louise Holborn, 'The Legal Status of Political Refugees, 1920–1938' (1938) 32(4) *The American Journal of International Law* 680, and Report by the Secretary-General on the Future Organisation of Refugee Work LN Doc 1930.XIII.2 (1930), 3 in James Hathaway, *The Rights of Refugees under International Law* (CUP 2005) 84; Claudena Skran, 'Historical Development of International Refugee Law' in Andreas Zimmermann (ed.), *The 1951 Convention Relating to the Status of Refugees and its 1967 Protocol: A Commentary* (OUP 2011) 7.
49 Louise Holborn, 'The Legal Status of Political Refugees, 1920–1938' (1938) 32(4) *The American Journal of International Law* 680, and Report by the Secretary-General on the Future Organisation of Refugee Work LN Doc 1930.XIII.2 (1930), 3 in James Hathaway, *The Rights of Refugees under International Law* (CUP 2005) 84.
50 *Ibid.*
51 James Hathaway, *The Rights of Refugees under International Law* (CUP 2005) 86.
52 *Ibid.*
53 League of Nations, Arrangement Relating to the Issue of Identify Certificates to Russian and Armenian Refugees, 12 May 1926, League of Nations, Treaty Series Vol. LXXXIX, No. 2004; League of Nations, Arrangement Relating to the Legal Status of Russian and Armenian Refugees, 30 June 1928, League of Nations Treaty Series, Vol. LXXXIX, No. 2005.
54 Atle Grahl-Madsen, *The Status of Refugees in International Law, vol. 1* (A. W. Sijthoff 1966).
55 A League of Nations, Arrangement Relating to the Issue of Identify Certificates to Russian and Armenian Refugees, 12 May 1926, League of Nations, Treaty Series Vol. LXXXIX, No. 2004: 'any person of Russian origin who does not enjoy or who no longer enjoys the protection of the Government of the Union of Socialist Soviet Republics and who has not acquired another nationality'. Supplementing and Amending the previous arrangements dated July 5th, 1922 and May 31st, 1924.
56 Sir Guy Goodwin-Gill and Jane McAdam, *The Refugee in International Law* (3rd edn, OUP 2007) 16.
57 *Ibid.*
58 Arrangement Relating to the Issue of Identify Certificates to Russian and Armenian Refugees, 12 May 1926, included one provision relating to children: 4. 'The Conference agree that children under 15 years of age should be included on the identity certificates of their parents'.
59 James Hathaway, *The Rights of Refugees under International Law* (CUP 2005) 86; Claudena Skran, 'Historical Development of International Refugee Law' in

Andreas Zimmermann (ed.), *The 1951 Convention Relating to the Status of Refugees and its 1967 Protocol: A Commentary* (OUP 2011) 14.

60 Claudena Skran, 'Historical Development of International Refugee Law' in Andreas Zimmermann (ed.), *The 1951 Convention Relating to the Status of Refugees and its 1967 Protocol: A Commentary* (OUP 2011) 24.

61 The 1933 Refugee Convention entered into force June 13 1935; James Hathaway, 'The Evolution of Refugee Status in International Law' *ICLQ* 33 (1984).

62 Work of the Inter-Governmental Advisory Commission for Refugees during its Eighth Session LN Doc. C.17.1936.XII (1936) 159.

63 Sir Guy Goodwin-Gill and Jane McAdam, *The Refugee in International Law* (3rd edn, OUP 2007) 201.

64 Report Submitted to the Sixth Committee to the Assembly of the League of Nations: Russia, Armenia, Assyrian, Assyro-Chaldean, Saar and Turkish Refugees LN Doc. A.45.1935.XII (1935).

65 Claudena Skran, 'Historical Development of International Refugee Law' in Andreas Zimmermann (ed.), *The 1951 Convention Relating to the Status of Refugees and its 1967 Protocol: A Commentary* (OUP 2011) 15.

66 *Ibid*, 27 and 28.

67 For more information: *Ibid*, 30–35.

68 1938 Convention concerning the Status of Refugees coming from Germany: 191 LNTS No. 4461 & Additional Protocol, 14 Sept. 1939: 198 LNTS No. 4634 (expansion of Convention to include Austria after Anschluss).

69 Bermuda Conference 1943 in Sir Guy Goodwin-Gill and Jane McAdam, *The Refugee in International Law* (3rd edn, OUP 2007) 18.

70 *Ibid*, 19.

71 Louise Holborn, *The International Refugee Organization: A Specialized Agency of the United Nations. Its History and Work 1946–1952* (OUP 1956).

72 See: Sir Guy Goodwin-Gill and Jane McAdam, *The Refugee in International Law* (3rd edn, OUP 2007) 19.

73 Louise Holborn, *The International Refugee Organization: A Specialized Agency of the United Nations. Its History and Work 1946–1952* (OUP 1956).

74 Sir Guy Goodwin-Gill and Jane McAdam, *The Refugee in International Law* (3rd edn, OUP 2007) 20.

75 Erika Feller, 'The Evolution of the International Refugee Protection Regime' (2001) 5 *Journal of Law and Policy* 134.

76 Memorandum by the Secretary-General to the Ad Hoc Committee on Statelessness and Related Problems UN Doc. E/AC.32/2 3 January 1950, 6–7 in James Hathaway, *The Rights of Refugees under International Law* (CUP 2005) 93.

77 International children's rights are described as rights based in international treaties, such as the Convention on the Rights of the Child 1989. Jane Fortin, *Children's Rights and the Developing Law* (3rd edn, CUP 2009) 31–68.

78 Jane Fortin, *Children's Rights and the Developing Law* (3rd edn, CUP 2009) 35.

79 This movement was spearheaded by Eglantyne Jebb and the Save the Children [Fund]. See: Clare Mulley, *The Woman who Saved the Children: A Biography of Eglantyne Jebb, Founder of Save the Children* (Oneworld Publications 2009, 2011 ebook reprint).

80 Jane Fortin, *Children's Rights and the Developing Law* (3rd edn, CUP 2009) 35.

81 Anthony Grenville, 'The Kindertransport: An Introduction' in Andrea Hammel and Bea Lewkowicz (eds), *The Kindertransport to Britain 1938/39: New Perspectives* (Brill 2012).

82 Sir Guy Goodwin-Gill, 'Unaccompanied Minors: The Role and Place of

International Law in the Pursuit of Durable Solutions' (2005) *International Journal of Children's Rights* 413.

83 Jane McAdams, 'Seeking Asylum under the Convention on the Rights of the Child: A Case for Complementary Protection' (2006) 14 *International Journal of Children's Rights* 251.

84 These children were granted entry on the condition that there stay in the UK would not be permanent and that they would eventually return to Spain. Jane McAdams, 'Seeking Asylum under the Convention on the Rights of the Child: A Case for Complementary Protection' (2006) 14 *International Journal of Children's Rights* 251.

85 Hansard Bd 341 Sp. 1471 ff (21 November 1938), cited in Rebekka Göpfert (1999) *Der judische Kindertransport von Deutschland nach England 1938/39: Geschichte und Erinnerung* (Campus Verlag 1999) p. 57 in McAdam (2006).

86 Anthony Grenville, 'The Kindertransport: An Introduction' in Andrea Hammel and Bea Lewkowicz (eds), *The Kindertransport to Britain 1938/39: New Perspectives* (Brill 2012).

87 Sir John Hope Simpson, *The Refugee Problem: Report of a Survey* (OUP 1939) 343 in Jane McAdams, 'Seeking Asylum under the Convention on the Rights of the Child: A Case for Complementary Protection' (2006) 14 *International Journal of Children's Rights* 251.

88 Anthony Grenville, 'The Kindertransport: An Introduction' in Andrea Hammel and Bea Lewkowicz (eds), *The Kindertransport to Britain 1938/39: New Perspectives* (Brill 2012).

89 United States Holocaust Memorial Museum, 'Kindertransport, 138–140' <www.ushmm.org/wlc/en/article.php?ModuleId=10005260> accessed 15 July 2016.

90 Jacqueline Bhabha, 'Demography and Rights: Women, Children and Access to Asylum' (2004) 16(2) *International Journal of Refugee Law* 229.

91 Atle Grahl-Madsen, *The Status of Refugees in International Law* vol. 1 (A.W. Sijthoff 1966) 35.

92 *Ibid.*

93 UN General Assembly, Statute of the Office of the United Nations High Commissioner for Refugees, 14 December 1950, A/RES/428(V) <www.refworld.org/docid/3ae6b3628.html> accessed 21 March 2015.

94 *Ibid.*

95 Universal Declaration of Human Rights 1948, Article 14.

96 UN General Assembly, Statute of the Office of the United Nations High Commissioner for Refugees, 14 December 1950, A/RES/428(V), available at: www.refworld.org/docid/3ae6b3628.html (accessed 21 March 2015) Chapter 1.

97 1951 Convention relating to the Status of Refugees, Article 1A(2).

98 1938 Convention concerning the Status of Refugees coming from Germany.

99 1967 Protocol relating to the Status of Refugees.

100 Sir Guy Goodwin-Gill and Jane McAdam, *The Refugee in International Law* (3rd edn, OUP 2007) 18.

101 Jacqueline Bhabha, 'Demography and Rights: Women, Children and Access to Asylum' (2004) 16(2) *International Journal of Refugee Law* 229.

102 1951 Convention relating to the Status of Refugees, Article 4.

103 Ad Hoc Committee on Statelessness and Related Problems, United States of America: Memorandum on the Definition Article of the Preliminary Draft Convention Relating to the Status of Refugees (and stateless Persons) (E/AC.32.2) Statelessness Conference, 18 January 1950 United States of America: Memorandum on the Definition Article of the Preliminary Draft

Convention Relating to the Status of Refugees (and Stateless Persons) (E/AC.32.2).

104 Jane McAdams, 'Seeking Asylum under the Convention on the Rights of the Child: A Case for Complementary Protection' (2006) 14 *International Journal of Children's Rights* 252.

5 A children's rights approach to refugee law?

Abstract

This chapter seeks to establish whether or not a children's rights approach to the interpretation of the Refugee Convention is possible. This chapter shows that there is a precedent for one human rights regime influencing another, generally, and international children's rights law influencing refugee law, specifically. This is done by looking at general rules of treaty interpretation. The object and purpose of both the Convention on the Rights of the Child (CRC) and the Refugee Convention are analysed to identify if there is scope for cross-treaty interpretation. Guidance from the Committee on the Rights of the Child and the United Nations High Commissioner for Refugees (UNHCR) are principal sources in the justification for the potential for a children's rights approach. Chapter 5 also looks at some key terminology relating to the interpretation of the Refugee Convention concerning children. The definition of 'refugee', the interpretation of persecution and the convention grounds in their application in children's cases are examined.

Introduction

Children have been recognised as refugees across the industrialised world for a variety of reasons. According to the UNHCR, also known as the United Nations Refugee Agency, children may fear or experience persecution on the basis of military conscription, trafficking, female genital mutilation, familial or domestic violence, forced marriage, labour and sexual exploitation, among other forms of persecution.[1] UNHCR referred to these examples of persecution as *child-specific*.[2] In articulating the different persecution experiences that children around the world may face, it is evident that UNHCR views the child as a person with a right to asylum in their own right if they, like their adult counterparts, meet certain criteria.[3] UNHCR also elaborated on the ways in which breaches in CRC rights may impact upon a child's application for refugee protection,[4] a step towards bridging the gap between children's rights law and refugee law. These developments and contributions signal the possibility of a nexus (or several nexuses) between both areas of international law.

The Refugee Convention is considered to form the foundation of international refugee law. It has informed practice and guidance produced by UNHCR and national governments. Yet, the Refugee Convention provides very little guidance on the *qualification* of refugees. Furthermore, the Refugee Convention does not explicitly mention children in Article 1A(2), which details those who may qualify as refugees. The substantive provisions of the convention deal with the rights of refugees once recognised. None of those provisions attribute rights to children *or* exclude them from those rights. Nevertheless, child refugee law has evolved since 1951. Guidance provided by UNHCR, the Committee on the Rights of the Child, the Convention on the Rights of the Child (CRC), national laws, regional laws and jurisprudence have resulted in refugee law's expansion, through the interpretation of the provisions of the Refugee Convention, to reflect the particular circumstances of children. Today, children have been recognised as refugees within the framework provided by the Refugee Convention. Some of these developments can be attributed to the interpretive guidance provided by UNHCR and the Committee following the publication of the CRC. These developments and influences are the focus of this chapter, as they make the best and most comprehensive case for the interaction between the two regimes – two regimes that have been and continue to be somewhat siloed.

The previous chapters discussed early children's rights and refugee law and the limited interplay between the two. The conclusion reached was that children, although an important part of the international discourse around protecting the vulnerable, in particular in times of conflict, did not feature significantly in mainstream international human rights law or refugee law. Children's protection needs were dealt with separately through the League of Nations (1924) and United Nations (1959) Declarations of the Rights of the Child or through once-off initiatives such as the *Kindertransport*. Therefore, further refugee law guidance in respect of children needed to come from another source in order to bridge the gap between the developing children's rights paradigm and refugee law.

The advent of the CRC and its impact on children's rights assisted the expansion of refugee law. The CRC changed the face of international children's rights law. It presents children as vulnerable persons in need of special protections *and* as rights' holders in their own right (as established in Chapter 3). As a result, other areas of law also evolved, including refugee law. It was not until after the CRC came into force that child refugee law began to develop with traceable momentum.

In light of the post-CRC developments, this chapter explores how the current refugee regime is positioned to continue to develop to take into account the different forms of child-specific persecution that are emerging through various fora. This book examines the potential for breaches of children's rights, including those not traditionally associated with refugee protection, to be considered within the refugee determination process. The overarching hypothesis is that where there are breaches in children's rights (and there is a link with a convention ground), there is scope to expand the definition of persecution taking into account the fact that all children have a universal right to positive development and a positive experience of childhood as set out in Article 6. This hypothesis is based not only in theory, but also reflects the evolution of refugee law in considering claims from children and the narrowing of the gap between children's rights law and refugee law (see Chapter 6).

This chapter takes another step towards answering the question set out in the introduction – when do violations of CRC-based rights, in particular where there is a link to development, or Article 6, amount to persecution in the context of refugee law? Part I seeks to establish whether or not a children's rights approach to the interpretation of the Refugee Convention is possible, considering contributions from guidance, jurisprudence and law. This chapter aims primarily to show that there is a precedent for one human rights regime influencing another, generally, and international children's rights law influencing international refugee law, specifically, building upon discussions in Chapter 4.

Key terminology and aspects of the Refugee Convention framework in its application to children are introduced in Part II. This includes a discussion on persecution, actors of persecution and protection and the five convention grounds, with a particular focus on the particular social group ground, as it is the most developed in the context of children. This chapter concludes with reflections on universality and the dichotomy between children's rights and refugee law.

Part I

Context setting

Not identifying children in the Refugee Convention as possible beneficiaries of international protection, likely delayed the development of child refugee law until the drafting and subsequent ratification of the CRC. It was not until 1987 that guidance was produced to assist States in dealing with refugee claims from children.

The relationship between violations of children's rights and persecution therefore must be unpacked. The systemic problem, as dealt with by Foster, of refugee grants being more commonly awarded to those whom have been denied civil and political rights than those denied social and economic rights also compounds the problem of fitting children's rights into the refugee framework as there is a reluctance to attribute agency to children in law generally (see Chapters 2 and 3). This chapter and Chapter 6 show that this reluctance also applies in the case of refugee law. As discussed in previous chapters, children have traditionally been conceived of as objects of the law, rather than subjects, despite the fact that the literature supports the view that the modern child is both object *and* subject.[5] Some commentators and the literature argue that children are now primarily subjects of law,[6] however, in practice the categorisation of children as objects of law is still dominant in international law, including refugee law. The question must therefore be asked: Are children, inherent to the system, less likely to be recognised as refugees when compared with their adult counterparts?

These matters are explored herein considering the advances in refugee law relating to children in the past two decades. The refugee paradigm indeed has evolved through guidance, regional and national policy and legislation, and jurisprudence. Decision-makers, States and regional bodies have been increasingly aware of developments in the area of human rights and children's rights law and that awareness has influenced refugee decisions. This indicates the flexibility of the Refugee Convention and its capacity to evolve reflecting developments in other areas of law and the ever-changing face of conflict, persecution and persistent harm.[7] Human rights law has increasingly had an influence on the definition of persecution. This has led to the expansion of the term to include various harms that affect children (among others), such as female genital mutilation, economic exploitation including trafficking, domestic violence, underage marriage and underage military recruitment.[8] This expansion has been the result of relying upon and referencing key human rights treaties, most notably the Universal Declaration of Human Rights (UDHR), but also the CRC. Due to the comprehensive nature of the CRC, which includes both civil and political and social and economic rights, there is arguably scope for even further development of the interpretation of persecution considering children's rights, including those rights where a child's development is affected and where there is a link with a convention ground. There remains potential for the Refugee Convention to expand to include more claims based on denial of rights considered to be children's rights, or even the establishment of a children's rights approach.

The rapid development in children's rights law has had an impact on refugee law. In recent decades, there has been a push to not only make children's rights visible, but to prioritise children's rights in the development of research, law, policy and practice. The Committee on the Rights of the Child (the committee with responsibility for monitoring the implementation of the CRC)[9] (Committee) has provided guidance on the interpretation of the treaty including in the specific case of children seeking protection (the guidance focused on separated children, but the section on child-specific forms of persecution can be and is seen as relevant to all children, discussed below).[10] Most significantly, UNHCR has published a number of materials to assist States in the determination of child claims, which also drew on and made explicit reference to the CRC. The Committee also drafted optional protocols to the CRC that dealt with the sexual exploitation of children[11] and underage military recruitment,[12] two forms of child-specific persecution as established by UNHCR.[13]

The appointment of Special Rapporteurs on education, housing, food and health and other UN initiatives have also impacted upon the interpretation of the provisions contained within the CRC and how they relate to general human rights law.[14] These developments have also helped pave the way for their inclusion in refugee law. The interconnectedness of children's rights law and refugee law has been exhibited at various levels of the human rights machinery (to which both children's rights law and refugee law belong).[15] In addition, the acceptance that children are unique within the law has added an awareness to the different and nuanced forms of persecution and harm children face compared with their adult counterparts. The acknowledgement that children are different also brought to light the fact that children are affected both directly and indirectly by conflict, environmental conditions including famine, poverty and access to economic and social services.[16]

Additionally, there is increased awareness around the domestic abuse children may suffer, where the home may be the locus of persecution, and where the State may not intervene for cultural, religious or legal reasons bringing the role of the family (as protector and/or as persecutor) into focus.[17] Lastly, there is also growing awareness of the fact that children have views, beliefs and can act in their own right making them actors in their own experience of persecution, not just bystanders exposed to indiscriminate violence or harm.[18] The following section begins the justification for a children's rights approach, an approach that is needed based on the fact that children are different and their needs are different, including in the context of refugee law.

Children within the Refugee Convention and the need for a cross-treaty interpretive approach: some assumptions

As defined in the previous chapter, refugees are persons who: (1) are outside of their country of origin, (2) cannot or are unwilling to seek the protection of their country or place of residence and (3) have a well-founded fear of persecution with a link to one of the five convention grounds.[19] A child, in order to qualify as a refugee would need to satisfy these criteria as well. In respect of point (1), it is assumed that children are mobile either in the company of their families or able to travel on their own. Point (2) assumes that children have legal agency, with rights in their own right. Point (3) assumes that children can exercise their agency and act autonomously and are thus able to substantiate a claim of a well-founded fear relating to one or more of the five grounds: race, nationality, religion, membership of a particular social group or political opinion.

The reality is that children are often unable to travel without the assistance of adults. That does not necessarily mean that they cannot meet the criteria in point (1), but that there is an added barrier to accessing asylum. Additionally, and in relation to point (2), children are often not consistently considered as rights holders around the globe.[20] Lastly, and in relation to point (3), children are persons in a developmental stage in their lives where their ability to reason is evolving. Children are not always able to communicate their fears in the same way as an adult or they may be perceived to be unable to do so.[21] Additionally over the years, UNHCR and adjudicators began to argue that children also have fears that are different from that of adults and a lower threshold to persecution and benefit-of-the-doubt should be applied in the determination of their claims.[22] This book does not address these points, however, as they are procedural.[23] Based on these contributions and guidance provided by UNHCR and others, it is nevertheless clear that the Refugee Convention is not an adequate framework for child applicants *on its own* as it did not sufficiently consider their particular needs, abilities and circumstances.

Before, looking to the interpretation of the Refugee Convention through a children's rights lens, the following sections discuss whether or not this is possible. The following sections look in brief at the general rules that govern international human rights law treaty interpretation. This discussion is then applied to the interpretation of the Refugee Convention in light of developments in the area of international children's rights law.

Bridging the gap: treaty interpretation

Much of the key terminology in the refugee definition is not defined in any other area of international law, including persecution and the particular social group. As a result, the aforementioned terms have only been defined in respect of refugee law. For example, the CRC did not define persecution in the context of violations of rights contained within the CRC itself. It merely stated that the rights contained within the CRC belong to all children, including those seeking refugee protection or who are refugees.[24] The CRC never made a link between the rights contained within the CRC and qualifying for international protection. This presents a challenge for those responsible for interpreting the Refugee Convention in the case of child applicants. The same applies to adults as the International Bill of Rights (IBR) does not provide a definition of persecution. This may account for the inconsistent application of human rights and children's rights law in the context of refugee law (developed in Chapter 6).[25] The terminology has not been universally defined in a way that would allow for consistent application and interpretation of human and children's rights violations in the context of refugee law. Nevertheless, there is considerable overlap in content and objectives within all human rights treaties.

The need for a cross-treaty interpretative approach has been debated in the literature,[26] stemming from the inconsistency in which the refugee definition is applied in the case of all applicants, including children.[27] However, States and decision-making authorities face some challenges in making this a reality. The International Law Commission noted that when interpreting one treaty, the relevant party may need to justify the referencing of another treaty if used in the interpretation process.[28] However, there is a trend to reference other treaties and developments within other areas of law in the interpretation of a particular area of law, including in the context of children. The Court of Justice of the European Union also reiterated this point in relation to the need for a holistic approach to treaty interpretation, specifically referencing the CRC in a case relating to the right to family reunification. In *Case C-540/03 – European Parliament v Council of the European Union*, the Grand Chamber of the Court of Justice of the European Union stated that:

> The court has already had occasion to point out that the International Covenant on Civil and Political Rights is one of the international instruments for the protection of human rights of which it takes account in applying the general principles of community Law. [That] is also true of the Convention on the Rights of the Child [which], like the Covenant, binds each of the Member States[29]

This case does not deal with the matter of refuge, but it demonstrates that human rights, albeit in the context of Article 8 of the European Convention on Human Rights, may interact with the CRC.

The Vienna Convention on the Law of Treaties (VCLT) did not include reference to the interaction of various treaties in respect of the interpretation of one. The most widely referenced and most applicable provision in the VCLT is Article 31 which states that a 'treaty shall be interpreted in good faith in accordance with the ordinary meaning to be given to the terms of the treaty in their context and in the light of its object and purpose'.[30] Hathaway noted that the general approach in common law jurisdictions is to undertake holistically any interpretation of international law in light of contemporary interpretations of Article 31 of the VCLT and this has indeed been the case,[31] including in the case of children's rights.[32]

The challenge of implementing international law

International laws are inherently different from national laws, which are written by a consortium of States for all States. States, then, must assume responsibility for ensuring that international laws are respected and implemented within their own borders.[33] However, States did not and do not easily reconcile the potential for their sovereignty to be undermined by an international legal regime.[34] The rights afforded citizens were long thought to be the responsibility of the sovereign State alone.[35] International law brought about two key shifts in governance. Firstly, the global community had a responsibility to enact laws to guide States to prevent abuses of human rights. Secondly, the global community had a responsibility to act or intervene when a State infringes upon the fundamental rights of those within their territory.[36]

This balance of responsibility is also embedded in contemporary refugee law and children's rights law. The definition of 'refugee' includes the element of State protection. The State must be found to be unwilling or unable to protect the applicant from a violation of their rights. This establishes a condition that may protect the applicant while respecting the country's statehood. In respect of children's rights, the CRC places the obligation to ensure access to the rights contained within the treaty on the State, and also the family to some degree. International laws therefore set a standard to which States must aim to fulfil or must fulfil in the case of non-derogable[37] rights (discussed below). The individual therefore benefits from the States' fulfilment of their obligations under international law. However, individual recourse where a State does not fulfil their obligations is not straightforward. For children, who are also often dependent on adults to realise their rights, it is even less straightforward.

Fundamentally, the challenge of implementing international laws relates to oversight and enforcement. International laws operate *in addition* to national laws. Although States may be able to easily access recourse when one State breaches international law, for example in the case of a breach in international trade law,[38] avenues to access recourse may be more challenging for an individual who has suffered a breach in their human rights. International law, in relation to the individual, is sometimes described as a sort of rulebook for States, which, from time to time, also affects the individual either through the rights bestowed upon them or the responsibilities imposed upon them.[39] This means that the implementation of international law presents additional challenges as it may occur in the space between States and in the space between the State and the individual, and in the case of children – in the space between the child and the responsible adult(s).

In the case of children, the parents or responsible adults may be viewed as the first benefactor of individual rights under international law. This includes those rights attributed specifically to children. This is because adults are often viewed as the first party with responsibility in realising children's rights, regardless of whether or not rights are aimed at the protection or promotion of the interests of the child or if the rights are in fact the child's right in their own right, reminiscent of the position of Locke and Rousseau and those that followed. The ability of children to access their rights therefore depends on national laws on parental and guardianship roles and responsibilities. Furthermore, and as discussed in Chapter 3, the literature in a variety of disciplines tells us that the age and level of maturity of children may affect the child's ability to understand their rights and thus understand possible avenues for recourse where a right is breached. The role of adults and children's capacity as they are relevant to discussions on a children's rights approach to the interpretation of the Refugee Convention are revisited in Chapter 6.

This challenge also exists in the context of refugee law. Simply put, the proportion of child refugees (compared with their adult counterparts) is higher in refugee camp settings than the proportion of child asylum seekers in the Global North.[40] This indicates that children are unable to or prevented from accessing this potential avenue for protection. While this book does not ask questions around why children are not proportionally represented in refugee applications, this discrepancy brings to light a potential reason for the limited development around child refugee law – there are simply very few cases due to their underrepresentation. In addition, children are often subsumed within head-of-household claims. Chapter 2 identified as problematic the secondary position children hold within the family unit and the reluctance to attribute rights to children, in particular participation rights. The secondary position and the reluctance persists in international law, despite the contributions of the CRC. This is developed in Chapter 6.

International law as national guidance

Despite difficulties in the implementation and enforcement of international law, without it, States would not have a framework from which they could borrow. And despite early and ongoing resistance, international legal provisions have begun to be regularly referred to in national and regional court judgments and in legislation, thus integrating human rights norms domestically in a way that offers a direct line of recourse for violations of those rights.[41] This may mean that although international human rights law itself may not always be enforceable at the international level, international law has become more integrated into national and regional legal structures. This is also true in the case of children's rights and refugee law. Innumerable countries include the exact or near exact definition of 'refugee' as contained within the Refugee Convention.[42] A number of countries also include a provision on the 'best interests principle', among other CRC provisions, in child care law and in some cases in constitutions.[43] Even where there is reluctance to reference international law in case law and in national legislation, there are still transpositions of international principles drawing on the Refugee Convention and the CRC, among other treaties.[44] The best examples are States whose immigration legislation also includes provisions from the CRC and vice versa. For example, the UK Border, Citizenship and Immigration Act 2009 Section 55 provided:

> Duty regarding the welfare of children
> (1) The Secretary of State must make arrangements for ensuring that—
> (a) the functions mentioned in subsection (2) are discharged having regard to the need to safeguard and promote the welfare of children who are in the United Kingdom, and
> (b) any services provided by another person pursuant to arrangements which are made by the Secretary of State and relate to the discharge of a function mentioned in subsection (2) are provided having regard to that need.
> (2) The functions referred to in subsection (1) are—
> (a) any function of the Secretary of State in relation to immigration, asylum or nationality;

(b) any function conferred by or by virtue of the Immigration Acts on an immigration officer;
(c) any general customs function of the Secretary of State;
(d) any customs function conferred on a designated customs official.[45]

This is an example of the transposition of a children's right in the context of immigration and a recognition that these two areas of law overlap and influence each other.

The notion of legal norms also emerged as a result of the mainstreaming of human rights law. Peremptory Norms, or *jus cogens*, are laws that, although perhaps also difficult to enforce, have been accepted by the international community as a standard where derogation is prohibited.[46] Freedom from torture, genocide[47] and *non-refoulement* are among those considered *jus cogens*.[48] Norms assist in the implementation of international law or the transposition of international law at national level. Chapter 3 asked which children's rights are considered to be norms. Chapter 6 then asks which children's rights norms, if any, when violated amount to persecution in the context of refugee law. These questions are addressed in this chapter and Chapter 6.

The object and purpose of the Refugee Convention

Michelle Foster in her book, *International Refugee Law and Socio-Economic Rights*, provided a detailed case for the use of human rights treaties in the interpretation of the Refugee Convention. She analysed the object and purpose of the Refugee Convention in order to ask whether or not it is capable of accommodating 'more nuanced' asylum claims. Her reasoning is referred to throughout this section and the approach is also applied to the analysis of the object and purpose of the CRC in the following section.

Some of the literature has argued that there are conflicting objects and purposes reflected within the preamble itself. One view is that the purpose of the Refugee Convention is to provide international protection to those who fit the definition. Another view is that the purpose relates to fundamental rights and freedoms as established by the UDHR.[49] The view of some decision-makers has been that this indicates that the Refugee Convention was 'written against the backdrop of international human rights law'.[50]

The other perspective is that the convention serves to provide support to States, rather than individuals in working towards solving a difficult and cross-border problem. This view derived from one statement in the preamble that refers to the 'unduly heavy burden' granting asylum may have on some countries, also referring to the importance of international co-operation.[51] This objective is also reflected in UNHCR's mandate.[52] The view within the higher courts has not reflected this sentiment as discussed below.

Foster also reiterated Klabbers' assessment that the content of the treaty may also indicate its object and purpose.[53] Foster applied this approach to the

Refugee Convention and found that the content focused on human rights overwhelmingly, noting that Articles 2–34 'are concerned with the clarification of the rights to which those falling within the definition are entitled'.[54] Although the analysis herein did not look at the rights of refugees after recognition, the balance of provisions nevertheless indicates that the existing human rights framework informed the drafting of the Refugee Convention.

Foster showed that the dominant view of the courts and UNHCR has been that the Refugee Convention's object and purpose is to provide international protection to those in need and to protect and promote the rights and freedoms of refugees.[55] The Australian High Court further noted that the convention was designed to ensure mistakes of the middle of the twentieth century were not repeated, referring to various countries not providing refuge to those persecuted in the Second World War.[56]

UNHCR described the object and purpose as a combination of the two perspectives: 'to ensure the protection of the specific rights of refugees, to encourage international cooperation in that regard, including through UNHCR, and to prevent the refugee problem from becoming a cause of tensions between states'.[57]

UNHCR referred to the VCLT and its role in the interpretation of the treaty and reiterated the significance of the relationship between human rights and refugee protection.[58] In fact, UNHCR's *Interpreting Article 1 of the 1951 Convention Relating to the Status of Refugees* explicitly made this connection noting that:'Refugees are owed international protection precisely because their human rights are under threat'.[59]

This supports the view that the refugee test must be holistic and that the Refugee Convention established a system for States to provide protection 'because their human rights are under threat'.[60]

This section did not deal with the CRC as it was not mentioned in any of the sources discussed herein. Nevertheless, it is clear that: (a) children are not extensively referred to in the UDHR, but they are not excluded, (b) the CRC is now considered to form part of the international human rights framework, despite having been published after the drafting of the Refugee Convention and (c) there is an established approach which reflects the holistic nature of human rights law as argued by Foster. It follows that the CRC can form part of the holistic approach to the intepretation of the Refugee Convention. The following section turns to the object and purpose of the CRC.

The object and purpose of the Convention on the Rights of the Child

The preamble of the CRC makes a number of references to human rights and fundamental freedoms. The first three recitals of the preamble refers to principles contained within the Charter of the UN, the UDHR, the International Covenant on Civil and Political Rights (ICCPR) and the International

Covenant on Economic, Social and Cultural Rights (ICESCR) acknowledging their contributions in recognising 'the inherent dignity and the equal and inalienable rights of all members of the human family'; the 'human rights … dignity and worth of the human person' and that 'everyone is entitled to all the rights and freedoms set forth' within the IBR 'without distinction'. This indicates that the CRC also builds upon the human rights framework: 'Recalling that, in the Universal Declaration of Human Rights, the United National has proclaimed that childhood is entitled to special care and assistance'.

The CRC in this way also refers to the 1924 (League of Nations) and 1959 (United Nations) Declarations of the Rights of the Child (discussed in Chapter 3). These references indicate that the CRC's object and purpose in one respect is to ensure that children have access to the extensive rights associated with the human person as previously developed within the UN treaty system, reminiscent of the liberationist approach discussed in Chapter 2. The preamble also states outright that children are subjects of individualised rights:

> Considering that the child should be fully prepared to live an individual life in society, and brought up in the spirit of the ideals proclaimed in the Charter of the United Nations, and in particular the spirit of peace, dignity, tolerance, freedom, equality and solidarity.

This recital emphasises the right to develop as an important element of the experience of childhood. This recital therefore indicates that within the CRC, children were considered by the drafters to be subjects of human rights law, not merely objects. Chapters 2 and 3 discussed the children's rights movement. This movement led to a paradigm shift in children's rights law. Children were subsequent to the movement considered more and more to be subjects of law. This notion, now arguably normative in nature, is reflected in the CRC.

However the preamble also establishes that children required *special care and assistance*, as provided for in the 1959 Declaration of the Rights of the Child: 'the child, by reason of his physical and mental immaturity, needs special safeguards and care, including appropriate legal protection, before as well as after birth'. The preamble emphasises that children need assistance and protection to ensure full access to those rights. This indicates that under the CRC children are not only subjects of the laws relating to their own development and experiences of childhood, they are also objects of the law in the case of protection rights, reminiscent of the protectionist approach.

The preamble also contains some conflicting references that confuse the object and purpose of the CRC. Firstly, there are two recitals that refer to the importance of family life and the child's right to a family environment. The first recital provides that the family unit is the fundamental group in society, which requires protection:

> Convinced that the family, as the fundamental group of society and the natural environment for the growth and well-being of all its members and particularly children, should be afforded the necessary protection and assistance so that it can fully assume its responsibilities within the community[61]

This recital perhaps reflects the difficulty in balancing the rights of the child with the rights of the family unit. Placing the family unit to the fore suggests that that unit has rights within the construct of children's rights as established by the CRC. This paradox has been present in debates since the beginning of the children's rights movement, as discussed in Chapters 2 and 3. This also undermines, in some way, Goodwin-Gill's assertion that children are 'subjects, not objects' of international human rights law. The literature suggested that the CRC had to strike the right balance between acknowledging the inherent rights of children, while recognising the important role of the family and indeed the rights of the family unit, including rights relating to privacy.[62] The reluctance to attribute rights to children identified across centuries in Chapter 2 persists into the drafting phase of the CRC.

The second recital provides: 'that the child, for the full and harmonious development of his or her personality, should grow up in a family environment, in an atmosphere of happiness, love and understanding'.[63]

This recital arguably constructs the family from the child's perspective and how the family should benefit the child. This introduced scope for intervention where the family environment fails to provide 'happiness, love and understanding'. This also indicates that the drafters recognised that although the parents play an important role in protecting children, children also have rights separate to that family unit.[64] This recital also underlines the importance of the right to develop – 'full and harmonious development' – demonstrating that Article 6 forms part of the overall object and purpose of the CRC.

Overall, the preamble suggests that the object and purpose of the CRC is to ensure the protection of children and facilitate their growth into adulthood considering the volume of human rights that already apply to children as human beings. The CRC places this obligation not only on States to oversee the implementation of protection rights, but also family units as the potential mechanism through which protection is delivered. This is consistent with the conceptualisation of childhood in international law as established in Chapter 3.

The Refugee Convention is not referred to in the preamble, but the content, as Foster and Klabbers argued, also informs the object and purpose of a given treaty. There is one provision, Article 22, which relates specifically to seeking refugee protection (discussed in Chapter 3). However, it does not state that children have the right to seek asylum or provide guidance as to the CRC rights violations that may invoke the Refugee Convention. It merely states that all children should have access to CRC rights, including child refugees and children seeking refugee protection. There is nevertheless a wealth of provisions that relate to protecting children from: violence, abuse, neglect,[65] child labour,[66] drug abuse,[67] sexual exploitation, trafficking, sale, abduction,[68] torture and inhuman treatment[69] and underage military recruitment.[70] These provisions reinforce the notion that children need extra support and protection without making a link with qualification as a refugee.

There is also an international element to the rights contained within the CRC, reflected in the final recital of the preamble: 'Recognizing the importance of international co-operation for improving the living conditions of children in every country, in particular in the developing countries'.

Conclusion on objects and purposes

The object and purpose of the CRC relates primarily to protecting and promoting the fundamental rights and freedoms of children in particular their development. Although it is not possible to suggest that the object and purpose of the CRC is to provide refugee protection to children, the content of the convention indicates that there is the potential for the CRC to be read in conjunction with the Refugee Convention. This case is best made by referring back to the Refugee Convention and the strong presence international human rights law has within that framework. It is possible to suggest that the CRC is now part of the human rights regime and that there is therefore scope for it to be considered within refugee determinations following the human rights argument set out by Foster and outlined in Chapter 1. The following section looks at UN soft law guidance that was produced by UNHCR and the Committee to bridge the gap between refugee law and children's rights following the adoption of the CRC.

A children's rights approach – justification through UN Guidance

Before turning to a discussion on what a children's rights approach to the interpretation of the Refugee Convention might look like, it is important to justify its legitimacy. Chapter 3 briefly mentioned the difficulty in advocating for a children's rights approach – an approach that would effectively allow for the rights outlined in the CRC to be used as part of the mechanism to interpret the Refugee Convention in the case of child applicants. However, the response in guidance, law and jurisprudence has been that such an approach is possible. Let us not forget also that all human rights instruments discussed in Chapter 3 and herein in their preambles called upon States to consider other areas of law and the rights therein. For example, both the preambles in the CRC and the Refugee Convention draw the readers' attention to the State's already existing obligations under the UDHR. The need for consistency in the application of the Refugee Convention has been expressed in case law[71] and also by UNHCR.[72] In light of these insights, it is possible to see a justification for a uniform children's rights approach in the assessment of refugee claims. There is also a need to 'bridge the gap' between the two areas of law described in the previous chapters as representing a dichotomy.

While children's rights have been referred to in refugee case law, international guidance and some domestic policy and legislation, a universal approach does not exist. The CRC is applied in refugee law inconsistently across jurisdictions, with some countries more likely than others to regard human rights treaties as having a role in decision-making and adjudication. There have only been sparse references to the CRC in national frameworks for asylum determinations, leaving the interpretation of the Refugee Convention in reference to children's rights up to the decision-makers, tribunals and courts. This has resulted in the disordered application of children's rights in the interpretation of the Refugee Convention. There is nevertheless evidence to suggest that a children's rights approach is possible. This section seeks to further demonstrate this possibility through an examination of key guidance materials.

There are two significant sources of soft law guidance, which have responded over the years to children's rights law and refugee law together. The first source is UNHCR, which has issued guidance and guidelines and produced research addressing the particular needs of child refugees. The second source is the Committee on the Rights of the Child (Committee). The Committee monitors the implementation of the CRC and three Optional Protocols on the involvement of children in armed conflict, on the sale of children, child prostitution and child pornography and on a communication procedure.[73] The Committee issues General Comments that provide guidance to States Parties on the interpretation of the CRC. The Committee has mentioned refugee children in a number of General Comments. The Comments serve as a primary source for the interpretation of the CRC. They have also impacted upon the interpretation of other areas of law where children are concerned. However, neither source produced binding guidance. This section looks at the contributions made by UNHCR and the Committee towards bridging the gap between refugee law and children's rights law. This section seeks to ascertain to what degree UNHCR and the Committee have provided guidance that would suggest that a children's rights approach is possible and indeed necessary.

United Nations High Commissioner for Refugees

UNHCR's *Guidelines on International Protection: Child Asylum Claims under Articles 1(A)2 and 1(F) of the 1951 Convention and/or 1967 Protocol relating to the Status of Refugees* (Guidelines) was published in December 2009. The Guidelines, like all guidelines published by UNHCR, provides 'legal interpretive guidance for governments, legal practitioners, decision makers and the judiciary, as well as UNHCR staff carrying out refugee status determination in the field'.[74]

The Guidelines mentioned the CRC in the introduction, noting that 'a child-sensitive application of the refugee definition would be consistent with the [CRC]'.[75] UNHCR reiterated the Committee's guidance on interpreting the refugee definition, which stated that it

> must be interpreted in an age and gender-sensitive manner, taking into account the particular motives for, and forms and manifestations of, persecution experienced by children. Persecution of the kin; under-age recruitment; trafficking of children for prostitution; and sexual exploitation or subjection to female genital mutilation, are some of the child-specific forms and manifestations of persecution which may justify the granting of refugee status if such acts are related to one of the 1951 Refugee Convention grounds. States should, therefore, give utmost attention to such child-specific forms and manifestations of persecution as well as gender-based violence in national refugee status determination procedures.[76]

In 1987, UNHCR's Executive Committee published a Conclusion on Refugee Children. The Committee noted that children 'constitute approximately one half of the world's refugee population' and reiterated their position that children need special protection and assistance. In this Conclusion, the Committee 'called upon' the High Commissioner to develop guidelines 'in consultation with concerned organizations' to promote co-operation to improve the protection, security, well-being and psychological development of refugee children. The Committee also called upon the High Commissioner to establish a working group on child refugees.[77] The Guidelines on Refugee Children were then published one year before the adoption of the CRC in 1988, followed by a reviewed version, updated and published in 1993, as the UNHCR Policy on Refugee Children.[78] The 1993 Policy referred to the CRC noting that it 'codified standards for the rights of all children, including those who are refugees'.[79] The Policy also noted that the CRC

> provides a comprehensive framework for the responsibilities of its States Parties to all children within their borders, including those who are of concern to UNHCR. Moreover, as a United Nations convention, it constitutes a normative frame of reference for UNHCR's action. The policy which follows, therefore, is consistent with the Convention on the Rights of the Child. It also provides parameters for action which supplement those contained in this Convention and which aim to ensure appropriate protection and assistance of children of concern to the High Commissioner.

This development indicated that the CRC is relevant in the context of refugee law and that the UNHCR viewed the CRC as a normative instrument that should be used when developing laws and policies. This also showed that immediately following the adoption of the CRC, UNHCR began to respond (and even during its drafting, see the above 1987 Conclusion on Refugee Children). This supports the idea that the CRC as a 'United Nations convention'[80] forms part of the broader human rights framework.

The 1994 *Refugee Children: Guidelines on Protection and Care* continued in this vein and stated from the outset that the book 'came to be written' on the basis of historical developments including the 'most recent forebear' of human rights, the CRC.[81] In fact, the first substantive chapter of the Guidelines was entitled 'Refugee Children and the Rights of the Child'. The authors referred to the CRC as important to refugee children as 'it sets comprehensive standards' and it has 'gained importance' to refugee children due to 'it's near universal ratification'.[82] However, these insights do not suggest that the CRC can be used as an interpretive tool as to children's eligibility for protection, just that the CRC articulated a host of rights relevant to refugees.

UNHCR in 1997 expanded upon their guidance in relation to refugee children with the publication of their *Guidelines on Policies and Procedures in dealing with Unaccompanied Children Seeking Asylum*. The 1997 Guidelines referred to the CRC reiterating that 'in the treatment of issues concerning unaccompanied children seeking asylum' the CRC should be taken into account as one part of the framework of international standards. In addition to describing the ways in which the CRC was relevant for procedures, the Guidelines also provided a clear statement on the way the CRC is relevant in the determination of child asylum claims

> It should be borne in mind that, under the Convention on the Rights of the Child, children are recognized certain specific human rights, and that the manner in which those rights may be violated as well as the nature of such violations may be different from those that may occur in the case of adults. Certain policies and practices constituting gross violations of specific rights of the child may, under certain circumstances, lead to situations that fall within the Scope of the Refugee Convention. Examples of such policies and practices are the recruitment of children for regular or irregular armies, their subjection to forced labour, the trafficking of children for prostitution and sexual exploitation and the practice of female genital mutilation.

The 1997 guidance therefore suggested, nine years on, that the CRC is an instrument through which the Refugee Convention should be interpreted 'under certain circumstances'. This brings this discussion up to date with the 2009 UNHCR Guidelines discussed at the introduction to this section.

The 2009 Guidelines have been referred to in higher courts in respect of child asylum seekers, for example in the case of *DS (Afghanistan) v. Secretary of State for the Home*, discussed in detail in Chapter 6. Lord Justice Pill referred to the Guidelines in response to the submission of various passages[83] by the Queen's Counsel (QC) for the appellant.[84]

There is extensive guidance on the relevance and the application of the CRC in the field of refugee protection provided by UNHCR. The reference to UNHCR guidelines in case law indicates an acknowledgement by decision-makers of the relevance of the CRC in the interpretation of the Refugee Convention, and the relevance of the guidelines, despite the fact that they are non-binding. The 2009 Guidelines are referred to throughout Chapter 6 alongside children's rights discussed in the context of refugee law. The Guidelines act as a conduit between the two areas of law in some cases.

Before moving on to the Committee, it is important to note that there are limitations to the UNHCR guidance. In the first instance, the materials stem from the definition of refugee as we are accustomed to it, in an adult context. Although attempts were made to reduce the threshold and provide for certain extra safeguards, the UNHCR guidance materials do not originate from a children's rights perspective. Furthermore the guidance materials are heavily focused on protection-based rights (discussed in Chapter 6), which is not reflective of the three categories of rights that children have under the CRC or indeed the characteristics that we typically attribute to childhood, such as the right to positive development. This research seeks to provide further insight into a children's rights approach to the interpretation of the Refugee Convention by starting from an analysis of the rights children possess and identify which rights are so fundamental that when they are breached may amount to persecution. Although it is not proposed that the any violation of a children's right amounts to persecution, it is suggested that the efforts taken by the UNHCR were refugee law centric and not children's rights centric and that there is indeed scope for a widening of the approach taken in the case of child applicants to reflect the Three Ps and the right to *life, survival and development*. This is developed in Chapter 6.

Committee on the Rights of the Child

The Committee also began referring to the case of refugee children soon after the publication of the CRC.[85] The first comprehensive example of guidance to this effect was General Comment No. 6 *on the treatment of unaccompanied and separated children outside their country of origin* (Comment No. 6). However, General Comment No. 5 *General measures of implementation of the Convention on the Rights of the Child (arts. 4, 42 and 44, para. 6)*[86] assisted in making the argument that there is a relationship between the CRC and the Refugee Convention. Comment No. 5, reiterating CRC Article 41(b),[87] stated:

> As part of its consideration of general measures of implementation, and in the light of the principles of indivisibility and interdependence of human rights, the Committee consistently urges States parties, if they have not already done so, to ratify the two Optional Protocols to the Convention on the Rights of the Child (on the involvement of children in armed conflict and on the sale of children, child prostitution and child pornography) and the six other major international human rights instruments. During its dialogue with States parties the Committee often encourages them to consider ratifying other relevant international instruments. A nonexhaustive list of these instruments is annexed to the present general comment, which the Committee will update from time to time.[88]

The Committee emphasised the interdependence of human rights treaties and encouraged States to ratify other human rights instruments. This is an important statement as it came from the Committee with responsibility for the CRC – the most ratified UN convention.

Comment No. 6 went into greater detail on interpreting the CRC, in light of the situation of unaccompanied and separated children. Comment No. 6 reiterated the principle articulated in Comment No. 5 and CRC Article 41(b) (as above).[89] Although the Comment did not frame itself as a tool for the interpretation of the Refugee Convention, it is a useful tool through which to do so. The failure to refer directly to the Refugee Convention in the 'objectives'[90] on the one hand does not support the contention that the CRC is a framework to apply in the interpretation of the Refugee Convention. On the other hand, it indicates that the rights of unaccompanied children and separated children exist in a space bigger than the narrow refugee framework. Sir Goodwin-Gill also referred to this paradox in his assessment of the utility of the CRC in the context of durable solutions for refugee children: 'Here, the Convention on the Rights of the Child (CRC) offers substantial general support for a comprehensive approach to durable solutions, but in a sense wider than is normally understood with respect to refugees'.[91]

The other reason the Refugee Convention is not referred to, to the exclusion of other international treaties, in the 'objectives' relates to the simple fact that not all unaccompanied and separated children are refugees or persons seeking international protection.[92] The Refugee Convention is nevertheless referred to alongside various other relevant international legal instruments under the section titled 'Applicable Principles'.[93]

Comment No. 6 referred to the Refugee Convention on eight occasions in the body of the text.[94] Most significantly, the Comment included the principle of *non-refoulement* as contained within Article 33 of the Refugee Convention (and Article 3 of the Convention against Torture and Other Cruel, Inhuman or Degrading Treatment or Punishment)[95] within the list of six General Principles. The other five are those designated General Principles by Comment No. 5: best interests, non-discrimination, the right to be heard, the right to survive and develop (as discussed in Chapter 3)[96] and the right to confidentiality, another principle arising from the CRC.[97] This indicates the Committee's view that a principle commonly attributed to refugee law is as important as the General Principles identified initially by the Committee in the application of the CRC at least in the case of separated and unaccompanied children.[98]

Following the publication of Comment No.6, the Committee discussed child refugees in a more substantive way.[99] General Comment No. 9 *the rights of children with disabilities*, for example, referred not only to the Refugee Convention, but also to the various UNHCR child-specific guidance as well as Comment No. 6.[100] General Comment No. 17 *on the right of the child to rest, leisure, play, recreational activities, cultural life and the arts (art. 31)* referred heavily to refugee children and the particular challenges they face in accessing CRC Article 31. These comments, among others, indicate that efforts were made by the Committee to suggest ways to interpret the Refugee Convention and to influence the treatment of child refugees globally in light of developments in the area of children's rights.

Most recently, the Committee on the Elimination of Discrimination against Women and the Committee (CEDAW) published a joint 'general recommendation/general comment'[101] 'on harmful practices'.[102] The Joint Recommendation/Comment provided guidance to assist States in their efforts to eliminate harmful practices. It referred directly to the qualification of children as refugees,[103] noting that 'asylum officials should be aware that women and girls may be fleeing their country of origin to avoid undergoing a harmful practice'.[104] This example shows that not only are two human rights bodies collaborating thus showing the interdependence of human rights instruments and fields, the two regimes pointed to their direct relationship with the Refugee Convention. In other words, the Joint Recommendation/Comment provided guidance for the interpretation of the Refugee Convention through the lens of two other human rights instruments: the CRC and the CEDAW.

The Committee stated that the obligation to ensure access to the asylum procedure, legal safeguards and rights in asylum begins with Article 22 of the CRC, which requires States to take 'appropriate measures' to ensure eligible children receive appropriate protection.[105] The Committee argued that States should take into account existing international standards including those deriving from international refugee law when implementing Article 22. The Committee therefore acknowledged that those interpreting the CRC must consider the refugee framework. However, Article 22 does not refer to the qualification of children as refugees. This is a significant challenge to the children's rights approach. However, developments in courts have shown that it is not insurmountable (see also Chapter 6). This is evidenced by the fact that the Comments of the Committee have been referred to in case law around the world,[106] including in the case of refugee law.[107]

The Committee provided a wealth of guidance in respect of child refugees and children engaged in the asylum process. The fact that the Committee's comments, including Comment No. 6, have been used in legal submissions in applications for international protection and appeals and are sometimes referenced in judgments arising from higher courts[108] indicates the CRC's relevance in the interpretation of the Refugee Convention. However, much like the UNHCR guidance, the Committee's efforts to elaborate on child refugees, in particular in relation to their qualification, do not provide all the answers. No 'comment' was drafted to specifically address the matters related to qualification as a refugee, i.e. in which instances a violation of a CRC right might amount to persecution or have a nexus with the Refugee Convention. Most of the guidance provided by the Committee in respect of child refugees and asylum seekers relates to procedural rights, safeguards and care.

Part II looks to the detail of persecution and how UNHCR, the Committee and the CRC have influenced the qualification of children-as-refugees. Before discussing developments in respect of child persecution, the following section examines the challenges inherent in applying the children's rights regime in the context of refugee law. The same section also looks at the limitations associated with the guidance discussed in this section.

Challenges in the interpretation of the Refugee Convention in respect of children's rights

A 'children's rights approach' to the interpretation of the Refugee Convention is not explicitly mentioned or defined in the literature. The literature, guidance, law and case law, however, indicate that in interpreting the Refugee Convention in the case of children, a different approach is required. The abovementioned sources outlined the ways in which CRC and children's rights more generally impact upon the Refugee Convention. The Committee has also consistently recommended to States to give legal effect to the CRC.[109] This means that there is a framework for the interpretation of the Refugee Convention considering child-specific rights. However, a number of matters remain to be resolved.

Firstly, not all State Parties have transposed or given legal effect to the CRC. Some States or courts may be reluctant to engage with the CRC due to the fact that it is not transposed into their national law.[110] This is typically explained away as CRC rights are widely considered to be normative in nature, as discussed in Chapter 3. Nevertheless, the different approaches nationally to transposing or relying upon the CRC have resulted in its inconsistent application, including in the context of refugee law.

Secondly, it is not clear which children's rights are applicable in the context of refugee law. Identifying these rights and analysing the law in practice to date is the focus of Chapter 6, which revisits the Three Ps Approach and the rights identified in Chapter 3 and their application in refugee law.

Thirdly, the guidance mentioned above is considered to be soft law. Soft law guidance, though useful, is not binding on States. It can therefore be seen merely as an interpretive tool States or decision-makers *may* use.[111] The absence of binding guidance has also contributed to the inconsistent application of children's rights in the interpretation of the Refugee Convention. This is of particular concern as there is no international treaty that deals with the specific circumstances of child refugees. There are, however, some regional examples of law, which have included child-specific forms of persecution as part of the definition of persecution.[112] European Union law, for example, provides for the inclusion of 'acts of a gender-specific or child-specific nature' within the definition of 'acts of persecution' in Directive 2011/95/EU of the European Parliament and of the Council of 13 December 2011 *on standards for the qualification of third-country nationals or stateless persons as beneficiaries of international protection, for a uniform status for refugees or for persons eligible for subsidiary protection, and for the content of the protection granted (recast)*.[113]

This section shows that guidance and the modern interpretation of the rules of treaty interpretation support the potential for a children's rights approach to the interpretation of the Refugee Convention. However, this chapter has not answered the question: is the Refugee Convention a sufficient framework for determining child refugee claims? The following chapter looks at this question and revisits the question of consistency given the absence of legal and binding guidance dealing with child refugee claimants. Chapter 6 also looks at how the law is applied in practice to examine to what extent the CRC has influenced refugee decision-making and if a children's rights approach is possible and whether or not it is needed.

The litmus test for tracking the progress of the children's rights approach lies with persecution. Persecution is central to the definition of 'refugee' as established in the previous chapter and developed below. Through the lens of persecution, we can see how children's rights have been considered and to what extent they form part of assessments for refugee protection. The following section therefore takes a closer look at persecution and the other key elements of persecution. This assists in our effort to elaborate on the possibility of a children's rights approach while keeping in mind the secondary objective, which is to establish a conceptualisation of the child refugee. The following section serves to look briefly at the definition of persecution and the ancillary elements of persecution as a backdrop to be built upon in Chapter 6.

Part II

A brief introduction to persecution

The question of persecution is central to refugee determinations;[114] however, persecution was not defined in the Refugee Convention. The definition has been left to decision-makers and courts to interpret.[115] Given the centrality of the discussions and debate around persecution, the way it is defined in the case of children is critical to the analysis herein. The term persecution has been grappled with in guidance and jurisprudence over the years, leading UNHCR to note: 'There is no universally accepted definition of "persecution", and various attempts to formulate such a definition have met with little success'.[116]

There have nevertheless been attempts to define it in law and literature. In 1953, Vernant described persecution as akin to: 'severe sanctions and measures of an arbitrary nature, incompatible with the principles set forth in the Universal Declaration of Human Rights'.[117]

From as early as 1953, it was suggested that the framework for human rights be the 'barometer'[118] for persecution.[119] In 1991, Hathaway described persecution as the 'sustained or systemic violation of a basic human right demonstrative of a failure of state protection'.[120] He also proposed that the IBR inform the examination of the nature and seriousness of the harm experienced or feared by an applicant to assess whether or not it amounted to persecution.

In 2012, the Court of Justice of the European Union Advocate General in *Germany v Y and Z* defined persecution as an 'act of the utmost gravity, because it sets out flagrantly and persistently to deny the most essential rights of the human person, on the basis of skin color, nationality, gender, sexual orientation, political beliefs or religious convictions'.[121]

In 2006, UNHCR in their *Master Glossary of Terms*, described persecution '*to comprise human rights abuses or other serious harm, often, but not always, with a systematic or repetitive element*'.[122]

The CRC was not mentioned in the analysis by Hathaway or others. Children were not extensively referred to in any key literature on refugee law as highlighted in Chapter 1. However, the approach put forward generally by Vernant, Hathaway and Foster highlighted the importance of considering the human rights framework. This is relevant in the case of children's claims in two respects. Firstly, some children's rights are included in the IBR *and* the CRC is informed by those rights. Secondly, the CRC is arguably considered another human rights treaty, as discussed in the previous section, and can therefore be assumed to play a role in a persecution barometer.[123] In general, the acceptance of the Hathaway approach has resulted in an expansion of the scope of persecution to include child-specific persecution.[124]

Persecution and children

Children are considered to be of the most vulnerable of the refugee demographic.[125] The existing literature referred to children fleeing for the same reasons as adults, for example, from war, conflict and civil unrest.[126] However, the literature also noted that children are subjected to other violations of human rights and child-specific rights, including: trafficking, bonded labour, forced military conscription, child abuse, gender-based violence, child prostitution and pornography and other forms of exploitation, forced marriage, religious servitude and female genital mutilation.[127] Bhabha and Young argued that children are *increasingly* 'themselves targets for human rights abuses'.[128] They categorised child refugee claims as: '(1) Situations which amount to 'persecution' for adult asylum seekers and for children, (2) Situations which are of a child-specific persecution that only arise in relation to children and (3) Situations which when applied to children (but not adults) amount to persecution'.[129]

The above guidance, literature and case law suggested that not only are there examples of persecution that are child-specific, the severity of the harm or ill-treatment does not need to reach the same threshold in the case of children as their adult counterparts. One example of applying a lower threshold[130] and a form of child-specific persecution referred to by UNHCR is the *witnessing* of violence, including domestic violence, considering the possibility of psychological harm.[131] UNHCR and others have contended that children are more sensitive to acts that target close relatives, including witnessing violence and experiencing fear even if the act was not perpetrated against them.[132] As Bhabha noted, 'There may be situations where children should be considered victims of persecution though they have suffered *less harm* than would be required for an adult', including separation from family in war, conflict or displacement, trafficking, gang violence and homelessness.[133] These examples are expanded upon in Chapter 6, but we can already see a strong protectionist presence in the literature and case law. Absence of family is also prominent and as discussed the role of family in the context of Article 6 is an important consideration in rights generally and refugee law specifically (also revisited in Chapter 6).

The abovementioned rights violations, for example, separation from family, displacement generally and homelessness, primarily fall within the provision and protection categories of the Three Ps Approach. Experiences arising from conflict, war, exploitation, violence, trafficking and gang violence also fall within the protection rights category. These are examples of child-specific forms of persecution discussed in the literature reinforcing the tendency to view children as victims and not persons with the capacity to exercise their agency (as discussed in Chapter 3).

Persecution in United Nations High Commissioner for Refugees Guidance

UNHCR, as mentioned above, acknowledged that persecution experienced or feared by children may differ from the experiences or fears of adults *and* that the scope of persecution should be widened by encouraging the consideration of the CRC. UNHCR in their Guidelines stated that 'persecution' in respect of children:

> can be considered to involve serious human rights violations, including a threat to life or freedom, as well as other kinds of serious harm or

> intolerable situations as assessed with regard to the age, opinions, feelings, psychological make-up of the applicant. Discrimination may amount to persecution in certain situations where the treatment feared or suffered leads to consequences of a substantially prejudicial nature for the child concerned. The principle of the best interests of the child requires that the harm be assessed from the child's perspective. This may include an analysis as to how the child's rights or interests are, or will be, affected by the harm. Ill-treatment which may not rise to the level of persecution in the case of an adult may do so in the case of a child.[134]

UNHCR suggested that persecution must consider the child's rights reflected in the CRC and the child's interest in accordance with the best interests principle. UNHCR also noted that 'a contemporary and child-sensitive understanding of persecution encompasses many types of human rights violations, including violations of child-specific rights' arguing that it is 'essential to analyse the standards of the CRC'.[135]

The Committee emphasised that in interpreting persecution within the context of the Refugee Convention, the State must consider the differences in the experiences and manifestations of persecution in the case of children. The Committee listed a number of examples that are also grounded in protection rights, where children are more often considered as objects of law: 'persecution of the kin; under-age recruitment; trafficking of children for prostitution; and sexual exploitation or subjection to female genital mutilation'.[136] UNHCR noted that these reasons must have a link to one of the five convention grounds.[137]

Kilkelly noted that 'The CRC, rather than contributing to the disaggregation of international human rights law, has led to a cross-fertilisation of children's rights within and between differing domestic, supra-national and international legal systems'.[138] This cross-fertilisation also applies to persecution. There is a wealth of guidance, literature, legislation and case law reflecting the developments in the interpretation of the term persecution in the case of children. Indeed, some of these developments reflected guidance of the CRC, as discussed in this section. Some countries have introduced child-specific guidelines. And in some countries these developments are reflected in a body of case law.[139]

Persecution in practice

In *AA (unattended children) Afghanistan*, for example, the UK Upper Tribunal found that a child applicant who left Afghanistan at 14 was entitled to recognition as a refugee due to the child's well-founded fear of being persecuted on the basis of his membership of his family and being associated with their political opinions (discussed in further detail in Chapter 6). The applicant challenged the original decision to refuse refugee protection and grant discretionary leave on the basis that there were no suitable care arrangements available for the child if returned.[140] The Tribunal therefore had to consider whether or not the persecution feared rose to the level of persecution, referred to as an 'up-grade appeal'.[141] The Tribunal concluded that the applicant's political opinion ('whether actual, or imputed by reason of family membership')[142] did indeed rise to the level of persecution and the appeal was successful.

In relation to the CRC, the Upper Tribunal in *AA (unattended children) Afghanistan* held that in determining the viability of internal relocation they had an obligation to consider the provisions of the CRC in accordance with recital 20 of the Qualification Directive: 'It is necessary, when assessing applications from minors for international protection, that Member States should have regard to child-specific forms of persecution'.[143]

The Tribunal also referred to *R (on the application of Howard League for Penal Reform) v Secretary of State for the Home Department & Anor* and the observations made by Munby J:

> The European Convention is, of course, now part of our domestic law by reason of the Human Rights Act 1998. Neither the UN Convention [on the Rights of the Child] nor the European Charter is at present legally binding in our domestic law and they are therefore not sources of law in the strict sense. But both can, in my judgment, properly be consulted insofar as they proclaim, reaffirm or elucidate the content of those human rights that are generally recognised throughout the European family of nations, in particular the nature and scope of those fundamental rights that are guaranteed by the European Convention.[144]

This section highlights the existing discourse on child-specific persecution. This brief introduction to persecution and child-specific forms of persecution indicates the willingness of the international community, legislators and decision-makers to interpret the Refugee Convention differently in the case of children's claims compared with their adult counterparts, including by referring to the CRC and other guidance. The developments in relation to persecution are discussed at length in Chapter 6. Chapter 6 seeks to establish a conceptualisation of the child refugee, among other objectives described throughout this book, and persecution is central in doing so. The following sections look at other elements of the definition of persecution which aid us in conceptualising child refugees.

Actors of persecution and protection and the role of the family

The agents or actors of persecution are typically conceived of as State actors – either agents of the State or agents acting on behalf of the State. However, under the Refugee Convention, actors of persecution may also be individuals with no affiliation to the State itself.[145] Child applicants must nevertheless prove that the feared or experienced persecution would be/was at the hands of the government, or an agent of the government or another person or persons.[146] The applicant must show that they sought protection unless seeking protection from the government would have put the applicant at risk or would have been futile based on a history of inaction.[147] Assessments include looking at the existence of legal systems that criminalise and sanction acts of persecution and evidence to suggests acts would be prosecuted.[148] The applicant must also be able to demonstrate that the State facilitates, encourages or tolerates the acts of persecution in question *or* is unable or unwilling to intervene on behalf of the persecuted.[149] For example, the State may not be in a position to protect the individual if the country is in the middle of civil-conflict or civil-unrest or where the State lacks the infrastructure to protect the applicant. Both the actors of persecution and the applicants' inability or unwillingness to seek protection from the State must relate to one of the five convention grounds.[150] This also applies in the case of children.[151]

A child's access to State protection may also depend on the ability and willingness of the child's parents or other caregivers to intervene on behalf of the child and/or seek protection from the State on behalf of the child.[152] It is also possible that the home may be the locus of the persecution. Some examples of the parent-as-persecutor dynamic are female genital mutilation, forced child marriage or domestic abuse.[153] In any of these examples, the family may act as a barrier to accessing adequate protection. This is particularly true in countries where States do not intervene in family affairs.[154] Parents or carers may also fail to seek protection on behalf of their children.

This dilemma is central to debates around the child-as-rights-holder. This relationship dynamic impacts upon children's access to all three categories of rights. National laws, international laws and the majority of the discourse on children and childhood identify the parents or responsible adults as the main source of protection (as developed in Chapters 2 and 3). It is when this relationship does not serve to protect children and/or harms children, that is of interest in this context. Chapter 6 also discusses parents as persecutors and parents as protectors.

Children who are not eligible for protection: exclusion

Exclusion forms part of the determination process – once an applicant is found to qualify as a refugee, grounds for exclusion are then also considered as part of the qualification process. The Refugee Convention does not apply to three categories of persons. Article 1D states that persons already in receipt of protection through the United Nations Relief and Works Agency for Palestine are excluded from the provisions contained within the Convention.[155] Additionally, Article 1E excludes persons who can avail of protection in another jurisdiction other than their country of origin where they are already resident.[156] Lastly, Article 1F excludes any person believed to have: committed a war crime or a crime against peace or humanity; committed a serious non-political crime prior to applying for protection; or been found guilty of committing acts contrary to the principles of the UN.[157]

The same exclusions apply to children[158] in particular where they have attained the age of criminal responsibility and are considered to have capacity to commit crimes and understand the consequences of their actions. Exclusion therefore has a link to child agency and participation rights. An assessment of the child's capacity is often an attribute of cases where exclusion is invoked. Recently, case law relating to exclusion and former child soldiers has emerged. The UK Border Agency, for example, rejected an application from a 16-year-old boy from Afghanistan who killed a family member in self-defence. However, the High Court found that 'the primacy of welfare consideration should be manifest … What might be regarded as the right approach for an adult is not always the right approach for a child or young person'.[159]

The UK Border Agency was found to have erred in their decision.[160] More exclusion cases are discussed in Chapter 6.

UNHCR in a letter to legal counsel regarding the International Standards for Exclusion from Refugee Status as Applied to Child Soldiers noted:

> Any exclusion analysis regarding the acts of child soldiers must be undertaken with great care. The use of child soldiers in armed conflict is a practice of increasing international concern and has been condemned by the international community on legal, moral and ethical grounds. Children are often targeted for forcible conscription into military service due to their young age and vulnerability. Many are forced to commit crimes, as well as witness the crimes of others, and as a result are left psychologically and emotionally scarred for years. Access to rehabilitation and social services once a conflict ends is often limited, if not non-existent.

The letter further stated that 'In the case of child soldiers, issues such as age, mental and emotional maturity, voluntariness of service, and treatment by other military personnel, all factor heavily in determining whether exclusion from refugee protection is appropriate'.[161]

The role of the right to participation, or the exercise of choice or agency (as discussed in Chapters 2 and 3) has arisen in child refugee cases dealing with involvement in gang, military or other illicit activities. There is very limited case law dealing with exclusion and very infrequent mention of exclusion in the literature on child refugees, but it is, as said, an emerging issue and one worthy of further comment (see Chapter 6).

Convention grounds

Children as a particular social group

Theorists and child and refugee rights commentators often capture the conceptualisation of a legal framework for the refugee child within the minority construct.[162] Locke, Rousseau, Ariès and contemporary theorists and academics, as well as international law, identify children and the period of childhood as distinct from adulthood. The literature and law also attribute characteristics specific to children, such as a difference in 'capacity' compared with adults. Lastly, it is also largely agreed that children depend on adults to ensure their rights and livelihoods during childhood are protected and promoted. Children are considered in the sociological discourse to represent a unique social group in society based on the aforesaid characteristics.[163] Bhabha and Young, in their article 'Not adults in miniature: unaccompanied child asylum seekers and the new U.S. guidelines', also argued that children can form a particular social group on the basis of a shared 'child-specific' form of persecution.[164] The development of guidance and law in the area of asylum has reflected Bhabha's and Young's view.

Children and the attributes and experiences of childhood are considered to reflect the general meaning and current understanding of the concept of the particular social group as set out in *LQ (age: immutable characteristics) Afghanistan* [2008] UK AIT 00005:

> Age is immutable. It is changing all the time but one cannot do anything to change one's own age at any particular time. [Membership of a particular social group depended on his being a child.] At the date when the appellant's status has to be assessed he is a child and although, assuming he survives, he will in due course cease to be a child, he is immutably a child at the time of assessment.[165]

UNHCR noted that membership of a particular social group 'normally comprises persons of similar background, habits or social status. A claim of a fear of persecution under this heading may frequently overlap with a claim of a fear of persecution on other grounds, i.e. race, religion or nationality'.[166]

The Guidelines emphasised that being a child is 'directly related' to the child's identity and the way their identity is perceived by society.[167] The Guidelines characterised children by their 'innocence, relative immaturity, impressionability and evolving capacities', reminiscent of early theorising and underscored by protection rights. Additionally the Guidelines noted that children can be identified as a social group by their shared experience of childhood: 'children share a common socially-constructed experience, such as being abused, abandoned, impoverished or internally displaced'.[168] The Guidelines also noted that children can be considered a member of a particular social group not related to childhood, or being children, but as a result of another common experience or aspect of their identity for example, 'former child soldiers'.[169] In *MJZ,* the Canadian Convention Refugee Determination Division in 1999 considered abandoned children from Mexico as a particular social group under international law.[170]

There are now innumerable examples of child applicants' cases considered in the context of the particular social group or groups all over the world. In the US in *Matter of S-E-G*, the BIA stated that

> the mutability of age is not within one's control and that if an individual has been persecuted in the past on account of an age-described particular social group, or faces such persecution at a time when that individual's age places him within the group, a claim for asylum may still be cognizable.[171]

There are examples of national guidance that describe instances where children may be considered as members of a particular social group as well. The UK, for example, provided some clarification for case owners responsible for determining children's cases. The guidance entitled 'Processing an asylum claim from a child' noted that:

> Age groupings such as 'children' or 'young men', or 'young girls' may constitute a particular social group; depending on the specific country context and the treatment of this group and how they are perceived within that society and the laws of the relevant country. Case owners should bear in mind that at any given point, a child's age may be considered an immutable characteristic (for example, notwithstanding the fact that the child will ultimately grow out of his/her present age grouping).

It further noted that 'Case owners should also be aware that other particular social groups may be identifiable, such as street children, HIV/AIDS-affected children, children in armed forces or lesbian, gay, bisexual and transgender children'.[172]

UNHCR also highlighted that an adult applicant may still invoke the particular social group ground as its relevance does not necessary cease when childhood ends. Past shared experiences that are unchangeable and historic may also fall within the scope of the ground, for example: former child soldiers or persons who were trafficked as children.[173]

Villarreal in 2004, drawing on the findings in *Sanchez-Trujillo*, considered a landmark case in interpreting the particular social group at the time, and *Matter of Sanchez and Escobar*, also noted, however, that

> Possession of broadly-based characteristics, such as youth, is usually insufficient for a classification in a social group. This is because the term "particular social group" does not "encompass every broadly defined segment of a population, even if a certain demographic division does have some statistical relevance".[174, 175]

In other words, although childhood indicates membership of a particular social group, there must also be a reason for migration that is based on an experience or a well-founded fear of persecution.

The particular social group is the most developed ground in refugee law in the context of children. UNHCR in their *Guidelines on International Protection No. 2: 'Membership of a Particular Social Group' within the context of Article 1A(2) of the 1951 Convention and/or its 1967 Protocol Relating to the Status of Refugees* published in 2009 noted that 'children's claims to refugee status most often have been analysed in the context of the Convention ground of "membership of a particular social group"', while also acknowledging that other grounds may be relevant or invoked.[176]

The case law and guidance established the particular social group ground as the most relevant as it is linked directly to age and to the characteristics associated with age, innocence and vulnerability. Some characteristics, experiences and rights related to childhood are also linked to other convention grounds. They are introduced below in the context of refugee law and guidance and they are also discussed further in Chapter 6.

Race and nationality

Persecution based on race is a common reason for seeking international protection, including in the case of children. Goodwin-Gill and McAdam argue that persecution on grounds of race should take account of Article 1 of the Convention on the Elimination of All Forms of Racial Discrimination.[177] Article 1.1 provided

> the term "racial discrimination" shall mean any distinction, exclusion, restriction or preference based on race, colour, descent, or national or ethnic origin which has the purpose or effect of nullifying or impairing the recognition, enjoyment or exercise, on an equal footing, of human rights and fundamental freedoms in the political, economic, social, cultural or any other field of public life.[178]

UNHCR in the Handbook contended that persecution on grounds of race, in the broadest sense including ethnicity and other minority categorisations, occurs when 'a person's human dignity is affected to such an extent as to be incompatible with the most elementary and inalienable human rights, or where the disregard of racial barriers is subject to serious consequences'.[179]

According to UNHCR, nationality does not only relate to citizenship, but it has also been interpreted to include other minority groups. Goodwin-Gill and McAdam highlighted that this ground may apply in a given State where distinctions are drawn on ethnic, religious, cultural or linguistic lines.[180] For this reason, UNHCR stated that nationality may overlap with the race ground. Additionally, UNHCR acknowledged that the nationality ground may overlap with the political opinion ground in circumstances where two nationality groups in a given country are in conflict and the conflict also manifests in political movements. By this argument, there may also be an overlap with the religion ground. The Handbook clarified that persecution on nationality grounds 'may consist of adverse attitudes and measures directed against a national (ethnic, linguistic) minority and in certain circumstances the fact of belonging to such a minority may in itself give rise to well-founded fear of persecution'.[181]

The Guidelines categorised race, ethnicity and nationality together. The Guidelines described a number of scenarios where the race or nationality ground may be relevant, emphasising the relevance of policies that prohibit children of a particular race from registering at birth or being deprived of nationality.[182] Additionally, it elaborated on policies that block children from a particular race from accessing education[183] or health services[184] as having the potential to amount to persecution. For example, in *D. v Refugee Appeals Tribunal*, (introduced in Chapter 1 and discussed in detail in Chapter 6) the Irish High Court heard a case submitted on behalf of a child who would be denied access to education due to his ethnicity. Justice Hogan noted that the applicant would 'effectively be excluded from any meaningful participation' in society.[185] The Guidelines also highlighted the systematic targeting of girls from particular race or ethnic groups or nationalities for the purposes of trafficking or exploitation.[186]

The race and nationality grounds are discussed further in the following chapter. The discussions surround children's rights as they relate to provision, protection and participation rights and the interactions these rights have with refugee law in particular as they arise in the context of discrimination. The relationship between these convention grounds and the CRC-based rights is also discussed in Chapter 6.

Religion and political opinion

Religious persecution has been a central feature throughout history on every continent. The persecution of the Jews in Europe leading up to and during World War II, the Ahmadis in Pakistan and various other Muslim countries and the Baha'is in Iran are just a few examples of widespread religious persecution.[187] Based on the presumption that all human rights treaties influence each other, Goodwin-Gill and McAdam argued that decision-makers should take account of Article 18 of the ICCPR,[188] which provided that 'Everyone shall have the right to freedom of thought, conscience and religion'.[189] This has also been interpreted to mean that a religion cannot be forced upon someone, nor can a person's right to adopt a religion be violated.[190]

The Handbook provided that 'prohibition of membership of a religious community, of worship in private or in public, of religious instruction, or serious measures of discrimination imposed on persons because they practise their religion or belong to a particular religious community' may amount to persecution.[191] The Handbook emphasised the relevance of the rights to freedom of thought and to practice one's religion, as set out in the UDHR. The Guidelines commented that this convention ground also applies to children in the same way as adults, however, noting that children are not always able to influence their religion. This ground may also relate to circumstances where children do not adhere to set gender roles or fulfil gender-based obligations, discussed below and in Chapter 6.[192]

One point worth brief discussion is the mention of religious education in the Refugee Convention (and the UDHR[193] and the CRC).[194] The Refugee Convention in Article 4 provides that it is the right of the parent to determine the religious education of their children once recognised as refugees. This does not sit easily with a claim from a child based on religious persecution where the locus of the persecution is the home, or where guardians limit access to protection from persecution. For example, where a girl child refuses to wear a burqa due to her religious or political opinion and as a result suffers abuse amounting to persecution in the home. This example does not refer to education, but it highlights the conceptual conflict inherent in Article 4 of the Refugee Convention and how it might influence the child's right to exercise agency in respect of religion or politics. It points to a wider conceptual challenge in the application of refugee law.

The right to one's political opinions exists in international law in the UDHR and the ICCPR. The UDHR in Article 19 and Article 19 of the ICCPR provide that everyone has the right to 'freedom of opinion and expression'. The CRC provides this right in Article 14 (freedom of thought and religion).[195] The political opinion ground relates to opinions held or attributed to, or actions taken by, the applicant 'critical of polices, traditions or methods', which are 'not tolerated by the authorities or society'. Goodwin-Gill and McAdam described political opinion as 'any opinion on any matter in which the machinery of State, government, and policy may be engaged'.[196] The Handbook noted that persecution on this ground may also include opinions relating to gender roles or (and perhaps linked to) non-conformist behaviour.[197] It may also arise in the context of an opinion that was not voiced, but was attributed based on family, race or nationality.[198]

The Guidelines also provide for a multitude of situations and circumstances where the religious and political opinion grounds may become relevant in the case of children. On the one hand, children may be perceived as holding religious beliefs or political opinions based on the views of their parents or their ethnic or racial group. On the other hand, children may in fact hold their own views, which may come into conflict with the views of society, the government or even their own community and family. Regardless of the way this form of persecution may manifest, UNHCR recognised that these convention grounds apply to children in the same way as adults.

The religion and political opinion grounds are discussed in the following chapter in sections dealing with provision, protection and participation rights. The discussions in the provision and protection rights sections surround instances where religion and/or political opinions, which are *imputed* onto the child, affect the child's access to rights and engage the

Refugee Convention. The religion and political opinion grounds are then discussed in the context of participation rights where children exercised or are perceived to have exercised their agency.

Conclusions

This chapter discussed UN soft law guidance that indicated that there is scope for the CRC to influence the treatment of children seeking refugee protection *and* the qualification of child refugees. Additionally, case law has developed which references the provisions of the CRC and as a result impacts on the outcome of refugee decisions. Case law has also emerged that shows that provisions of the CRC have formed part of the analysis of persecution. This is discussed in detail in Chapter 6.

As discussed in the previous chapter, children were largely invisible in refugee discourse before the publication of the CRC and the guidance that followed. This chapter demonstrated that there is considerable justification for the creation of a children's rights approach. The developments relating to treaty interpretation also support this. Although the children's rights regime emerged decades after the publication of the Refugee Convention, guidance considering the contributions made by the CRC on child refugees followed shortly thereafter. The considerable amount of guidance provided by the Committee and UNHCR on the application of the CRC at all levels of the process of seeking refuge, qualifying as a refugee, and the needs of child refugees after formal recognition provides a clear indication that children's rights are influencing refugee law and therefore that there is scope for a formalised children's rights approach.

The literature, guidance, law and case law show that persecution, the central element of determining eligibility for refugee protection, is different in the case of children. The expansion of the interpretation of the term persecution to include breaches in children's rights is gaining ground. UNHCR made clear that the definition for persecution is different for children. It encompasses a wider array of abuses and forms of harm than that experienced by adults. UNHCR provided a requirement that the State determination body apply a lower threshold when considering what amounts to persecution in the case of children. UNHCR also argued that persecution must be considered in line with the standards established by the CRC. These insights indicate the possibility that violations of CRC-based rights may amount to persecution and that a children's rights approach can develop within the framework for the Refugee Convention.

However, this chapter, in discussions on persecution, also brought out the prominence of protection-based rights in particular when captured within the particular social group, which has developed with the idea that children are inherently vulnerable in mind. This illustrated the continued tendency to see children as vulnerable and the reluctance to attribute rights, in particular participation rights, to children (developed in Chapter 6).

Chapter 6 reflects on these discussions and looks at examples in case law where violations of the children's rights identified in Chapter 3 have been found to amount to persecution. Persecution and within that the convention grounds, actors of persecution and protection, and other relevant elements are remarked and expanded upon. Chapter 6, however, is structured in line with the framework established in Chapters 1, 2 and 3. Chapter 6 follows a children's rights approach to refugee law rather than a refugee law approach to children's rights. Chapter 6 looks to bring together discussions on children's rights set out in Chapters 2 and 3 and discussions on refugee law in Chapter 4 and herein to analyse the extent to which the two legal regimes have influenced each other and to take stock of where we are now in the application of children's rights in the context of refugee law.

The Three Ps Approach is not developed in this chapter, but it is the framework for the analysis in Chapter 6. This chapter indicates that a children's rights approach is possible and Chapter 6 builds upon this work to measure the impact children's rights has had in the context of refugee law. Chapter 6 also seeks to determine where we are now in terms of the potential for a children's rights approach and what that approach might look like based on existing case law.

Notes

1 United Nations High Commissioner for Refugees, 'Guidelines on International Protection: Child Asylum Claims under Articles 1(A)2 and 1(F) of the 1951 Convention and 1967 Protocol relating to the Status of Refugees' HCR/GIP/09/08 22 December 2009.

2 United Nations High Commissioner for Refugees, 'Guidelines on International Protection: Child Asylum Claims under Articles 1(A)2 and 1(F) of the 1951 Convention and 1967 Protocol relating to the Status of Refugees' HCR/GIP/09/08 22 December 2009.

3 Convention relating to the Status of Refugees 1951, Article 1A2. For the purposes of the present Convention, the term 'refugee' shall apply to any person who:… (2) As a result of events occurring before 1 January 1951 and owing to well-founded fear of being persecuted for reasons of race, religion, nationality, membership of a particular social group or political opinion, is outside the country of his nationality and is unable or, owing to such fear, is unwilling to avail himself of the protection of that country; or who, not having a nationality and being outside the country of his former habitual residence as a result of such events, is unable or, owing to such fear, is unwilling to return to it.

4 United Nations High Commissioner for Refugees, 'Guidelines on International Protection: Child Asylum Claims under Articles 1(A)2 and 1(F) of the 1951 Convention and 1967 Protocol relating to the Status of Refugees' HCR/GIP/09/08 22 December 2009, para 5: 'A child-sensitive application of the refugee definition would be consistent with the 1989 Convention on the Rights of the Child (hereafter "the CRC")'.

5 See Chapters 2 and 3.

6 Sir Guy Goodwin-Gill, 'Unaccompanied refugee minors: The role and place of international law in the pursuit of durable solutions' (1995) 3 *International Journal of Children's Rights* 405. See also Chapters 2 and 3.

7 See Chapter 4.
8 Michelle Foster, *International Refugee Law and Socio-Economic Rights: Refugee from Deprivation* (CUP 2007).
9 United Nations Human Rights Office of the High Commissioner, 'Committee on the Rights of the Child' <www.ohchr.org/EN/HRBodies/CRC/Pages/CRCIndex.aspx> accessed 15 July 2016.
10 UN Committee on the Rights of the Child, *General comment No. 6 (2005): Treatment of Unaccompanied and Separated Children Outside their Country of Origin* CRC/GC/2005/6.
11 Optional Protocol to the Convention on the Rights of the Child on the sale of children, child prostitution and child pornography A/RES/54/263 of 25 May 2000 entered into force on 18 January 2002.
12 Optional Protocol to the Convention on the Rights of the Child on the involvement of children in armed conflict A/RES/54/263 of 25 May 2000, entry into force 12 February 2002.
13 United Nations High Commissioner for Refugees, 'Guidelines on International Protection: Child Asylum Claims under Articles 1(A)2 and 1(F) of the 1951 Convention and 1967 Protocol relating to the Status of Refugees' HCR/GIP/09/08 22 December 2009 para 4. See also Chapter 6.
14 UNICEF, *The State of the World's Children: A fair chance for every child* (UNICEF 2016).
15 As established in Chapter 4.
16 For information about children affected by conflict, see, for example: Graca Machel, *Impact of Armed Conflict* (UN 1996) <www.un.org/ga/search/view_doc.asp?symbol=A/51/306> accessed 15 July 2016.
17 United Nations High Commissioner for Refugees, 'Guidelines on International Protection: Child Asylum Claims under Articles 1(A)2 and 1(F) of the 1951 Convention and 1967 Protocol relating to the Status of Refugees' HCR/GIP/09/08 22 December 2009 para 33.
18 United Nations High Commissioner for Refugees, 'Guidelines on International Protection: Child Asylum Claims under Articles 1(A)2 and 1(F) of the 1951 Convention and 1967 Protocol relating to the Status of Refugees' HCR/GIP/09/08 22 December 2009 paras 42–47.
19 1951 Convention relating to the Status of Refugees, Article 1A(2).
20 See Chapter 3 on the 'global child'.
21 UN High Commissioner for Refugees, *The Heart of the Matter – Assessing Credibility when Children Apply for Asylum in the European Union* (UNHCR 2014) 66–76.
22 *Ibid.*
23 For more information on procedural matters, see UN High Commissioner for Refugees, *The Heart of the Matter Assessing Credibility when Children Apply for Asylum in the European Union* (UNHCR 2014).
24 Convention on the Rights of the Child, Article 22. See Chapter 3.
25 Michelle Foster, *International Refugee Law and Socio-Economic Rights: Refugee from Deprivation* (CUP 2007).
26 Michelle Foster, *International Refugee Law and Socio-Economic Rights: Refugee from Deprivation* (CUP 2007) 35.
27 Jacqueline Bhabha and Wendy Young, 'Not Adults in Miniature: Unaccompanied Child Asylum Seekers and the New U.S. Guidelines' (1999) 11 (1) *International Journal of Refugee Law* 91.
28 International Law Commission, *Fragmentation of International Law: Difficulties Arising from the Diversification and Expansion of International Law*, Report of the Study Group of the International Law Commission (A/CN.4/L.682 4 April

2006) at 175 in Michelle Foster, *International Refugee Law and Socio-Economic Rights: Refugee from Deprivation* (CUP 2007) 35.

29 This case, *Case C-540/03 – European Parliament v Council of the European Union*, was brought by the European Parliament against the Council of Europe asserting that a section of Council Directive 2003/86/EC on the right to family reunification breached the requirement to respect fundamental rights, referencing Article 24 of the Charter on Fundamental Freedoms and the CRC. In UNICEF and the United Nations Human Rights Office of the High Commissioner European Regional Office, *Judicial Implementation of Article 3 of the CRC in Europe* (UNICEF and the United Nations Human Rights Office of the High Commissioner European Regional Office 2012) 17.

30 Vienna Convention on the Law of Treaties 1969, Article 31.

31 James Hathaway, *The Rights of Refugees under International Law* (CUP 2005) 49–51.

32 For example, *Case of Neulinger and Shuruk v Switzerland* Application No. 41615.07, para 131; *Case of Nunez v Norway* Application No. 38058/09 para 84. These are not asylum cases, but they demonstrate that the CRC has been used in regional courts in Europe.

33 Javaid Rehman, *International Human Rights Law: A Practical Approach* (Longman 2003); John Torpey, *The Invention of the Passport: Surveillance, Citizenship and the State* (CUP 2000).

34 Claudena Skran, 'Historical Development of International Refugee Law' in Andreas Zimmermann (ed.), *The 1951 Convention Relating to the Status of Refugees and its 1967 Protocol: A Commentary* (OUP 2011) 43.

35 Antonio Cassese, *Human Rights in a Changing World* (Temple University Press 1990).

36 Gareth Evans, 'The Responsibility to Protect: From an Idea to an International Norm' in Robert Cooper and Juliette Voinov Kohler (eds), *Responsibility to Protect* (Palgrave 2009)

37 Vienna Convention on the law of treaties 1969, Article 53 Treaties Conflicting with a Peremptory Norm of General International Law ('Jus Cogens'). A treaty is void if, at the time of its conclusion, it conflicts with a peremptory norm of general international law. For the purposes of the present Convention, a peremptory norm of general international law is a norm accepted and recognised by the international community of States as a whole as a norm from which no derogation is permitted and that can be modified only by a subsequent norm of general international law having the same character.

38 See, for example: Daniel Bethlehem et al. (eds), *The Oxford Handbook of International Trade Law* (OUP 2009).

39 Sir Robert Jennings and Sir Arthur Watts, *Oppenheim's International Law: Volume 1 Peace* (9th edn, Longman 1992) 4.

40 See also: Jacqueline Bhabha, 'Demography and Rights: Women, Children and Access to Asylum' (2004) 16(2) *International Journal of Refugee Law* 227.

41 See, generally: Javaid Rehman, *International Human Rights Law: A Practical Approach* (Longman 2003).

42 See, Irish example: International Protection Act 2015, Section 2 'refugee' means a person, other than a person to whom section 10 applies, who, owing to a well-founded fear of being persecuted for reasons of race, religion, nationality, political opinion or membership of a particular social group, is outside his or her country of nationality and is unable or, owing to such fear, is unwilling to avail himself or herself of the protection of that country, or a stateless person, who, being outside of the country of former habitual residence for the same reasons as mentioned above, is unable or, owing to such fear, unwilling to return to it.

43 Thirty-first Amendment of the Constitution Act, 2012, Article 42A 1(2). Provision shall be made by law for the adoption of any child where the parents have failed for such a period of time as may be prescribed by law in their duty towards the child and where the best interests of the child so require.
44 See for example: UK Borders Citizenship and Immigration Act 2009, Section 55.
45 UK Borders Citizenship and Immigration Act 2009, Section 55.
46 See: Vienna Convention on the law of treaties 1969, Article 53 and Andrea Bianchi, 'Human Rights and the Magic of Jus Cogens' (2008) 13(3) *European Journal of International Law* 491.
47 See, for example: Statute of the International Tribunal for the Former Yugoslavia, 1993 and Statute for the International Tribunal for Rwanda 1994.
48 Jean Allain, 'The jus cogens Nature of non-refoulement' (2001) 13(4) *International Journal of Refugee Law* 533.
49 1951 Convention relating to the Status of Refugees, Preamble: Recital 1 Considering that the Charter of the United Nations and the Universal Declaration of Human Rights approved on 10 December 1948 by the General Assembly have affirmed the principle that human beings shall enjoy fundamental rights and freedoms without discrimination; Recital 2 Considering that the United Nations has, on various occasions, manifested its profound concern for refugees and endeavored to assure refugees the widest possible exercises of these fundamental rights and freedoms.
50 See: *Minister for Immigration and Multicultural Affairs v. Mohammed* [2000] 98 FCR 405 at 421. Other judgments reiterating this point: *Applicant A* [1996] 190 CLR 225 at 296–7 (Kirby J); *Wang* [2000] 105 FCR 548 at 74–81 (Merkel J); *Shah* [1999] 2 AC 629 at 639 (Lord Steyn); *Premalal* [1993] 41 FCR 117 at 138 in Michelle Foster, *International Refugee Law and Socio-Economic Rights: Refugee from Deprivation* (CUP 2007).
51 1951 Convention relating to the Status of Refugees, Preamble: Recital 4. Also referred to in *Applicant A* (1996) 190 CLR 225 at 247–248 (Dawson J) & *MMM v. Minister for Immigration and Multicultural Affairs* (1998) 90 FCR 324 in Michelle Foster, *International Refugee Law and Socio-Economic Rights: Refugee from Deprivation* (CUP 2007).
52 UN High Commissioner for Refugees, 'About Us' <www.unhcr.org/pages/49c3646c2.html> accessed 15 July 2016.
53 Jan Klabbers, 'Some Problems regarding the Object and Purpose of Treaties' (1997) 8 *The Finnish Yearbook of International Law* 138.
54 Michelle Foster, *International Refugee Law and Socio-Economic Rights: Refugee from Deprivation* (CUP 2007) 45.
55 Michelle Foster, *International Refugee Law and Socio-Economic Rights: Refugee from Deprivation* (CUP 2007) 40–49.
56 *Chen Shi Hai v. Minister for Immigration and Multicultural Affairs* (2000) 201 CLR 293 at 308 (Kirby J).
57 UN High Commissioner for Refugees, *Interpreting Article 1 of the 1951 Convention Relating to the Status of Refugees* (UNHCR 2001) 2.
58 *Ibid.*
59 *Ibid.*
60 *Ibid.*
61 Convention on the Rights of the Child 1989, Preamble Recital 1.
62 See Chapter 3.
63 Convention on the Rights of the Child 1989, Preamble Recital 2.
64 As established in Chapter 3.
65 Convention on the Rights of the Child 1989, Article 19.

66 *Ibid*, Article 32.
67 *Ibid*, Article 33.
68 *Ibid*, Article 35.
69 *Ibid*, Article 37.
70 *Ibid*, Article 38.
71 See: Reference V94/01570, RRT 28 February 1995 at 4; R v. Secretary of State for the Home Department, ex parte Robinson [1998] QB 929, [1997] 4 All ER 201, [1997] 1 WLR 1162, [1997] Imm AR 568; Horath v. Secretary of State for the Home Department [2000] Imm AR 205 (Ward LJ).
72 See: UN High Commissioner for Refugees, *Report on International Protection* UN Doc. A/AC.96/527 (1996).
73 United Nations Human Rights Office of the High Commissioner, 'Committee on the Rights of the Child' <www.ohchr.org/EN/HRBodies/CRC/Pages/CRCIndex.aspx> accessed 15 July 2016.
74 UNHCR, *Guidelines on International Protection No. 8: Child Asylum Claims under Articles 1(A)2 and 1(F) of the 1951 Convention and/or 1967 Protocol relating to the Status of Refugees*, 22 December 2009, HCR/GIP/09/08, 1.
75 UNHCR, *Guidelines on International Protection No. 8: Child Asylum Claims under Articles 1(A)2 and 1(F) of the 1951 Convention and/or 1967 Protocol relating to the Status of Refugees*, 22 December 2009, HCR/GIP/09/08, para 5.
76 UN Committee on the Rights of the Child, General Comment No. 6 (2005): Treatment of Unaccompanied and Separated Children Outside Their Country of Origin, CRC/GC/2005/6, Sep. 205 para 74.
77 UNHCR Executive Committee Conclusion No. 47 on Refugee Children (XXXVIII) 1987.
78 UNHCR Executive Committee, October 1993 as Document EC/SCP/82, in UN High Commission for Refugees, *Refugee Children: Guidelines on Protection and Care* (UNHCR 1994) Preface, Introduction and Annex A.
79 I UNHCR Executive Committee, October 1993 as Document EC/SCP/82, in UN High Commission for Refugees, *Refugee Children: Guidelines on Protection and Care* (UNHCR 1994) para 8.
80 Taken from above quote.
81 UN High Commission for Refugees, *Refugee Children: Guidelines on Protection and Care* (UNHCR 1994) 11.
82 Refers to the figure to 155 States parties by March 1994.
83 *DS (Afghanistan) v SSHD [2011] EWCA; LQ (age: immutable characteristics) Afghanistan* [2008] UK AIT 00005 referring to United Nations High Commissioner for Refugees, 'Guidelines on International Protection: Child Asylum Claims under Articles 1(A)2 and 1(F) of the 1951 Convention and 1967 Protocol relating to the Status of Refugees' HCR/GIP/09/08 22 December 2009 paras 65 (age and procedural and evidentiary safeguards); 68 (separated children and the initiation of family tracing efforts); 73 (burden of proof).
84 *DS (Afghanistan) v SSHD [2011] EWCA; LQ (age: immutable characteristics) Afghanistan* [2008] UK AIT 00005.
85 The three earliest General comments refer to refugee children: General Comment No. 2 (2002) The role of independent national human rights institutions in the promotion and protection of the rights of the child CRC/GC/2002/2 in the context of encouraging national human rights institutions to reach out to vulnerable children, including refugees, General Comment No. 3 HIV/AIDS and the rights of the child CRC/GC/2003/3 in the context of the particular vulnerability of children in refugee camps, paras 30

and 37 and General comment No. 4 (2003) Adolescent health and development in the context of the Convention on the Rights of the Child CRC/GC/2003/41 in the context of data collection. Refugee children are also mentioned in various comments after Comment No. 6: General Comment No. 7 *Implementing child rights in early childhood* CRC/C/GC/7/Rev.120 September 2006, which emphasises the need to pay special attention to vulnerable groups of children including refugees; General Comment No. 10 Children's rights in juvenile justice CRC/C/GC/10 in relation to fair trials.

86 General comment No. 5 General measures of implementation of the Convention on the Rights of the Child (arts 4, 42 and 44, para 6) CRC/GC/2003/527 para 12.

87 Convention on the Rights of the Child 1989, Article 41 Nothing in the present Convention shall affect any provisions which are more conducive to the realization of the rights of the child and which may be contained in: (a) The law of a State party; or (b) International law in force for that State.

88 The annex includes the Convention and Protocol relating to the Status of Refugees 1951 and 1967.

89 UN Committee on the Rights of the Child, *General comment No 6 (2005): Treatment of Unaccompanied and Separated Children Outside their Country of Origin* CRC/GC/2005/6 para 15.

90 UN Committee on the Rights of the Child, *General comment No. 6 (2005): Treatment of Unaccompanied and Separated Children Outside their Country of Origin* CRC/GC/2005/6 paras 1–4.

91 Sir Guy Goodwin-Gill, 'Unaccompanied refugee minors: The role and place of international law in the pursuit of durable solutions' (1995) 3 *International Journal of Children's Rights* 406.

92 Separated Children in Europe Programme, *SCEP Statement of Good Practice* (4th edn, Save the Children 2010).

93 UN Committee on the Rights of the Child, *General comment No. 6 (2005): Treatment of Unaccompanied and Separated Children Outside their Country of Origin* CRC/GC/2005/6 para 15.

94 The 1951 Convention is referred to in the context of: applicable international legislation (para 15); *non-refoulement* (para 26); in the context of prevention of trafficking (para 53); child-specific persecution (para 59); prevention of deprivation of liberty (para 62); child-sensitive assessment of protection needs (para 74); full enjoyment of all international refugee and human rights by children granted refugee status (para 76); and children benefiting from complimentary forms of protection (para 77).

95 Convention against Torture and Other Cruel, Inhuman or Degrading Treatment or Punishment Adopted and opened for signature, ratification and accession by General Assembly resolution 39/46 of 10 December 1984 entry into force 26 June 1987, in accordance with article 27 (1). Article 3: 1. No State Party shall expel, return ("refouler") or extradite a person to another State where there are substantial grounds for believing that he would be in danger of being subjected to torture. 2. For the purpose of determining whether there are such grounds, the competent authorities shall take into account all relevant considerations including, where applicable, the existence in the State concerned of a consistent pattern of gross, flagrant or mass violations of human rights.

96 See also Chapter 3 discussions on 'General Principles'.

97 Convention on the Rights of the Child 1989, Article 16; UN Committee on the Rights of the Child, *General comment No. 6 (2005): Treatment of Unaccompanied and Separated Children Outside their Country of Origin* CRC/GC/2005/6 paras 29–30.

98 Develop further in context of persecution refers to 'risk of irreparable harm to the child, such as, but by no means limited to, those contemplated under articles 6 and 37 of the Convention'.
99 Comment No. 11 (2009) Indigenous children and their rights under the Convention CRC/C/GC/11; GENERAL COMMENT No. 12 (2009) The right of the child to be heard CRC/C/GC/12; General comment No. 13 (2011) The right of the child to freedom from all forms of violence CRC/C/GC/13; General comment No. 14 (2013) on the right of the child to have his or her best interests taken as a primary consideration (art. 3, para. 1) CRC/C/GC/14; General comment No. 17 (2013) on the right of the child to rest, leisure, play, recreational activities, cultural life and the arts (art. 31) CRC/C/GC/17.
100 Committee on the Rights of the Child, General Comment No. 9 (2006) The rights of children with disabilities CRC/C/GC/9, Section IX. Special Protection Measures (arts 22, 38, 39, 40, 37 b–d and 32–36), para F.
101 'General Recommendation' is the term used by the Committee on the Elimination of Discrimination against Women and 'General Comment' is the term used by the Committee on the Rights of the Child in their guidance.
102 Joint general recommendation/general comment No. 31 of the Committee on the Elimination of Discrimination against Women and No. 18 of the Committee on the Rights of the Child on harmful practices CEDAW/C/GC/31-CRC/C/GC/18.
103 Joint general recommendation/general comment No. 31 of the Committee on the Elimination of Discrimination against Women and No. 18 of the Committee on the Rights of the Child on harmful practices CEDAW/C/GC/31-CRC/C/GC/18 para 54(m).
104 Joint general recommendation/general comment No. 31 of the Committee on the Elimination of Discrimination against Women and No. 18 of the Committee on the Rights of the Child on harmful practices CEDAW/C/GC/31-CRC/C/GC/18 para 53.
105 Convention on the Rights of the Child 1989, Article 22.
106 See, for example: *S.L. and J.L. v. Croatia* – 13712/11 – Legal Summary [2015] ECHR 540 (07 May 2015) (refers to Comment Number 14).
107 See, for example: *A,B,C and Norwegian Organization for Asylum Seekers (NOAS) v. The State*, HR-2012-2399-P (Case No. 2012/1042), Norway: Supreme Court, 21 December 2012.
108 See *AA (unattended children) Afghanistan CG [2012] UKUT 00016 (IAC).*
109 See, for example: Committee on the Rights of the Child, *Concluding Observations on Ireland's record on children's rights* 1 March 2016 CRC/C/IRL/CO/3–4.
110 Law Society Law Reform Committee, 'Rights-based Law: The case of reform' (Law Society 2006) 7.
111 Law Society Law Reform Committee, 'Rights-based Law: The case of reform' (Law Society 2006) 7.
112 See: Directive 2011/95/EU of the European Parliament and of the Council of 13 December 2011 *on standards for the qualification of third-country nationals or stateless persons as beneficiaries of international protection, for a uniform status for refugees or for persons eligible for subsidiary protection, and for the content of the protection granted (recast).*
113 Directive 2011/95/EU of the European Parliament and of the Council of 13 December 2011 *on standards for the qualification of third-country nationals or stateless persons as beneficiaries of international protection, for a uniform status for refugees or for persons eligible for subsidiary protection, and for the content of the*

protection granted (recast), Article 2(f). The Qualification Directive in the Preamble (Recital 28) also notes that '*It is necessary, when assessing applications from minors for international protection, that Member States should have regard to child-specific forms of persecution*'.

114 For further reading on the definition of persecution, see: James Hathaway, *The Rights of Refugees under International Law* (CUP 2005) and Sir Guy Goodwin-Gill and Jane McAdam, *The Refugee in International Law* (3rd edn, OUP 2007).

115 See Michelle Foster, *International Refugee Law and Socio-Economic Rights: Refugee from Deprivation* (CUP 2007).

116 UNHCR (re-issued 2011) *Handbook and Guidelines on Procedures and Criteria for Determining Refugee Status under the 1951 Convention and the 1967 Protocol relating to the Status of Refugees*, para 51.

117 Jacques Vernant, *The Refugee in the Post-War World* (YUP 1953) 8, quoted in A. Grahl-Madsen, *The Status of Refugees in International Law* (A.W. Sijthoff 1996) 193. See Michelle Foster, *International Refugee Law and Socio-Economic Rights: Refugee from Deprivation* (CUP 2007).

118 See Michelle Foster, *International Refugee Law and Socio-Economic Rights: Refugee from Deprivation* (CUP 2007) 16.

119 See Michelle Foster, *International Refugee Law and Socio-Economic Rights: Refugee from Deprivation* (CUP 2007).

120 James Hathaway, *The Law of Refugee Status* (Butterworths 1991) 104–105.

121 1 C-71/11, C-99/11 *Bundesrepublik Deutschland v Y and Z* (CJEU, 5 Sept 2012) para 56. This was the first case which dealt with the interpretation of the term persecution in the context of the Qualification Directive. See Julian M. Lehmann (2014) Persecution, Concealment and the Limits of a Human Rights Approach in (European) Asylum law – The Case of *Germany v Y and Z* in the Court of Justice of the European Union, *International Journal of Refugee Law* 26:1 65–81.

122 UN High Commissioner for Refugees (UNHCR), *UNHCR Master Glossary of Terms*, June 2006, Rev.1 p 16.

123 See Michelle Foster, *International Refugee Law and Socio-Economic Rights: Refugee from Deprivation* (CUP 2007) 16.

124 See, for example: Jacqueline Bhabha, 'Boundaries in the Field of Human Rights' (2002) 15 *Harvard Human Rights Journal* 157.

125 E.F. Abram, 'The Child's Right to Family Unity in International Immigration Law' (1995) 17(4) *Law & Policy* 397–439, 398.

126 Jacqueline Bhabha and Wendy Young, 'Not Adults in Miniature: Unaccompanied Child Asylum Seekers and the New U.S. Guidelines' (1999) 11 (1) *International Journal of Refugee Law* 86; K. Halvorsen (2002) Separated Children Seeking Asylum: The Most Vulnerable of All *Forced Migration Review* 34:12 in Danuta Villarreal, 'To Protect the Defenceless: The Need of Child-Specific Substantive Standards for Unaccompanied Minor Asylum-Seekers' (2004) 26(3) *Houston Journal of International Law* 744.

127 Jacqueline Bhabha and Wendy Young, 'Not Adults in Miniature: Unaccompanied Child Asylum Seekers and the New U.S. Guidelines' (1999) 11 (1) *International Journal of Refugee Law* 86; Danuta Villarreal, 'To Protect the Defenceless: The Need of Child-Specific Substantive Standards for Unaccompanied Minor Asylum-Seekers' (2004) 26(3) *Houston Journal of International Law* 745.

128 Jacqueline Bhabha and Wendy Young, 'Not Adults in Miniature: Unaccompanied Child Asylum Seekers and the New U.S. Guidelines' (1999) 11 (1) *International Journal of Refugee Law* 86.

129 Jacqueline Bhabha and Wendy Young, 'Not Adults in Miniature: Unaccompanied Child Asylum Seekers and the New U.S. Guidelines' (1999) 11 (1) *International Journal of Refugee Law* 104.
130 UNHCR, *Guidelines on International Protection No. 8: Child Asylum Claims under Articles 1(A)2 and 1(F) of the 1951 Convention and/or 1967 Protocol relating to the Status of Refugees*, 22 December 2009, HCR/GIP/09/08 para 15.
131 UNHCR, *Guidelines on International Protection No. 8: Child Asylum Claims under Articles 1(A)2 and 1(F) of the 1951 Convention and/or 1967 Protocol relating to the Status of Refugees*, 22 December 2009, HCR/GIP/09/08 para 16.
132 UNHCR, *Guidelines on International Protection No. 8: Child Asylum Claims under Articles 1(A)2 and 1(F) of the 1951 Convention and/or 1967 Protocol relating to the Status of Refugees*, 22 December 2009, HCR/GIP/09/08 para 17.
133 Jacqueline Bhaba and Mary Crock, *Seeking Asylum Alone – a Comparative Study: Unaccompanied and Separated Children and Refugee Protection in Australia, the UK and the US* (Themis Press 2007) 161.
134 UNHCR, *Guidelines on International Protection No. 8: Child Asylum Claims under Articles 1(A)2 and 1(F) of the 1951 Convention and/or 1967 Protocol relating to the Status of Refugees*, 22 December 2009, HCR/GIP/09/08 para 10.
135 UNHCR Guidelines on International Protection No. 8: Child Asylum Claims under Articles 1(A)2 and 1(F) of the 1951 Convention and/or 1967 Protocol relating to the Status of Refugees, 22 December 2009, HCR/GIP/09/08 para 13.
136 UN Committee on the Rights of the Child, *General comment No. 6 (2005): Treatment of Unaccompanied and Separated Children Outside their Country of Origin* CRC/GC/2005/6 para 74.
137 UNHCR Guidelines on International Protection No. 8: Child Asylum Claims under Articles 1(A)2 and 1(F) of the 1951 Convention and/or 1967 Protocol relating to the Status of Refugees, 22 December 2009, HCR/GIP/09/08 para 74.
138 Ursula Kilkelly quoted in Alice Diver, Eugene McNamee, Liam Thornton, '21 Years of the Convention on the Rights of the Child: A Coming of Age?' *The Children's Convention at 21: The Rights of the Child Come of Age? Conference*, Derry/Londonderry, 19 and 20 June 2010, University of Ulster.
139 Jacqueline Bhabha, *Child Migration and Human Rights in a Global Age* (PUP 2014) 223.
140 *AA (unattended children) Afghanistan CG [2012] UKUT 00016 (IAC)*.
141 *AA (unattended children) Afghanistan CG [2012] UKUT 00016 (IAC)* para 3.
142 This point is discussed further in Chapter 6, Section 6.5 in the context of participation rights and their nexus with the political opinion ground.
143 *AA (unattended children) Afghanistan CG [2012] UKUT 00016 (IAC)*.
144 R (on the application of Howard League for Penal Reform) v Secretary of State for the Home Department & Anor [2002] EWHC 2497 (Admin) in *AA (unattended children) Afghanistan CG [2012] UKUT 00016 (IAC)* at 55.
145 1951 Convention relating to the Status of Refugees, Article 1A(2).
146 *Ibid.*
147 *Matter of Juan Carlos Martinez-Meija*, A 76 312 250–256 (BIA Jan. 20 1999) (unpublished) in Jacqueline Bhabha, *Child Migration and Human Rights in a Global Age* (PUP 2014) 107.
148 UNHCR, *Guidelines on Gender-Related Persecution*, para. 11. Para 38

149 1951 Convention relating to the Status of Refugees, Article 1A(2).
150 *Ibid.*
151 See Convention on the Rights of the Child 1989 Article 3, which imposes a duty on States Parties to ensure the protection and care of children in respect of actions by both State and private actors. See also: American Convention on Human Rights 1978, Articles 17 and 19; African Charter on Human and People's Rights, Articles 1(3), 81. See also UN High Commissioner for Refugees, *Handbook and Guidelines on Procedures and Criteria for Determining Refugee Status under the 1951 Convention and the 1967 Protocol relating to the Status of Refugees* (UNHCR 2011) para 65; UN High Commissioner for Refugees, *Guidelines on Gender-Related Persecution* (UNHCR 2002) para 19; *Advisory Opinion on Juridical Condition and Human Rights of the Child*, No. OC-17/02, IACtHR, 28 Aug. 2002 para 37.
152 Also mentioned in Jacqueline Bhabha, *Child Migration and Human Rights in a Global Age* (PUP 2014) 107.
153 See: United Nations High Commissioner for Refugees, 'Guidelines on International Protection: Child Asylum Claims under Articles 1(A)2 and 1(F) of the 1951 Convention and 1967 Protocol relating to the Status of Refugees' HCR/GIP/09/08 22 December 2009.
154 The role of the family in both scenarios: forced marriage, given away by fathers, state will not interfere with private family matters *Shah and Islam* identified Pakistan does not provide adequate protection to women and children.
155 1951 Convention relating to the Status of Refugees, Article 1D.
156 *Ibid*, Article 1E.
157 *Ibid*, Article 1F.
158 Detailed guidance on the application of Article 1F in cases involving children can be found in: UN High Commissioner for Refugees, UNHCR Guidelines on International Protection No. 8: Child Asylum Claims under Articles 1(A)2 and 1(F) of the 1951 Convention and/or 1967 Protocol relating to the Status of Refugees, 22 December 2009, HCR/GIP/09/08.
159 *ABC (A Minor) (Afghanistan) v. Secretary of State for the Home Department* [2011] EWHC 2937.
160 *Ibid.*
161 UNHCR letter to legal counsel regarding the International Standards for Exclusion from Refugee Status as Applied to Child Soldiers, 12 September 2005 Washington.
162 Josée Archambault, 'The Status Shift of Refugee Children in Settlement: An Analysis of the Norwegian Context' (2010) 18 *International Journal of Children's Rights* 440; Louis Wirth, 'The Problem of the Minority Groups' in Ralph Linton (ed.), *The Science of Man in the World Crisis* (Columbia University Press 1945) 347–372.
163 See, for example: David Archard, *Children: Rights and Childhood* (2nd edn, Routledge 2004).
164 Jacqueline Bhabha and Wendy Young, 'Not Adults in Miniature: Unaccompanied Child Asylum Seekers and the New U.S. Guidelines' (1999) 11 (1) *International Journal of Refugee Law* 766.
165 *LQ (age: immutable characteristics) Afghanistan* [2008] UK AIT 0C005.
166 United Nations High Commissioner for Refugees, *Handbook and Guidelines on Procedures and Criteria for Determining Refugee Status under the 1951 Convention and the 1967 Protocol relating to the Status of Refugees* (UNHCR 2011) para 77.
167 United Nations High Commissioner for Refugees, 'Guidelines on International Protection: Child Asylum Claims under Articles 1(A)2 and 1(F) of the 1951

Convention and 1967 Protocol relating to the Status of Refugees' HCR/GIP/09/08 22 December 2009 para 49.

168 United Nations High Commissioner for Refugees, 'Guidelines on International Protection: Child Asylum Claims under Articles 1(A)2 and 1(F) of the 1951 Convention and 1967 Protocol relating to the Status of Refugees' HCR/GIP/09/08 22 December 2009 para 49.

169 United Nations High Commissioner for Refugees, 'Guidelines on International Protection: Child Asylum Claims under Articles 1(A)2 and 1(F) of the 1951 Convention and 1967 Protocol relating to the Status of Refugees' HCR/GIP/09/08 22 December 2009 para 51.

170 *MJZ, V97-03500, 1999 CRDD 118 (Can.).*

171 *Matter of S-E-G-*, 24 I&N Dec. 579, 583–584 (BIA 2008)

172 Home Office, 'Processing children's asylum claims' Version 1.0 (Home Office 2016) 42.

173 United Nations High Commissioner for Refugees, 'Guidelines on International Protection: Child Asylum Claims under Articles 1(A)2 and 1(F) of the 1951 Convention and 1967 Protocol relating to the Status of Refugees' HCR/GIP/09/08 22 December 2009 para 51.

174 Danuta Villarreal, 'To Protect the Defenceless: The Need of Child-Specific Substantive Standards for Unaccompanied Minor Asylum-Seekers' (2004) 26(3) *Houston Journal of International Law* 771.

175 Sanchez-Trujillo v. INS, 801 F.2d 1571, 1576 (9th Cir. 1986) at 1576; Matter of Sanchez and Escobar, 19 I. & N. Dec. 276, 285–86 (rejecting as overly broad a social group consisting of young Salvadoran men, ages 18 to 30, who were urban, working class males of military age) in Danuta Villarreal, 'To Protect the Defenceless: The Need of Child-Specific Substantive Standards for Unaccompanied Minor Asylum-Seekers' (2004) 26(3) *Houston Journal of International Law* 771.

176 UN High Commissioner for Refugees, *Guidelines on International Protection No. 2: "Membership of a Particular Social Group" Within the Context of Article 1A(2) of the 1951 Convention and/or its 1967 Protocol Relating to the Status of Refugee* (UNHCR 2002) para 48.

177 Sir Guy Goodwin-Gill and Jane McAdam, *The Refugee in International Law* (3rd edn, OUP 2011) 70.

178 Convention on the Elimination of All Forms of Racial Discrimination, Article 1.1.

179 UN High Commissioner for Refugees, *Handbook and Guidelines on Procedures and Criteria for Determining Refugee Status under the 1951 Convention and the 1967 Protocol relating to the Status of Refugees* (UNHCR 2011) para 69.

180 Sir Guy Goodwin-Gill and Jane McAdam, *The Refugee in International Law* (3rd edn, OUP 2011) 73.

181 UN High Commissioner for Refugees, *Handbook and Guidelines on Procedures and Criteria for Determining Refugee Status under the 1951 Convention and the 1967 Protocol relating to the Status of Refugees* (UNHCR 2011) para 74.

182 Convention on the Rights of the Child 1989, Article 7.

183 Convention on the Rights of the Child 1989, Article 28.

184 Convention on the Rights of the Child 1989, Article 24.

185 *D. [a minor] v Refugee Appeals Tribunal & Anor* [2011] IECH 431 at 23.

186 See United Nations High Commissioner for Refugees, 'Guidelines on International Protection: Child Asylum Claims under Articles 1(A)2 and 1(F) of the 1951 Convention and 1967 Protocol relating to the Status of Refugees' HCR/GIP/09/08 22 December 2009 para 41.

187 For up-to-date information on religious persecution around the world see: US Department of State, Country Reports on Human Rights Practices,

www.state.gov/j/drl/rls/hrrpt/.

188 International Covenant on Civil and Political Rights 1966, Article 18.

189 In addition, the Declaration on the Elimination of All Forms of Intolerance and of Discrimination Based on Religion or Belief was adopted in 1981 that sets out the need for protection against the same. The drafting of this Declaration began in 1962.

190 See *Wang v MIM* (2000) 105 FCR 548; [2000] FCA 1599, the High Court of Australia held that fear of persecution or punishment for a breach of a law that sought to regulate the practice of religion may give rise to a well-founded fear of persecution.

191 UN High Commissioner for Refugees, *Handbook and Guidelines on Procedures and Criteria for Determining Refugee Status under the 1951 Convention and the 1967 Protocol relating to the Status of Refugees* (UNHCR 2011) para 72. See *NABD v. MIMA* (2005) 79 ALJR 1142, the High Court of Australia.

192 See United Nations High Commissioner for Refugees, 'Guidelines on International Protection: Child Asylum Claims under Articles 1(A)2 and 1(F) of the 1951 Convention and 1967 Protocol relating to the Status of Refugees' HCR/GIP/09/08 22 December 2009 paras 42–44.

193 Universal Declaration of Human Rights 1948, Article 18.

194 Convention on the Rights of the Child 1989 Article 14.

195 Convention on the Rights of the Child 1989, Article 14.1 States Parties shall respect the right of the child to freedom of thought, conscience and religion.

196 They note that his wording was endorsed by the Supreme Court of Canada in *Attorney General v. Ward* [1993] 2 SCR 689.

197 UN High Commissioner for Refugees, *Handbook and Guidelines on Procedures and Criteria for Determining Refugee Status under the 1951 Convention and the 1967 Protocol relating to the Status of Refugees* (UNHCR 2011) para 32.

198 Sir Guy Goodwin-Gill and Jane McAdam, *The Refugee in International Law* (3rd edn, OUP 2011) 87.

6 Constructing a children's rights approach

The application of children's rights in refugee law

Abstract

Chapters 2 through 5 assist in creating a blueprint of the children's rights approach to the interpretation of the Refugee Convention through analysis of childhood studies, children's rights law and the historical trajectory of children in refugee law. This blueprint stems from the perspective of children's rights law, rather than refugee law. Chapter 6 therefore looks to analyse how refugee law has dealt with children through case law. The purpose of this chapter is to identify trends in the recognition of child refugee applicants. These decisions indicate which rights when violated may amount to persecution.

Introduction

The notion of *child refugee claimants* is not new. Children have benefitted from refugee protection prior to the Refugee Convention. However, the ways in which children have qualified and the reasons for granting international protection have evolved. The key development in respect of children within refugee law has been a shift from considering children as either beneficiaries within families or children indiscriminately affected by war to children being targets of persecution themselves, in their own right. This shift owes itself to the general evolution of children's rights and child and childhood theorising and studies. Children in all areas of study, society and law are increasingly seen as subjects, agents, or rights holders, including in the context of international protection.

In the past, children were seen as bystanders in war and conflict. Conflict was seen as directed at others, namely the adult population.[1] However, as the UN reported in 1996, the nature of conflict began to change, with children more frequently being the target of persecution and harm, or indeed participants in conflict,[2] subjected to *inter alia* genocide, forced military conscription, gender-based violence, torture and exploitation. In addition, there is increasing acceptance that children are capable of forming views and opinions and thus behaving in a way that is contrary to State or religious institutions that may place them *individually* at risk of persecution. This chapter looks at the influence the children's rights regime has had on refugee law, looking at international case law available on the qualification of child refugees.

This chapter also suggests where breaches of rights not dealt with in refugee law may or should amount persecution. The purpose of this chapter is to conceptualise children within refugee law and further develop a framework for a children's rights approach to the interpretation of the Refugee Convention. These discussions assist in the assessment of the ability of the Refugee Convention to accommodate a children's rights approach or child claims more generally. This chapter suggests where a children's rights approach may be beneficial in determining child claims, while recognising that a violation of a children's right does not automatically amount to persecution. The rights violations must not only amount to persecution, but must be characterised by differential impact on the basis of discrimination.

Challenges to consistency in the interpretation of child refugee claims

Three main challenges to designing a children's rights approach are: the limited number of applications made by children, the tendency for children's applications to be subsumed within head-of-household applications and the trepidation with which determination bodies approach claims from children. These three points are introduced here and discussed throughout the remainder of this chapter.

The increase in separated children seeking asylum globally has led to an increase in case law and guidance, despite still only amounting to approximately 4 per cent of the total global number of persons seeking asylum in 2010.[3] This has increased again in recent years. In Europe, for example, applications from separated children reached 7 per cent (93,925) of the total number of asylum applications submitted in the EU Member States and Norway (1,321,600) in 2015. The share is even larger in some countries. In Sweden, for example, separated children accounted for 38 per cent of the total.[4] Bhabha argued that invisibility, as mentioned above, is no longer the principal issue.[5] Bhabha, like Foster, in the case of the human rights approach,[6] argued that inconsistency in the application and interpretation of refugee law in the case of children is now a 'major part of the problem'.[7]

Accompanied children's claims can often be subsumed within the family application.[8] Children have often been conceived of as beneficiaries of head-of-household applications. For example, in Ireland, the International Protection Act 2015 provides: 'a person who makes an application under subsection (1)(a) shall be deemed to also have made an application for international protection on behalf of his or her dependent child where the child is not an Irish citizen'.[9]

These practices may be one reason for the low number of cases that are submitted by or on behalf of children in their own right. The way children have been dealt with within head-of-household claims compounds this challenge. In Ireland, for example, decisions that relate to a negative determination have often dealt with the adult claimant comprehensively and only included a brief analysis of the situation of dependent children.[10]

Bhabha described child persecution as a contradiction in terms as children may not be perceived as political actors significant enough to be persecuted *or* that persecution is a child welfare issue and of domestic rather than international concern.[11] Bhabha described two conceptualisations of child refugees. The first was the traditional child-welfare approach where children are seen as passive victims of harm inflicted by others. Children meeting this description may be perceived as needing protection on account of their vulnerability. Bhabha referred to this as the 'child as victim' approach. The other approach Bhabha referred to was the 'child as juvenile' approach to describe 'nonconforming adolescents'.[12] This was developed further on in her book to include transgressions of norms relating to *inter alia* political views and religion.[13] Bhabha described 'child-specific attitudes' as relating to: 'suspicion, condescension, and a patriarchal perspective that denies the significance of children as political agents while highlighting their culpability as irresponsible and irregular migrants'.[14] Bhabha also referred to the low recognition rate concerning unaccompanied minors.[15] Unaccompanied minors, as noted by Singh Juss in the case of Afghan unaccompanied minors, also found that they 'have been finding it particularly difficult to secure protection'.[16]

Although procedural aspects of refugee status determination are not discussed in this book, the insights mentioned briefly in this section highlight some of the reasons there is limited higher courts case law that deals specifically with the interpretation of persecution in child cases. There is however a wealth of case law and some literature dealing with procedural elements, such as credibility and burden of proof.[17]

Part I

Provision rights and refugee protection

Chapters 2 and 3 described childhood as a period where the human person is an *adult in becoming*.[18] The literature dating back to the seventeenth century described certain conditions that must be in place to ensure development. These conditions are reflected in Article 6 of the CRC. These conditions include: the role of the parent as protector, educator and provider of emotional support;[19] health;[20] and standard of living[21] as prerequisites to accessing other rights and opportunities for growth and education. All of these rights were set out in the CRC and various other international treaties as discussed in Chapter 3. These are all provision rights that paint a

Rousseauian, or romanticised, picture of childhood. They also relate mostly to social and economic rights. The abovementioned rights clusters are discussed below as they have developed in refugee case law.

Family

The role of the family has been both instrumental and contentious in the development of children's rights. In the ongoing debates, the family has at sometimes been invisible, or assumed, and at times considered as the sole provider and protector of children's rights. The role of the family in the context of protection is discussed in Part II. This section looks at the role of the family as a provision right and as a source of the realisation of Article 6, the right to survival and development, which, when satisfied, facilitates access to other rights. Children are both subject and object in the context of the right to protection and care provided by a family environment. Children are subjects insofar as the right to family is a vessel through which they may develop and self-actualise (discussed below and in Part III) and they are objects insofar as this right provides a vehicle for protection from harm (discussed in Part II).

Although the conceptual evolution of children's rights within the liberationist discourse was to focus more on the child as an agent of rights, international children's rights law still identified families and the wishes of the parents as paramount, unless, as introduced in the CRC, actions are not consistent with the child's best interests.[22] The Universal Declaration of Human Rights (UDHR), International Covenant on Civil and Political Rights (ICCPR), International Covenant on Economic, Social and Cultural Rights (ICESCR) and the UN Committee on the Rights of the Child (CRC) all recognise the family unit as 'the natural and fundamental group unit of society… entitled to protection by society and the State' (as discussed in Chapter 3).[23]

In the context of children on the move, the CRC *General Comment No. 6 on the treatment of unaccompanied and separated children outside their country of origin* (Comment No. 6) also dealt with the right to family from the understanding that the child concerned is at least temporarily 'deprived of their family environment' and therefore requires an alternative care arrangement. Comment No. 6 describes alternative care as: *inter alia*, foster placement, kafalah in Islamic law, adoption or, if necessary, placement in suitable institutions for the care of children as defined in Article 20.3 of the CRC. However, Comment No. 6 also stated that

> When selecting from these options, the particular vulnerabilities of such a child, not only having lost connection with his or her family environment, but further finding him or herself outside of his or her country of origin, as well as the child's age and gender, should be taken into account. In particular, due regard ought to be taken of the desirability

> of continuity in a child's upbringing and to the ethnic, religious, cultural and linguistic background as assessed in the identification, registration and documentation process.[24]

The abovementioned guidance demonstrates the importance of family, whether biological or otherwise, in respect of the child's development. The above example also shows that the child, although an object to be protected by family, is the subject of rights relating to identity deriving from such an environment. The child as subject or object should thus be considered somewhat fluid within this right.

Chapter VI of the *Handbook and Guidelines on Procedures and Criteria for Determining Refugee Status* (Handbook) dealt with family unity noting that the Refugee Convention did not include this principle in the definition of 'refugee'.[25] However, it was referred to in the recommendations that prefaced the Refugee Convention.[26] The purpose of Chapter VI was to reiterate the importance of maintaining family unity for those recognised as refugees, relating to other rights, such as family reunification.[27] It does not equate to a right to family unity in the context of qualifying as a refugee. The content in the Handbook is useful in that it emphasised the fundamental right of family unity, ableit without reference to family as a children's right in and of itself.

The Guidelines, on the other hand, outlined the ways in which the status, circumstances, beliefs or activities of the family may put children at risk of persecution. Additionally, the Guidelines described instances where the family may be the locus of persecution,[28] as discussed in Part II. However, like the Handbook, it did not deal with the child's *right* to their family or 'a family environment'.

No international treaty or guidance material in the area of asylum attributed the right to family or a family environment to children, with the exception of Comment No. 6. Comment No. 6 reiterated that the right to family is enshrined in the CRC and brings it into the rights discussion in relation to unaccompanied and separated children. However, it referred to this right in the context of finding suitable accommodation and care arrangements for those already 'deprived of their family environment'.[29] There is therefore no specific refugee guidance referring to the positive right to family that would assist in bridging the gap between children's rights law and refugee law – in terms of the qualification of refugee children. However, all guidance recognised the importance of family unity, including the Refugee Convention. Family unity is therefore still relevant and important in the context of refugee qualification.

In refugee case law, the right of the child to a family environment relates to two scenarios: (1) a structural barrier, or unjust State intervention, which creates circumstances preventing children from remaining with their families; for example, in the case of children who are recruited into the military, (2) an individual barrier such as when children face return to their country of origin without the possibility to be cared for in a family environment. For example, in the United Kingdom protecting Afghan children from returns that would place them at risk of 'irreparable harm' due to deprivation of family life is a trend.[30] These cases arise where the relevant persons in the receiving State, and or the child themselves, are unable to locate family in the country of origin.[31] These cases are discussed in Part II in the context of protection rights, though they also relate to this particular provision right. Another example is the case of children born in contravention of China's one child rule – children who might be separated from their family and/or face risk of infanticide.[32] However, these cases tend to focus on other provision rights such as the right to an adequate standard of living, see below.

In some jurisdictions there is an over-reliance on secondary forms of protection or regularisation in this area.[33] For example, in *AA (unattended children) Afghanistan*, the UK Home Office originally granted an unaccompanied minor applicant 'discretionary leave to remain' in accordance with the Home Office Policy Instruction on Discretionary Leave – an example of an alternative and temporary form of protection that often expires at 17.5 years[34] – on grounds that the minor did not have a secure family environment to return to.[35] The applicant challenged this decision and was ultimately granted refugee protection. This case is discussed in Part III, as the applicant was recognised as a refugee on the basis of political opinion.

A children's rights approach, as argued throughout, would rely upon the CRC (and other children's rights in international law) as a tool to interpret the Refugee Convention. This book has shown that not only are family rights dominant in the discourses (legal and otherwise), but the right to a family environment underscores *every* children's right as the family is the conduit to access and realise rights and developmental potential. Given the primacy of the role of the family in international law it is difficult to see how a violation of the right to a family environment would not amount to persecution, given also that the child could be (and has been in the case of *AA (unattended children) Afghanistan*) considered to form a particular social group on the basis of being an unattached child or child deprived of a family environment. Yet, in refugee case law, this rights violation is underdeveloped.

A children's rights approach to the interpretation of the Refugee Convention could thus not ignore the weight placed on this right across all sectors and all disciplines, but in particular international law and should form part of a 'persecution barometer' concerning children. The right to family is revisited in the context of protection and participation rights.

Right to the highest attainable standard of health

Health was a key feature of international law from the 1920s. The right to health is embedded in the International Labour Organization (ILO) Conventions,[36] the ICESCR,[37] the UDHR[38] and the CRC[39] as influenced by its predecessors (the 1924 and 1959 Declarations). The right to health is therefore enshrined in international law, generally, and international children's rights law, specifically. The CRC requires States to provide services to *all* children where services or interventions exist within the country. It has been established that when services or treatments are not accessible as a result of a form of structural discrimination on the basis of race or religion, for example, refugee law may become engaged. However, this right also leads us to wonder: how do refugee determination bodies deal with this right when the services in the country of origin merely do not exist? These two examples are dealt with below.

The Guidelines emphasised the right of the child to the highest attainable standard of health in a number of different contexts. The guidelines reiterated the view taken by the Committee, relating the right to health to Article 6: 'the right to survival and development can only be implemented in a holistic manner, through the enforcement of all the other provisions of the Convention, including rights to health, adequate nutrition, social security, an adequate standard of living, a healthy and safe environment, education and play'.[40]

The Guidelines noted that health is a factor that may increase children's vulnerability to persecution.[41] The United Nations High Commissioner for Refugees (UNHCR) gave the example of children with a disability who may be denied necessary treatment or may be ostracised by family.[42] The Handbook also noted that discrimination on the basis of religion may include barriers, or 'serious restrictions' to accessing healthcare, while reiterating the requirement that discrimination must rise to the threshold of persecution in respect of the Refugee Convention. The Guidelines cited some examples of health and access to health services considered to amount to a threat to life,[43] but not refugee protection.

The Guidelines also[44] recognised the role the CRC has in defining child-specific rights, referring to Article 24 'protection from traditional practices prejudicial to the health of children'.[45] The Guidelines also reiterated that the denial of access to health services for children from 'particular ethnic groups' may amount to persecution. The underlying feature of the right to health in the context of the Guidelines, and by extension refugee law, is that it is secondary to the reason of persecution, and not necessarily a reason in and of itself. In other words, it is considered persecution but it is linked with non-discrimination based on a social category such as race, nationality or religion.

The right to health and other rights and protections that impact upon a person's health can be found in refugee case law in the case of adult applicants. For example, in *RRT Case No. N94/04178*, the Australian Refugee Review Tribunal found that the adult applicant, who was diagnosed with an AIDS defining illness on arrival to Australia, would face persecution if returned home due to the lack of expert medical care in the area of HIV:[46]

> access to medical care and treatment is a fundamental human right and that active denial, or actions amounting to an effective denial, may

> constitute persecution. This is particularly so, in my view, in the Applicant's case in which he is suffering from a progressive, ongoing and life-threatening illness for which ongoing medical care is needed to maintain life itself.

The threshold was therefore interpreted in this case as equating to threat to the right to life and inhuman and degrading treatment.[47] However, there are many other cases where the court did not find in the applicant's favour.[48]

An example of a health-related child-specific form of persecution, as identified in the Guidelines, which is also present in case law is female genital mutilation (FGM).[49] It is linked with the right to the highest attainable standard of health, but it also relates to protection rights as it is a harmful practice, or as provided by the CRC, 'a traditional [practice] prejudicial to the health of children'.[50] There may also be a link with the political opinion ground or religion ground and thus may be considered a participation right – objecting to FGM may be seen as a political or religious[51] transgression. Despite the fact that it may come under a variety of headings, due to its close relationship with health, it is discussed here and revisited only briefly in the context of participation rights in Part III.

There are a number of refugee cases that have dealt with young girls facing persecution in the form of FGM.[52] For example, in 2011 the Australian Refugee Review Tribunal found that two female applicants from Uganda should be granted refugee protection based on their fear of FGM upon return. The Tribunal took the view that they were members of a particular social group. In this case, *RRT Case No. 1101038*, the Tribunal described the group as uncut 'female members of the Sabiny tribe'. The right to health was mentioned in the 'Findings and Reasonings'. The Tribunal accepted 'the individual evidence that Female Genital Mutilation exposes a woman to health hazards, including excessive bleeding, death, birth complications and exposure to illness'.[53]

No international treaties were referred to in respect of children's rights in this case.

In 1994, the Canadian Immigration and Refugee Board (Refugee Board) in *Khadra Hassan Farah, Mahad Dahir Buraleh, Hodan Dahir Buraleh*, held that a female child who was part of a family's asylum claim should be recognised as a refugee as it was likely that she would experience persecution in the form of FGM, outlining the short- and long-term health difficulties that typically follow the procedure. They cited the CRC as an instrument that the court was obliged to consider as the child was a minor, specifically Article 3. However, this case also referred to health difficulties *and* the potential long-term impact of the procedure. The right to health, as discussed throughout, is also considered within the canon of rights we associate with Article 6. A number of cases developed in this vein all over the world.[54]

The case law mentioned in this section relating to FGM indicates that the child is more an object of the right to the highest attainable standard of health. In the context of provision rights, children are perhaps more likely to be conceived of as objects. Alternatively, due to the often community (religious or cultural) nature of FGM it is possible that the child may also exercise their agency as a subject within this right by objecting to FGM. Part III revisits this form of persecution in cases where children are seen as asserting a political or religious opinion. Cases where the protection of children is at the fore are more commonly referred to in the literature, including in the context of protection from harmful traditional practices, and they are discussed, briefly, in Part II.

Further challenges associated with defining persecution in light of the right to the highest attainable standard of health are discussed below alongside discussions on the same in relation to the right to adequate standard of living. In this context, the right to the highest attainable standard of health, which includes adequate nutrition, for example, is discussed.

Adequate standard of living

The right to an adequate standard of living is also core to child development and the work of organisations such as Save the Children[55] and the United Nations Children's Fund (UNICEF).[56] The CRC provides that every child has the right to an adequate standard of living 'for the child's physical, mental, spiritual, moral and social development'.[57] This right is therefore linked not only to Article 6, but also to the right to health. Poverty and social exclusion are common themes in childhood literature.[58] There is a wealth of work and research available by advocates and global NGOs, and intergovernmental organisations that has contributed to the narrowing of the gap between the experiences of children in the developed world and those not in the developed world.[59] However differences in the experiences of childhood or childhoods due to economic conditions in respect of health and standard of living and development persist. The literature on refugee law emphasised that social and economic deprivation places children at greater risk of violations of other rights, in particular protection rights, such as protection from trafficking and other illicit activities (discussed in Part II).

To take an example, the CRC in 2011 published *Concluding Observations of the Committee on the Rights of the Child: Afghanistan*,[60] which provided a summary of the challenges faced by children in a country in conflict, where large parts of the population experience economic deprivation. It found that due to population displacement and settlement in Kabul, large numbers of 'unattached' or 'separated' children became 'street children'. It found that 54 per cent of the internally displaced persons were children and the report showed that 'young, displaced and unemployed men are particularly vulnerable to recruitment to the insurgency'.[61] In addition, an NGO shadow report to the Committee report found that 60 per cent of families in Afghanistan depended on their children for household income, noting also that there were 'tens of thousands of homeless children aged between five and 18 in

Kabul … The children work up to 16 hours a day selling anything from newspapers to plastic bags'.[62]

These reports showed that children living in these circumstances (characterised primarily by a violation of the provision right to an adequate standard of living) were not only vulnerable to exploitative and/or harmful labour practices, they were also at risk of becoming street children, losing the support of their family due to separation and risked being recruited into guerrilla and other militarised forces. This example shows the interconnectedness of all aspects of exploitation that may affect children living in a country experiencing conflict and social stratification. The reports also highlighted the link between the right to an adequate standard of living and protection rights. Afghanistan was chosen as an example as there is a wealth of case law available dealing with Afghan children, as discussed below.

There is a body of case law that has dealt with the right to an adequate standard of living,[63] but due to the overlap with protection rights, they are primarily discussed in Part II. There are nevertheless examples in case law where the standard of living was considered so dire that it amounted to persecution in and of itself. For example in *Cheung v. Canada,* which asked *inter alia* if a child born in contravention of China's one child policy may qualify for refugee protection,[64] the Canadian Federal Court of Appeal found that if the minor child, Karen Lee,

> were sent back to China, she would, in her own right, experience such concerted and severe discrimination, including deprivation of medical care, education and employment opportunities and even food, so as to amount to persecution. She was poignantly described as a "black market person," denied the ordinary rights of Chinese children. As such, she is a member of a particular social group, that is, second children, Karen Lee has already experienced certain deprivations and may be subject to further persecution should she be returned to China.[65]

Perhaps unsurprisingly, the right to develop and Article 6 were not mentioned in the judgment. However, like the FGM cases, survival and development were implicitly referred to. The judgment dealt with various elements of childhood and development that were likely to be impacted by destitution and limited access to education and medical care. This case arguably dealt with a breach of the child's Article 6 right as illuminated by Comment No. 5. – 'optimal development' could not be achieved under the circumstances outlined by the Court of Appeal.

In order to apply the notion of 'optimal development' in the context of refugee law, it is necessary to delineate parameters as the scope could be extensive considering the differences in developmental opportunities worldwide. The parameters must relate to the threshold and definition for persecution. In a children's rights approach, the 'persecution barometer' referred to in Chapter 5 merely includes assessing persecution considering the CRC and other relevant children's rights embedded in international law, in particular the well-established right to develop. *Cheung v. Canada* illustrates how this might work in practice. The child in this case would be denied optimal development *relative* to the wider population who were not born in contravention of the one-child policy. The nexus to the convention is still therefore relevant even in the case of Article 6. The nexus in *Cheung v. Canada* was with the particular social group ground. This case also shows the relevance of Article 2 (non-discrimination) in the adjudication of child refugee applications. Article 2 is therefore an important aspect of a persecution barometer concerning child refugee applicants.

Provision rights, one side of the Article 6 triangle of rights, as illustrated by this case and the FGM cases discussed in the previous section forms part of a road map to a children's rights approach to interpreting the Refugee Convention. The approach must nevertheless work within the existing parameters of refugee law, such as the requirement for the persecution feared and/or suffered to have a link with a convention ground as illustrated in *Cheung v. Canada*.

In a similar case in Australia, the High Court in *Chen Shi Hai* also found that the minor applicant would be subjected to severe economic deprivation and various violations of fundamental rights, including access to healthcare and food due to his unlawful birth.[66] Edstrom wrote that despite the precedent set in *Chen*, children claiming asylum on the basis of the one-child rule have not often been granted protection.[67] Applying a children's rights approach might assist in ensuring decisions in this particular area are more consistent. Part II further develops the point that social and economic disadvantage places children at greater risk of other rights violations.

The child is both object and subject within this provision right as well. Children born in contravention of the one-child rule, for example, were seen as objects experiencing fundamental violations of rights that should have been provided by others, such as medical care or subsistence. In addition, the case law highlighted that not having access to this provision right may impact upon the child's access to other rights including those relating to their identity and future development (ie education and employment) therefore crossing over into rights where children are often conceived of as subjects (see Part III). The following section looks at another provision, and arguably participation, right related to development – education.

Education

The right to education is firmly enshrined in international law and in the wider rights discourse as a development right. Education is often also considered to be an avenue through which other rights are accessed. Education is often held up as an intervention that assists in reducing the risk of experiencing other forms of persecution, for example child marriage and forced labour.[68] This right is therefore an important protection mechanism that assists in bringing all children around the world closer to a universal understanding of childhood.[69] Education is, as mentioned, at the crux of the modern conceptualisation of childhood and being a child (discussed in Chapters 2 and 3).

The CRC recognises that the right to develop must involve other rights, including education that assists in the mental and social development of children.[70] The Handbook stated that discrimination that amounts to persecution would occur

> if measures of discrimination lead to consequences of a substantially prejudicial nature for the person concerned, e.g. serious restrictions on his right to earn his livelihood, his right to practise his religion, or his access to normally available educational facilities.[71]

The Handbook clarified that the lack of an educational infrastructure, however, does not amount to persecution.[72] Instances whereby policy, whether written or effected, discriminates against *some* children in accessing education may amount to persecution. This is consistent with the other provision rights discussed herein.

UNHCR elaborated upon their position on education in their Guidelines noting that the level of education that the child has may indicate whether or not the child is more vulnerable to persecution.[73] The UN Committee on Economic, Social and Cultural Rights also noted:

> The lack of educational opportunities for children often reinforces their subjection to various other human rights violations. For instance, children who may live in abject poverty and not lead healthy lives are particularly vulnerable to forced labour and other forms of exploitation. Moreover, there is a direct correlation between, for example, primary school enrolment levels for girls and major reductions in child marriages.[74]

The Guidelines also reiterated the child's right to be protected from labour practices that may interfere with their right to education. This is discussed in Part II in the context of labour and protection rights.

UNHCR upheld the general and normative view that the right to education is a fundamental right and a well-developed one. Refugee case law in this vein has also emerged. The UNHCR Guidelines referred to two important cases that interpreted this right in the context of refugee protection. In *RRT Case No. V95/03256*, the Australian Refugee Review Tribunal in this case found that 'discriminatory denial of access to primary education is such a denial of a fundamental human right that it amounts to persecution'.[75] The Review Tribunal first established the applicant child as a member of the particular social group 'family members of HIV sufferers' as a member of a family forming the particular social group 'people with HIV and AIDS'[76] noting that in that society the disease was still seen as 'bewitchment'.[77] It was based on the child's affiliation with family with HIV that the applicant argued he would not be able to access primary education. The Tribunal was of the view, given the evidence provided, that this was indeed the case. The Tribunal noted that the right to education was a basic human right, citing Article 13 of the ICESCR.[78]

In Canada, the Refugee Board also held that 'education is a basic human right'. In *Ali v. Minister of Citizenship and Immigration*, a case which dealt with an Afghan family's claim for international protection, it was submitted that the girl child in the family could only 'avoid being persecuted' by not going to school. The Refugee Board did not cite any international treaties, but acknowledged that the right to education is fundamental and a legal norm.[79]

Neither development nor Article 6 were referred to in either *RRT Case No. V95/03256* or *Ali v. Minister of Citizenship and Immigration*. However, in line with the other provision rights discussed in Part I, education has a clear link with development, in particular optimal development that satisfies the child's 'mental, spiritual, moral, psychological and social development'.[80] A children's rights approach to refugee law must also consider the right to education as a pathway to develop into active citizens. However, as these cases noted, the right to education in the context of refugee law is limited by a link with a convention ground, such as the particular social group, race, nationality, etc., where it can be shown that a child is individually denied access to normally available educational services on account of their background – invoking non-discrimination rights, such as that provided for in Article 2 of the CRC.

In 2012, the Irish High Court in *D. v. Refugee Appeals Tribunal* also heard a challenge that dealt with a child's right to education.[81] The initial application was submitted on behalf of a child whose parents were from Serbia and of Ashkali ethnicity. It was asserted on behalf of the applicant that he would not be able to access education in Serbia as those considered to be Ashkali were discriminated against. The Refugee Appeals Tribunal found that although the applicant was likely to face discrimination, it did not amount to persecution. When the challenge reached the High Court, Judge Hogan found, however, that a breach of the right to education did in fact satisfy the threshold for persecution. Hogan J argued that persecution comprised 'something in the nature of systematic and pervasive infringements of a basic human right'.[82] Hogan J, on reflecting on the wealth of country of origin reports on Ashkali children who were considered Roma in Serbia, stated that it 'painted a picture of pervasive discrimination against Roma children … with regard to access to even basic education'.[83] He added that by denying access to education, the applicant would 'effectively be excluded from any meaningful participation in Serbian society',[84] reflecting the intention of the General Principle, the right to development (Article 6), and Locke's view that education served to prepare children for future participation in society. Hogan J also noted that the right to education was 'reflected in international agreements, such as Article 28 of the Convention on the Rights of the Child'.[85] The decision of the Tribunal was quashed.

The High Court decision referred explicitly to development, but not Article 6, in citing the infamous US education case *Brown v. Board of Education*.[86] The passage cited related to the compatibility of segregated education and the equality principle of the 14th Amendment to the US Constitution: 'Segregation with the sanction of law, therefore, has a tendency to [retard] the educational and mental development of negro children and to deprive them of some of the benefits they would receive in a racial[ly] integrated school system.'

Development was also referred to in the judgment as contained within a Committee report on Serbia in 2008. The Committee expressed concern:

> at the negative attitudes and prejudices of the general public and at the overall situation of children with minorities and, in particular, Roma children. The Committee is concerned at the effect this has with regard to discrimination and disparity, poverty and the denial of their equal access to health, education, housing, employment, non-enrolment in schools, cases of early marriage and decent standard of living. The Committee is also concerned at the very low levels of participation in early childhood development programmes and day care and the deprivation of education.

This case therefore established a link between development and the right to education.

This judgment provided four important contributions to this discussion: (1) it reiterated the effect the right to education, or the denial of that right, has on accessing other rights, (2) it assisted in defining persecution in relation to breaches in civil liberties, noting that the breach must be 'systematic and pervasive' (3) it highlighted the relevance of the right to education as enshrined in the CRC, even if it was not relied upon as anything more than an 'international agreement' and (4) it made a direct link with development even if Article 6 was not referred to. This case therefore demonstrated the potential for the application of a children's rights approach. A children's rights approach would involve considering the right to education and development as part of the 'persecution barometer' – in other words it would consider children's rights when assessing whether or not the rights violation under review amounted to persecution.

Despite the positive contribution this case has made to this field, it was challenged in the Supreme Court and was overturned. This shows that perhaps there is a reluctance to set this precedent, at least in Ireland.

This case and the cases highlighted above nevertheless show willingness amongst courts and decision-makers to engage with the right to education in respect of persecution. And indeed all three decisions referred directly to the right as contained within the CRC or other human rights instruments. Or, as was the case in *Ali v. Minister of Citizenship and Immigration*, the right was referred to as a norm (thus deriving from international law). It might also be noted that the right to education may have a nexus with a number of convention grounds including the particular social group, race, nationality, religion or even political opinion. Violations of this right, like all provision rights discussed in Part I, are linked with policies that are discriminatory in nature or where States are complicit in the denial of education as established in the case examples above.

It must be acknowledged that the right to education in the CRC strictly speaking only applies to primary education. The proportion of children affected would be very small amongst separated children (the largest group of child asylum applicants who submit applications in their own right).[87] This may account for the limited number of cases available via asylum law databases. In addition, cases dealing with this right may be found within head-of-household claims in respect of a secondary child applicant.

Although this is a provision right and a right that is prescribed in law as obligatory and thus choice on the part of the child is minimised, it is possible to view children as subjects of this right as it is part of the process of realising potential. Participating in education can be voluntary, can be political and can be forced. In the case of the former two options, it is possible to see children as subjects of the law and indeed this is the approach most often seen in refugee case law as the judgments mentioned above refer to positive development and future participation in society. The 'subject' within these assessments is the 'future adult' within the child applicant. Due to the age profile of those who come under this right (primary school age), it is also possible to conceive of children as objects of the right to education based on a presumed lack of capacity. This is another case where a fluid approach to conceptualising children as objects and/or subjects of law is observed.

Conclusion on provision rights

There is a reluctance to provide protection to applicants on the basis that their State has not met their obligations in accordance with provision rights generally. The provision rights relate often to public services and resources that have long been considered to be the competence of the sovereign State. One argument is that failure to provide public services may indicate social or economic deprivation rather than persecution, reflecting the historical divide between political and economic migrants and refugees.[88] This is reinforced by the education case. Child applicants must show that they are discriminated against in accessing education rather than merely showing that educational opportunities are not available in their country. This debate goes to the heart of the difficulty in determining the threshold of persecution in child cases.

Health, standard of living and education are all subjective and differ from country to country and culture to culture. However, where violations of these rights reach a certain threshold they may amount to persecution. The threshold as evidenced by some of the case law is set very high as captured in *RRT Case No. N94/04178* where it was recognised that the applicant had a 'life-threatening illness for which ongoing medical care is needed to maintain life itself'.[89] In the cases mentioned throughout relating to children, the threshold does not seem to be as high as a threat to life, necessarily, as we can see in the FGM case, education and perhaps in the case of a lack of a family environment. Nevertheless, the threshold seems to sit closer to the survival end of the spectrum, if we consider Article 6 as representing a spectrum of rights, which begins with survival and ends with optimal development.

The notion of an Article 6 spectrum is reinforced to some degree by the case of education as well. Education, given its primacy in our minds in respect of children's rights and its position as the cornerstone of civilisation, sits apart from survival rights and is deemed a slightly more sacred right. It is also, as referred to in Chapter 3, a right that is mentioned in all primary human rights treaties (UDHR, ICCPR, ICESCR and the CRC). Depriving a child of an education may result in hardship in the future, but not an immediate threat to life, yet a violation of this right may still amount to persecution.[90]

Article 6 was not referred to in any case discussed above. However, the right to development was either mentioned (for example in the Irish case) or it was implicit in the context of other rights which can be captured within a holistic interpretation of Article 6 as provided for by the Committee in Comment No. 5.

The best interests principle has been the main focus of research, policy and practice in the area of child refugee law and perhaps as a result other rights, such as Article 6, did not develop to the same extent. One reason for this could be that most of the research and policy on child refuge relates to matters of procedure. It is arguable that the best interests principle has mainly been utilised as a tool in the context of procedures as it requires a third party assessment (with participation from the child) and as a catch-all for all other rights, thus making the other rights, including the principle of survival and development, less visible.

Part I demonstrated that Article 6 must become more visible for a children's rights approach to refugee law to function. The right to development is core to our understanding of childhood and should provide the lens through which refugee law is applied in child cases. Research and guidance are required on Article 6 and its relationship with refugee law.

The right to participate, or have one's voice heard,[91] allows for the child to be considered a subject in respect of all rights contained in the CRC. The approach in respect of the limited developments in the area of provision rights indicates a fluid conceptualisation, children considered at times objects, at times subjects and at times both.

This section showed that there are few higher court child refugee cases dealing with violations of provision rights. The violations of provision rights often have a link with violations of other rights. As a result, many of these rights violations arise as secondary in the context of protection and participation rights (discussed in Parts II and III).

This section highlighted the possibility of violations of provision rights to amount to persecution, but also reluctance to engage with provision rights on their own (or to the exclusion of other categories of rights, in particular protection rights) by determination bodies. Part I nevertheless suggested that violations of the right to a family environment, to the highest attainable standard of health, adequate standard of living and to education, as fundamental children's rights, may amount to persecution where there is a convention nexus and where it is sanctioned, encouraged or facilitated by the State. These rights should thus form part of the 'persecution barometer', or the assessment of persecution in child cases. Part II outlines rights that relate to protection. The discussions on all three categories of rights are summarised in the conclusion to this chapter.

Part II

Protection rights and refugee protection

Childhood, as discussed in Chapters 2 and 3, was described as a permanent structure, a period characterised by learning, development ***and*** vulnerability. Chapter 2 established that childhood, as a period of development *en route* to adulthood, requires protection. Children require protection from harm, abuse, neglect, etc. in order to ensure their experience of childhood aids their development into productive adults. These rights relate to the provision rights discussed in Part I insofar as breaches of protection rights may also breach one or more provision right. For example, labour exploitation may affect the child worker's right to access education. Both sets of rights, provision and protection, associated with childhood fall under the umbrella of Article 6 as childhood and the right to develop are inextricably linked.

Protection rights relate to protection from *inter alia*: exploitation including labour and trafficking; forced military recruitment and participation in armed conflict; involvement in illicit activities; and other forms of harm, including indiscriminate violence and torture. This part elaborates on forms of persecution based on a violation of a protection right with a refugee nexus. The role of the family as-protector and as-persecutor is also discussed. The purpose of this exercise, consistent with the rest of this chapter, is to identify which rights violations deriving from children's rights law amount or may amount to persecution in the context of refugee law and how these cases relate to development. Part II, like Part I, seeks to show how the case law to date may assist in formulating a children's rights approach to refugee law.

Exploitation

Chapter 3 established that the earliest developments in children's rights law related to protecting children from exploitation. The prominence of the need to protect children from exploitation grew and expanded over the years, culminating in various provisions in the CRC and the ILO's Worst Forms of Child Labour Convention (WFCLC) (discussed in Chapter 3). In the context of refugee law, the Committee and the Guidelines included sexual abuse and exploitation in their respective definitions of child-specific forms of persecution.[92] Protection from sexual abuse and exploitation is mentioned throughout the Guidelines in respect of forced marriage,[93] military recruitment,[94] labour and trafficking,[95] domestic violence against children[96] and in the context of persecution on the basis of religion[97] or membership of a particular social group (such as street children, who may be more at risk of sexual abuse and exploitation due to their precarious situation and poverty).[98]

Labour and trafficking

It is easy to see a link between the provisions contained within the ILO Conventions and also the CRC in respect of 'other forms of exploitation' and refugee law, in particular where the CRC and the ILO refer to inter-country child migration. This area of children's rights concerning labour exploitation and traffickers elucidates some of the most fundamental examples of child-specific persecution.

Children in economically deprived circumstances may be required to work by their family or they may opt to work in order to survive. Accessing the labour market does not necessarily mark the end of childhood, but the characteristics of childhood change from being perhaps focused exclusively on education to either education and earning a living or merely earning a living. In the context of refugee law, it must be established that the work amounts to persecution by looking at, for example: the type of work, the age of the labourer and the hours of work (as outlined in Chapter 3).

The outcomes of labour exploitation and trafficking cases vary in refugee law. For example, in *Gomez-Guzmen v. Holder*, the US Court of Appeals upheld a decision by the Board of Immigration Appeals (BIA) in respect of an applicant who sought asylum on the basis of membership of a particular social group, 'Guatemalan children under age fourteen'. The applicant testified that he was forced to work in a job that was dangerous. His stepfather would beat him or withhold food if he did not go to work. He described one occasion where his stepfather 'beat him so badly that he could not breathe or go to work the next day'. The applicant earned two to three dollars per day and it was paid directly to his stepfather. He also testified that he never had any free time for friends as he had to do housework after work. The applicant's claim for refugee protection was premised on *Matter of Chen*, which held that 'in rare instances, an applicant may be eligible for asylum where he 'has suffered under atrocious forms of persecution,' even where there is little likelihood of future persecution'.[99] However, the Court of Appeals upheld the original decision finding that the applicant did not demonstrate 'that his persecution was so severe as to warrant asylum'.[100]

Although cases with a link to economic exploitation are determined inconsistently, it is nevertheless established that work that affects a child's positive growth and development is a breach of a fundamental children's right. It is arguable then that a violation of this protection right should amount to persecution where development is adversely impacted, it reaches a sufficient threshold, there is a convention nexus and there is no available recourse to protection. *Gomez-Guzmen*,[101] for example, may in another court or time be considered to amount to persecution.

Let us consider *Gomez-Guzmen* in the context of children's rights. The appellant, as set out above, a member of the particular social group 'Guatemalan children under age fourteen', was forced into labour. Without even looking to the WFCLC, the ILO in 1973 prohibited young people under the age of 15 to enter into the labour force: 'The minimum age specified in pursuance of paragraph 1 of this Article shall not be less than the age of completion of compulsory schooling and, in any case, shall not be less than 15 years'.[102]

In addition, it was submitted that the work was hazardous, thus invoking some of the rights discussed in Chapter 3 within the WFCLC. However, labour was just one aspect of *Gomez-Guzmen*. The appellant also testified that he suffered domestic abuse and could not enjoy leisure activities, both are aspects of childhood, and within that development, which are protected by the CRC.[103] This case therefore included violations of several children's rights. This is an instance where the determination of a child's refugee claim would have benefitted from a formalised children's rights approach where children's rights violations were explicitly considered in the assessment of persecution.

There is more literature and case law on child labour and exploitation where there is also a link with trafficking, and in particular the possibility of re-trafficking. In the United States, a child asylum applicant from India who was beaten by parents and sold to traffickers for domestic service in the US was found to belong to a particular social group of 'Indian children sold or abandoned by their parents'.[104]

There is growing momentum in respect of cases dealing with persecution and trafficking. This is evidenced not only by case law, but also by the uptake of the issue in asylum institutions, such as the European Asylum Support Office[105] and UNHCR, with the publication of their 2006 Trafficking Guidelines.[106] UNHCR in their Trafficking Guidelines describe the following serious violations of human rights that generally amount to persecution: abduction, incarceration, rape, sexual enslavement, enforced prostitution, forced labour, removal of organs, physical beatings, starvation and the deprivation of medical treatment.[107] A number of jurisdictions have recognised trafficking as a form of persecution.[108] The risk of re-trafficking has also been accepted as a form of persecution.[109]

In *Bian v. Canada*,[110] the Federal Court of Canada held that a 13-year-old boy from China along with some 200 other unaccompanied minors who were smuggled into Canada 'had a well-founded fear, both subjectively and objectively, that they would again be trafficked if they were returned to China, and are thus "Convention refugees"'.[111]

This decision focused on the debt that his family owed and the fact that the child would be put to work to repay that debt. The court found that the child was at risk of re-trafficking and at risk of persecution.[112] The court also found that he was not able to consent to trafficking.[113] This is an example where capacity was involved in the decision-making process. The conclusion was that the child lacked capacity to give consent, favouring a more paternalistic approach to this particular trafficking case, considering the child more as an object of law.

Trafficking is also relevant in the case of sexual exploitation and a similar approach has developed.[114] For example, a 16-year-old child who was trafficked from Nigeria to the UK for the purposes of sexual exploitation was recognised as belonging to a particular social group 'young girls from Nigeria whose economic circumstances are poor'.[115] This case made a link with the provision right to an adequate standard of living. The Canadian Convention Refugee Determination Division also recognised an applicant as a refugee belonging to the particular social group 'impoverished young women from the former Soviet Union recruited for exploitation in the international sex trade', emphasising the link between the right to an adequate standard of living and protection rights.[116]

Not having an adequate standard of living places children in a more vulnerable position in society – this line of cases reflects this. As stated in Part I, standard of living is frequently a factor in persecution, but infrequently the sole basis for protection.

This section highlighted that child applicants were largely considered to be objects to protect within this category of rights. It was not argued in any case that the child exercised their agency in either fleeing economic exploitation or choosing to engage in exploitative or indeed illegal labour.

This area of refugee law is underdeveloped given the large volume of labour laws relevant to children. However, it may also be the case that labour exploitation finds its way more often into criminal law spheres, where there is legislation protecting victims of organised crime, rather than the protection sphere.[117] Refugee case law on trafficking with a particular social group nexus nevertheless represents a slightly more optimistic prospect as regards accessing international protection.

International labour laws relating to children must also form part of the 'persecution barometer'. Children under the age of 15 who are economically exploited whether or not it is in an area of work considered to be one of the 'worst forms of child labour', may, where a link with a convention ground can be established, come within the scope of a children's rights approach to the interpretation of the Refugee Convention.

Forced military recruitment and protection of children during conflict

As described throughout, poverty, family separation and conflict can place children at risk of various forms of exploitation. Article 38 of the CRC established that children should be protected from involvement in the military and protected from the effects of armed conflicts.[118] Children are nevertheless involved in military activities across the world. Machel in the 1996 UN study, *Impact of Armed Conflict on Children*,[119] documented instances of 'calculated' genocide specifically targeting children during conflict, for example, in Srebrenica.[120] In 2011, Human Rights Watch reported a sharp rise in the use of children, some as young as seven years old, in suicide bombings by the Taliban.[121]

In the aforementioned UN study, Machel documented and described instances of the use of child soldiers, largely in the case of boy children, and the recruitment of girl children for the purposes of sexual exploitation or for other duties such as food prep or cleaning.[122] She noted that it was generally the poorest children who were at risk of recruitment, underscoring the role 'standard of living' plays in established forms of persecution. Children or families may volunteer their services as a way to escape poverty or hunger, or as a means of generating income.[123]

The Guidelines included under-age recruitment into the military as a child-specific form of persecution in the context of refugee law.[124] A number of cases involving recruitment or fear of recruitment into armed groups have been brought before higher courts, but the outcomes have varied.[125] The Quaker United Nations Office in a 2013 report, *Former Child Soldiers as Refugees in Germany*, estimated that there were 300 to 500 unaccompanied minors who were former child soldiers in Germany (at the time of the research). For the report, they interviewed 11 young people who identified as former child soldiers. They noted, however, that all applications for refugee protection from those interviewed were refused due to the 'unfoundedness' of their claim.[126] This study indicated that 'child-specific attitudes' played a role in these cases, to the disadvantage of the applicant children.[127]

In many countries, children are recruited and then forced to commit crimes and human rights abuses against their families or communities.[128] It is for this reason that cases in this particular area of refugee law may be dealt with in the context of Article 1F[129] of the Refugee Convention, or exclusion (see Chapter 5).[130] The Refugee Convention does not distinguish between adults and children.[131] The drafters may not have foreseen that Article 1F would be applied to children.[132] Goodwin-Gill argued that neither the

Refugee Convention nor the CRC provided an adequate legal basis for the interpretation of Article 1F.[133]

In one refugee case Article 1F was referred to in a positive decision of the National Asylum Court of France (CNDA). The applicant was from the DR Congo. At 15, he was forced to fight in the national armed forces and committed crimes against civilians. Two years later, he fled to France. The CNDA found that he had a well-founded fear of being persecuted based on imputed political opinions linked to being a former child soldier. The CNDA also found that Article 1F did not apply given his vulnerability and the forcedness of his actions.[134]

This case showed that the court engaged with the debate around criminal responsibility and exclusion in such a way that took account of the child's innate vulnerability. In this way, despite being an actor in the armed group, due to the forcedness of his actions, the child was seen as an object of the law.

As a form of exploitation and as a practice accepted to be harmful to children, underage military conscription may breach various rights including the right to be free from harm and the right to family unity. This practice would also breach Article 6 as illustrated by the Committee, by breaching children's rights relating to their 'physical, mental, spiritual, moral, psychological and social development'.[135] The one case example mentioned above did not refer to development or Article 6. The CRC, specifically Article 6, read along with Article 38, would however be a useful tool for interpreting the Refugee Convention from a children's rights perspective as argued in Part I. This section mentioned a procedural barrier to the assessment of these claims however. The Quaker study and Bhabha[136] argued that child soldiers' and former child soldiers' cases were often unsuccessful for reasons unrelated to an assessment of the substantive elements of the refugee application – namely, credibility. This research therefore needs to be read alongside contributions to children's rights approaches to the *processing* of asylum claims in order to achieve full CRC compliance. The aim of a children's rights approach would be to provide more consistency in child refugee determinations.

Involvement in illicit activities – gangs

Illicit activities such as the drugs trade are established enterprises involving children. The Guidelines also referred to the use of children in illicit activities as something that 'would be considered persecution, whether perpetrated independently or as part of a trafficking experience'.[137] Children often become subjected to such activities on the basis of gang recruitment. Recruitment is conceptually similar to conscription into armed forces[138] and the trafficking industry due to the sometimes forcedness of the recruitment process. And, as discussed above, young people may also be excluded where crimes were committed, satisfying the criteria set out in Article 1F of the

Refugee Convention.[139] This is particularly true where the crime was committed at an age that is consistent with the age of criminal responsibility in the receiving country.[140]

Children may be recruited to join gangs in situations of prolonged civil war and/or social and economic deprivation. Gang members may coerce or entice children to join by offering protection or material goods.[141] Persecution in this context may arise when a child either refuses to join a gang or when a child decides to leave a gang.[142] There is documented evidence of persecution that occurs within the gang, leading to persons escaping. Gangs are endemic in countries such as: Guatemala, Honduras, Mexico and El Salvador.[143]

However, as Bhabha described, determinations in this area have been 'disappointing'.[144] This is a sentiment shared by critics of adult claims of a similar description.[145] Bhabha referred to two cases dealt with by the BIA. In one case, *S-E-G*, two 16-year-old boys and their 19-year-old sister who resisted joining a gang were denied asylum on the basis that they could not show that they were any different to any other person in El Salvador who had crossed the gang. Furthermore, the BIA was not satisfied that the reason for resisting was due to an anti-gang political opinion.[146] The BIA held that there was no evidence of political or public activism.

The BIA in the second case referred to by Bhabha, *Matter of E-A-G*, reversed a decision to grant asylum to a young boy from Honduras whose brothers had been killed by gangs and resisted joining himself on the basis that resisting recruitment did not constitute a political opinion and that the social group to which he belonged was not visible.[147] The threshold is therefore quite high in that the child must express disdain for the gang and therefore become both political and visible. Bhabha argued that the threshold is therefore 'tantamount' to death.[148]

In *Canada (Minister of Citizenship and Immigration) v. X*, the Refugee Board found that children who lack maturity and capacity would normally not be considered to have voluntarily joined a gang.[149] However, the child applicant, although 14 at the time of joining the gang, was determined to have understood the decision and a deportation order was issued against him:

> In summary, he knew before he joined that the gang was involved in violent and illicit activities and that these activities were wrong. He joined voluntarily and he joined against the advice of adults.
>
> In my opinion, these findings support my determination that even at age 14, Mr. XXXXX had the knowledge and mental capacity to understand that he was joining the gang and that there were obligations and consequences that would flow. Obviously, the extent of those obligations and consequences were not fully known to him.[150]

The political opinion ground was invoked in these cases. As mentioned above, gang recruitment is similar to military recruitment and trafficking and other forms of exploitation. However, the approach relied upon in the previous section was largely to invoke the particular social group ground while also viewing the child as vulnerable and in need of protection. The decision makers in the trafficking cases held that the child could not give consent. From a children's rights perspective, the two violations of rights are somewhat similar, they are protection based and involve coercion, such as promises of a route out of poverty. However, they are dealt with differently in refugee law as discussed throughout.

Cases in the area of gang recruitment may benefit from adopting the approach used in trafficking cases – that is viewing the child as an object in need of protection rather than a subject in the context of political opinion, requiring the applicant to exercise their agency. This may indicate that within the protection rights category that portraying the child as an object of the law requiring protection may be more successful in attaining recognition as a refugee than portraying the child as a political actor expressing or acting on their views or opinions. This is revisited in Part III and in the conclusion to this chapter.

However, in utilising a children's rights approach it may be possible for a child to be a subject of the law and exercise their agency by expressing their political opinion relating to joining or leaving a gang *and* for that child to be considered in need of protection based on their vulnerability. The child could be seen as an object in need of protection due to the likelihood (dependent on individual circumstances) of the child to be coerced or forced into the gang or indeed persecuted for not joining the gang. The assessment would be based on their vulnerability and need to be protected from harm, considering the potential impact of their social and economic position in society. This line of cases therefore draws on a number of children's rights, including provision, protection and participation rights. A children's rights approach may allow for a more nuanced assessment of the protection needs of the child.

Other forms of harm: indiscriminate violence and torture

Protecting children from indiscriminate violence was part of the vision of Eglantyne Jebb[151] and the work of Save the Children in the early twentieth century. It was the backdrop of the international children's rights movement culminating in the 1924 Declaration. However, like all refugee applicants, children have to show that they are individually at risk of perscution in order to qualify for refugee protection. That is not to say that a person who suffers[152] indiscriminate violence is not eligible for protection, but as *Elgafaji* showed, subsidiary protection,[153] at least in the European Union, is beginning to fill this space – a space that used to belong to refugee protection during the times of the category approach.[154]

Due to the fact that more and more indiscriminate violence is conceived of within the subsidiary or complementary protection sphere and it is not mentioned in the Guidelines, it is not dealt with in any more detail in this chapter. Indiscriminate violence in and of itself should not be central to the assessment of children's claims when utilising a children's rights approach, however, the individual rights of children that may be violated *due* to indiscriminate violence should be central.

Freedom from torture is another example of a protection right provided for in the CRC,[155] the UDHR[156] and the ICCPR,[157] which has had implications in refugee law. Torture is an established form of persecution[158] and freedom from torture is an established children's right.[159]

As in the case of military conscription, there is a wealth of guidance and jurisprudence. However, it is less prevalent in the literature in respect of child refugees, despite being mentioned throughout the UN study on children in armed conflict. This may be due to the perception, as Bhabha noted, that children are not considered as political actors[160] and thus not at risk of torture on that basis. There are nevertheless some examples of refugee case law where torture forms part of the decision. For example, cases involving health may relate to inhuman and degrading treatment as established in Part I.

In *GH v Refugee Appeals Tribunal*, for example, the court reiterated the Guidelines'[161] position on the impact of torture on children and its relationship with persecution:

> Another principle is that actions which may not constitute persecution when experienced by an adult could satisfy the persecution element of the refugee definition when experienced by a child. Minor applicants are necessarily more vulnerable to the effects of torture and other forms of serious harm, in particular physical and psychological harm, and the principle of the best interests of the child require that the harm feared upon return be assessed from the child's perspective.[162]

This case dealt with an infant child and persecution based on her status as an Ahmadi in Pakistan. She witnessed her mother being harassed and threatened. The mother submitted on behalf of her child that she would be discriminated against in school and in the community.[163] The decision of the Refugee Appeals Tribunal was quashed and sent back to be reconsidered. The child was considered in this case to be an object of law. The rights to education and development were also considered in this particular judgement.

In *Juan Carlos Martinez-Mejia*, the BIA granted protection to a child who was subjected to abuse at the hands of his stepfather. The child would have otherwise faced returning to live as a street child in Honduras. The findings were based on a well-founded fear of persecution at the hands of the police in Honduras who were known to torture and kill street children, while also considering the fact that the child had no family environment to return to.[164] This can be seen as fitting within Bhabha's child welfare approach and the protectionist approach. It is also an example of the right to be free from torture applied in a case where the child was seen as an object of protection.

Therefore, the right to be free from torture has also been used as a mechanism through which to determine the severity of the persecution suffered in the case of children as well as in the case of adults.

There is limited case law dealing with torture and children, but when this right is breached it may amount to persecution and should therefore form part of the framework for a children's rights approach to the Refugee Convention. The developments relating to lowering the persecution threshold in the case of children (revisited in Part III in relation to participation rights) should form part of this approach as well. Uniquely, for the protection rights category, children may be considered subjects who must exercise their agency to become at risk of torture – rather than objects assumed to be in need of protection.

Family as persecutor and protector – unattached children

Case law, literature and guidance has suggested that when the family is absent from the child's life, the child would be at greater risk of harm *and* less likely to access their rights. Cases in this vein emphasised the role of the family in protecting the child from external harms, identifying the family as the primary access point to all other children's rights.[165] There are a number of decisions that have dealt with children who are in the receiving country and unaccompanied and thus without the protection of their family. For example, the Upper Tribunal (Immigration and Asylum Chamber) in the United Kingdom in *HK and Others (minors – indiscriminate violence – forced recruitment by Taliban – contact with family members) Afghanistan*[166] held that:

> children are disproportionately affected by the consequences of the armed conflict in Afghanistan' yet 'a distinction has to be drawn between children who were living with a family and those who are not.

The Tribunal also noted that:

> there are some risks to which children who will have the protection of the family are nevertheless subject, in particular the risk of land mines and the risks of being trafficked, they are not of such a level as to lead to the conclusion that all children would qualify for international protection.

Despite dismissing the appeals, concluding that the evidence did not show that the appellants faced a real risk on return,[167] the Tribunal found that children who were 'unattached' in Afghanistan depending on their individual circumstances 'may be exposed to risk of serious harm, inter alia from indiscriminate violence, forced recruitment, sexual violence, trafficking and a lack of adequate arrangements for child protection'.

In *HK and Others*, various UNICEF reports on the situation of minors in Afghanistan were referred to in submissions. UNHCR in their *Eligibility*

Guidelines for Assessing the International Protection Needs of Asylum-Seekers from Afghanistan in 2010 found that unaccompanied children, among other vulnerable persons in households with no adult male protection, would not be able to 'lead a life without undue hardship in areas with no social support networks, including in urban centres'.[168]

In a more recent case, *AA (unattended children) Afghanistan*, the UK Upper Tribunal found that the unaccompanied minor applicant was a refugee on grounds of his political opinion (this case is discussed in more detail in Part III), but also on the grounds that he would not have the protection of his family:

> We are further satisfied that the appellant would be at real risk of persecution as an unattached child from his particular home area who has lost all contact with his family, so that family protection will not be available to him.[169]

These cases show a willingness on the part of decision-makers and courts to interpret the Refugee Convention utilising this children's rights norm. There is therefore scope for the application of a children's rights approach in the context of unattached children. However, there is a trend to invoke other forms of protection, such as subsidiary protection or humanitarian permissions in these cases.[170]

'Unattached child' cases are also determined inconsistently, even within one jurisdiction as shown by the UK example. This line of cases might therefore be buttressed by a children's rights approach that would provide a 'persecution barometer' using development and the CRC rights that flow from it as the baseline. The result of which might be more predictability, or consistency, in the use of refugee protection and complementary forms of protection.

Another aspect of the role of the family is ensuring the child is protected from harm both domestic[171] and from the outside world,[172] which Rousseau argued was part of protecting the experience of childhood.[173] Domestic violence and forms of harm at the hands of family members are associated with protection rights in the CRC. As discussed in Part I, the family should serve as the protector and enforcer of children's rights, yet there has been some family-as-persecutor case law relating to child abuse at the hands of relatives,[174] incest is one example.[175]

The child is largely conceived of as an object in the consideration of their right to the protection of the family or to be free from persecution arising from the family environment. The discussions on the right to family in the context of provision rights highlighted the implications a lack of a family environment may have on the child and their future outcomes, or development. As established throughout, protection rights must be satisfied in order to access other rights and the family plays a key role in this process.

Conclusion on protection rights

There are a number of examples of protection rights with a Refugee Convention nexus mentioned herein. Examples discussed above range from labour exploitation to gangs to domestic violence. The approaches in the decisions in relation to this category, and the others, were inconsistent, however. This analysis nevertheless established, that CRC-based protection rights have been invoked in refugee determinations.

Cases that relate to the child as an object of law to be protected – characterised by youth and vulnerability – are more prevalent in the literature guidance and in the case law databases relied upon for this research. Protection rights are indeed most prominent in the UNHCR Guidelines as discussed in Chapter 5. Children are sometimes considered as not 'fully-formed' in the case law, reminiscent of the views of Locke and Rousseau and various sociologists who argued that the child is an adult-in-becoming, or incapable of giving consent; for example, in the case of trafficking or sometimes in the case of child soldiers. In these cases, this approach – the protectionist approach – has been shown to work to the advantage of the child applicant. In the examples discussed in this section, the child was an object to be protected.

In other cases, children were seen as unable to form political views, for example, as a result of their status as not-fully-formed and therefore were not perceived as persons who could have political opinions, for example, that would place them at risk of torture. In this example, children were conceived of as objects of the law and thus unable to invoke protection on this particular ground. In this line of cases, the conceptualisation of the child as an *adult-in-progress* worked to their disadvantage.

Lastly, this section discussed protection rights cases where children were seen to exercise their agency in respect of involvement in gangs or other illicit activities. In some of these cases, children were seen as responsible for their actions, aware of the impact of their actions. In these cases, where children were viewed as subjects of the law, the attribution of participation or agency rights onto the child worked to their disadvantage. Despite similarities between trafficking and gang cases, the outcomes have been different. This demonstrates a preference for protection rights cases where the child applicant was considered an object in need of protection. This is consistent with the current and inherent conflict in international children's rights as discussed in Chapters 1 through 3.

Part III

Participation rights and refugee protection

The international children's rights movement[176] has reinforced the consensus that children are not only seen as rights holders, but also as agents in reference to their rights, including rights to self-determination.[177] This includes the area of refugee law.[178] The way children are conceived of has an impact on many of their rights and their ability to access those rights. This includes their right to seek and access refuge in another country. In the case of international refugee law, agency is a crucial element of any protection claim. The applicant must prove that he or she has or is individually likely to suffer persecution for reasons of race, nationality, religion, membership of a particular social group or political opinion. They must also demonstrate that they cannot access, or are unwilling to seek, the protection of their own State.[179] Children therefore must not only have agency to be perceived as a subject of persecution, they must also have the capacity to seek protection and articulate their fears. As already mentioned, this book does not look at procedural law, but the matter of agency is relevant in the context of the qualification of child refugees because applicants are presumed to be able to exercise it in the pursuit of international protection. Part III and this book only look at the persecution of children based on exercising their agency rather than the way they exercise it in the context of making an application for asylum, however.[180]

Part III departs somewhat from the structure of this chapter and book. Parts I and II have used general children's rights subheadings to ensure that the analysis looks to children's rights first in an effort to analyse the current point of development of children's rights in the context of refugee law. However, and as Bhabha argued, children who act with their own agency are often typified as transgressors.[181] It is therefore common in refugee law to categorise children who transgress a societal norm, such as resisting child marriage, as children who are expressing an opinion that is either political or religious in nature. Cases that involve child agency, and where the exercise of agency is at the fore, are discussed therefore under two convention ground headings: religion and political opinion. Part III takes account of the possibility that other rights violations may be relevant including the example of involvement in illicit activities discussed in Part II. In addition, Part III takes into account the fact that religion and political opinion can be and are grounds cited in cases not involving children exercising their agency, including where religious or political beliefs or opinions are imputed onto them.

The most relevant CRC rights are those that provide individual and autonomous rights, such as: freedom of expression,[182] thought, conscience and religion,[183] freedom of association and peaceful assembly,[184] privacy[185] and the protection of the right to practice one's own religion and speak one's language.[186] These rights relate to the religion and political opinion convention grounds most closely. Part III therefore discusses these rights in the context of the two grounds. The following section looks first at imputed beliefs, though persecution on the basis of imputed beliefs most often invokes protection rights.

Imputed beliefs

The Handbook stated that it is not necessary for a child to be an active participant to be at risk of persecution. It stated that merely being perceived as holding certain opinions or beliefs or being a member of a particular religious or political group can result in persecution. This may be based on the beliefs or membership of the child's parents, community, race or ethnic group. UNHCR noted that this may be the case in circumstances where the child is not capable of articulating such views.[187] For example, in a case in Belgium, the Council for Alien Law Litigation reasoned that expressing a fear of FGM was considered to be a political opinion. The court found therefore that the nexus of the applicant's fear lay with the political opinion ground though it was attributed to the mother (the principal applicant).[188] The child was a secondary applicant.

This case does not necessarily conflict with a children's rights approach, despite failing to consider the child as a subject of the proceedings, rather it emphasised the child's innate vulnerability and at times incapacity to understand, or seek protection from, the harm that may be forced upon them. It also emphasised the role of the family in protecting the child from such harms. In this case, the mother argued that she would not be able to protect her child. Although this case did not deal with the child's expression of a political opinion, it did show that the protection rights prong of child development was considered. Even if a formal children's rights approach to the interpretation of the Refugee Convention was established and utilised by decision makers, there would continue to be cases where the parent is the principal applicant, asserting their right to protect their children. This line of cases does not fall within the context of participation rights, however, as children in this context are not the subjects of the law nor are they expressing their own views or beliefs.

UNHCR in their *Guidelines on International Protection No. 6: Religion-Based Refugee Claims under Article 1A(2) of the 1951 Convention and/or the 1967 Protocol relating to the Status of Refugees* addressed the possibility that parents may also have a role in the child's transgressions and/or beliefs. These guidelines noted that mandated religious education may not only come into conflict with the child's beliefs, but may also conflict with the beliefs of the parents. UNHCR reiterated the right of the parents to make decisions regarding the child's moral and religious education in the context of broader human rights. In this case it is possible that the parents may place the child at risk of persecution because of their choice to have the child educated in accordance with their own beliefs and values in cases where those beliefs come into conflict with that of the State or community, for example. This scenario was not addressed in UNHCR's Guidelines relating to children, but they were addressed in the context of religious persecution in the UNHCR Handbook.[189] This omission in UNHCR's Guidelines on child claims, indicates that the parents' right to educate their child in the way that they wish is a right that is not attributable to children necessarily. Examples in this vein relate to provision and protection rights, not participation rights however. It is nevertheless noteworthy that the right of the child to be free from religious persecution and the right of the parents to educate their children in respect of their religion can come into conflict. The following sections look at rights, which are autonomous in nature, where the child is seen as a subject of the law.

Religion

Article 14 of the CRC notes that: 'States Parties shall respect the right of the child to freedom of thought, conscience and religion'.[190] It can therefore be concluded that in the context of the CRC, children have the right to their beliefs and to practice their own religion. Children, as discussed above, may be subjected to persecution on the basis of their religious beliefs,[191] imputed religious beliefs and, as outlined in the Guidelines and Handbook, refusing to ascribe to religiously prescribed behaviours and norms.[192]

Although UNHCR noted that children have 'limited, if any, influence over which religion they belong to or observe',[193] the Guidelines highlighted that circumstances may arise where a child may not adhere to assigned roles or behaviours.[194] Children may refuse to: participate in religious practices, for example, FGM[195] or *sati*,[196] adhere to accepted codes of conduct such as wearing a veil, participate in forced military activities in the context of religious ideologies[197] or ascribe to gender roles, such as enslavement[198] or forced marriage.[199] The Guidelines give examples of serious restrictions on the right to earn a livelihood or to access normally available educational facilities or health care, ie provision rights, based on religious discrimination as well. Some specific examples where children's rights and refugee law intersect are discussed below. Some of the examples discussed below are also relevant in the context of the political opinion ground.

Female genital mutilation revisited

FGM was discussed in the context of health, but it has also been linked to religion as it is often carried out as a religious or cultural rite of passage, though it is not limited to one culture or one religion.[200] In the context of refugee law, resisting or advocating for the eradication of FGM may relate to a belief or opinion challenging the majority belief system, which could be considered within the frame of the religion or political opinion ground, and/or perhaps race, nationality and the particular social group grounds. In US courts, there has been a tendency, as Bhabha noted, to grant asylum on the basis of objecting to FGM due to the influence 'western freedom of conscience' has had on the applicant. Regardless of how this example is categorised or discussed in this chapter, FGM nevertheless relates to various protection rights, in particular Article 19, *protection from all forms of violence*.[201] As highlighted in the Belgian case in Part II, it is more common for the religious or political opinion to be attributed to the adult applicant attached to the child's claim.

Child marriage

Child marriage is more common among members of certain communities often characterised by race, ethnicity, religion or nationality.[202] The UK Foreign and Commonwealth Office Forced Marriages Unit described forced marriage as an arrangement where one or both parties do not give valid consent. They described it as 'an abuse of human rights, and a form of domestic violence and child abuse, when it involves young people'. The starting point for the UK guidance on child marriage was thus grounded in protection.

Child marriage may also relate to economic exploitation, a protection right,[203] as there is often an economic benefit to child marriage either through a dowry[204] or another form of payment from the groom's family to the bride's family, or it may serve to alleviate some financial pressure from the bride's family.[205] There may also be a link with religion or political opinion, as communities may justify child marriage through religious doctrine or cultural norms.[206]

A 2004 study carried out in Norway found that nine out of 26 refugee recognitions (of female applicants with the exception of one boy fearing persecution at the hands of his girlfriend's parents) were based on applicants fleeing forced marriages.[207] The majority were young girls forced to marry older men. Applicants also reported experiencing abuse or threats from the community.[208] However, overall, the study found that instances of forced marriage in asylum claims were generally low.

In 2004, in the UK, it was submitted in *NS (social group) Afghanistan CG (forced marriage)* that forced marriage 'was something that occurred quite frequently to women and young girls in Afghanistan' (see below).[209] The Immigration Appeals Tribunal allowed an appeal from a woman who feared persecution on the basis of a threat of forced marriage on return to Afghanistan. In their determination they noted that the applicant's two daughters were also at risk of forced marriage:

> Her daughters are themselves extremely vulnerable to being forced into marriage, as they approach puberty, and vulnerable to other sexual assault and abuse. In turn, their vulnerability placed the Appellant at increased risk as the sole protector of the girls.[210]

There have been examples of child marriage forming the basis for positive refugee recommendations in the US. For example, in *Matter of [name not provided]*, an immigration judge granted asylum to a 16-year-old from China who fled a forced, arranged marriage by her parents in exchange for money.[211] Bhabha argued that this case hinged on the 'family's commodification of their daughter into a capital-generating asset'. It was on this basis that the applicant was granted asylum. Bhabha also noted that this example of persecution concerned both family and societal circumstances.[212]

In the context of a children's rights approach and the discussions in this chapter more generally, not only did the child exercise her agency, the social and economic circumstances of the child played a role. In other words, this form of violence is also linked to child development and agency. Importantly, this case also looked at the role of the family and their failure to fulfil their duties as the protector of the child, also a provision right with links to protection rights. Here, in this case, we can see the intersection of all three categories of rights, all three which affect the child's development. This case showed that the period of childhood, which should seek to ensure 'optimal development', is undermined by forced marriage and the deprivation of the family environment. Furthermore, it undermines the child's right to participate in decision-making about their future.[213]

Other child marriage case law has indicated that children may be granted lesser forms of protection, such as subsidiary protection or leave to remain, rather than refugee protection.[214] For example, in Sweden, the Migration Court of Appeal granted a young couple subsidiary protection based on the female's avoidance of forced marriage and the ensuing harassment both parties endured as a result. Low numbers in refugee status granted on this basis may also relate to low numbers of claims being submitted by children on their own as it is likely difficult to do so as a minor who is forced into marriage. Alternatively, it may relate to decision-makers not taking cases involving children seriously and discriminating based on age, as Bhabha and others have argued, albeit not in the context of forced marriage.[215]

Sexual orientation and gender identity

Another example of a transgression that may amount to persecution relates to sexual orientation and gender identity. Children and young people, though frequently ignored in UNHCR guidance and national laws relating to sexual orientation and gender identity, may also fear or experience persecution on this basis.[216] Although the Refugee Convention does not explicitly refer to these reasons for persecution, evidence of their inclusion under the category of the particular social group exists in European law[217] and international case law.[218] However, the *Guidelines on International Protection No. 9 Claims to Refugee Status based on Sexual Orientation and/or Gender Identity within the context of Article 1A(2) of the 1951 Convention and/or its 1967 Protocol relating to the Status of Refugees* noted that sexual orientation and gender identity may also relate to the religion[219] or the political opinion ground.[220] A transgression of this societal norm may have a nexus with the religion ground where the religious community does not accept homosexuality. It may have a nexus with the political opinion ground, for example, where there are anti-gay laws, policies or where public/governmental figures make anti-gay statements.[221]

Although many commentators have reflected on the paradox of children and sexual orientation and gender identity in decision-making,[222] there are nevertheless examples where children have been recognised as refugees on this basis. Take the decision of *Hernandez-Montiel*, for example. At 16, Geovanni Hernandez-Montiel applied for asylum in the US. He identified as gay and as someone who expressed their gender identity by wearing clothing typically characterised as feminine. He claimed membership of the particular social group 'gay men with female sexual identities'[223] in Mexico. Despite being rejected by the BIA, the Ninth Circuit Court overturned the decision on appeal.[224] The Ninth Circuit Court argued that the BIA had erred in their assessments of *inter alia* the particular social group ground and persecution. In the first instance, the Court found that dressing as a female was an expression of the applicant's gender identity and that his gender identity and sexual orientation were considered to be immutable applying the reasonings of *Sanchez-Trujillo*, *Matter of Acosta* and others.[225] In addition, the Court held that the discrimination and sexual abuse suffered at the hands of the police constituted persecution. The case was remanded to the BIA with instructions to grant his asylum.

This was an important case in the context of sexual orientation and gender identity as it was the first instance that a US federal court of appeals had 'recognized homosexuality or sexual identity as a basis for protection under the INA asylum Statute'.[226] However, what is interesting about this case in the context of child refugees is that the applicant's age was not considered material or significant. In fact, capacity was assumed. On the one hand, this case could be seen as an example where children's capacity to exercise their agency, as subjects of law was accepted. On the other hand, it could be argued that the decision makers treated the applicant, who was a child at the time of persecution, but not at the time of appeal, as an adult – perhaps because decision makers may consider sexual orientation and gender identity as characteristics of adulthood, not childhood. A third possibility is that the court deemed the age of the applicant immaterial or insignificant. Many commentators have argued that children continue to be invisible in the legislation, guidance and case law in the context of sexual orientation and gender identity refugee claims.[227] This case would support this argument. In the future, if a children's rights approach were employed, the court in this case would have referred to the appellant as a child and as someone who was capable of exercising their agency and expressing their identity. In addition, the court would have acknowledged that child-specific rights were also breached, such as the right to be free from abuse,[228] sexual violence[229] and their right to their identity (among others).[230] There is limited literature in this area of law concerning children, and there is therefore a need for further research.

Political opinion

Locke, Rousseau and the liberationists and protectionists that followed, emphasised the fact that as children mature, their ability to articulate and develop opinions also matures. Children in the context of the CRC thus have the right to hold political opinions, express their opinions and convene discussions or meetings with others to discuss or express their views.[231] UNHCR in their Handbook described the potential for persecution on grounds of political opinion in the following way: 'A claim based on political opinion presupposes that the applicant holds, or is assumed to hold, opinions not tolerated by the authorities or society and that are critical of generally accepted policies, traditions or methods'.[232]

Political opinion may apply therefore where the applicant expresses or makes their views known. However it is also possible, as UNHCR noted, that the applicant may not have expressed their views, but due to the strength of the applicant's convictions those views are likely to become known.[233] The Guidelines stated that this convention ground 'is not limited to adult claims':[234] 'It is important to acknowledge that children can be politically active and hold particular political opinions independently of adults and for which they may fear being persecuted'.[235]

UNHCR therefore made clear that children may be the subjects of laws in the context of seeking protection from persecution on the basis of their political opinions. In case law, political opinions have also been imputed onto children.[236]

This area of refugee law (concerning religion and political opinion) is the closest reflection of the liberationist approach discussed in Chapter 2. This area is also where we can see the biggest leap in the *idea* of children's rights, from Locke's view that children could not exercise civil and political rights and Rousseau's view that they were unable to hold views (which applied to religion) to today where children, at least in international law,[237] have the right to express their views.

Children commonly play a role in national protests and movements in their own right.[238] Children may be involved in political activities through distributing pamphlets, acting as couriers or participating in demonstrations.[239] There have been several specific examples of student activism, for example: the Soweto school children, Muslim children in France protesting against the prohibition of the veil in French schools and young labourers protesting working conditions in India and Pakistan.[240]

In the UK the Upper Tribunal in *AA (unattended children) Afghanistan* found that a child applicant who left Afghanistan at 14 was entitled to recognition as a refugee due to the child's well-founded fear of being persecuted on the basis of political opinion:

> He fears persecution by the Taliban by reason of his membership of his family, and therefore being associated with their political opinions, and by reason of his own political opinions as demonstrated from his actions at the Teachers' Day ceremony[241]

Whether or not the child is capable of holding a political opinion, or indeed religious convictions, is often determined by a third party assessment of the child's maturity and development, including their level of education and their ability to articulate their views.[242] Studies, commentators and the judgments discussed herein have illustrated that decision-makers are often not likely to see children as capable of holding views or political opinions.[243] This is a matter of procedure, but it brings to light some challenges that present to children in substantiating their claims.

In Germany, for example, in *BVerwG*, a child had applied for asylum at the age of 15 based on his political opinions. This application was rejected. He applied again a year later on the basis of his membership of the 'Constitutional Party of Iran' and the 'Organisation for the Protection of the Iranian Christians' Rights'. This was also rejected. He made a subsequent application after having been involved in a play that was critical of the regime in Iran. After a further series of appeals, the case ended up at the Federal Administrative Court. The Court held that the applicant should be considered as an exception to the rule that excluded applications on the basis of post-flight reasons, which were created based on the decision of the applicant (*selbstgeschaffene Nachfluchtgründe*). The justification for the application of this exception was due to the age of the applicant. It was reasoned that the applicant was not of legal age prior to expressing these most recent political opinions. This decision was remanded to the High Administrative Court Bayern for a new decision.[244]

This decision showed that those involved at various stages of the determination process did not view political activity as significant or intentional when the young person was a minor. However, once the young person reached the age of majority and exercised his right to express his political views, the court reasoned that the decisions could be re-considered on the basis that his views were made manifest on account of his participation in the play *as an adult*. This case demonstrates the bias inherent in child asylum claims in relation to agency. Determination bodies and courts have infrequently viewed the child as incapable of exercising their agency and forming political views (as discussed in Part II in relation to torture).

In a 2004 Norwegian country report for a pilot study, which looked at *Asylum Decisions on Child Applicants*, it was noted that asylum officials, judges, etc. were not likely to consider children capable of holding their own political opinions. The study quoted one decision-maker stating to the applicant:

> You have testified that you together with your friend, zy(name), have written and distributed pamphlets against the regime. The response to that is that this statement with reference to your young age – you are 15 years old – is not credible. It is not plausible that you at an age of 15 years together with your friend – who is the same age as you – independently and on your own account wrote and distributed pamphlets in mail-boxes up to three times a month and that you ie. and your friend have driven around in a car in your town to distribute these pamphlets.[245]

In this example and in the example from the German court, agency was not attributed to the child applicants. The abovementioned study found that only one out of 26 Norwegian cases was granted on the basis of political opinion.[246] A children's rights approach to the interpretation to the Refugee Convention could perhaps provide a pathway, or link, from, for example, Article 15 (freedom of association) of the CRC, to the political opinion ground in the context of the Refugee Convention.

Case law where children are depicted as unable to exercise their agency based purely on the fact that they are children may not be considered CRC compliant. Viewed through the lens of the CRC, decision makers should recognise that during the process of childhood, children begin to form their own views and develop the ability to express those views and act in a way consistent with those views (as established in Chapters 2 and 3).

This section shows that qualifying for refugee status on the basis of political opinion is not straight forward in the case of children. There is a well-documented reluctance to attribute the ability to act in a political way or to express political views to children. This reflects the uneasiness society still has with attributing agency to children, uneasiness that had emerged in the literature of the seventeenth century. The rights relating to protection are still the most developed and the least contested of the three rights groupings – in the context of international children's rights *and* refugee law. The tendency is still to view children as vulnerable and in need of protection and less likely to view them as having agency. Successful cases, as Bhabha's research also showed, depend on acknowledgement of children's distinctive dependence on adult protection, a dependence that makes them more vulnerable.[247] As discussed in Part II, often attributing agency works to the disadvantage of child applicants. These points are discussed below in the conclusion.

Conclusions: participation rights

There are a number of examples of participation rights with a Refugee Convention nexus. There have been times where violations of participation rights in the case of children who have views that run contrary to the State or surrounding society have been recognised as refugees and instances where they have not. These examples include both religious and political opinions, beliefs and indeed behaviours classified as transgressions.

UNHCR in their Guidelines acknowledged that children do have agency in respect of their religious beliefs. In refugee law, and specifically in relation to the religion ground, children can be considered as subjects of law, with the ability to make decisions about their own life. UNHCR clarified that children have a right to protection from persecution in their own right on the basis of their own religious views or transgressive behaviours if they fulfil the criteria set out in the Refugee Convention. It is therefore established in both children's rights law and refugee law that children can be considered as subjects of the law in relation to their religion. Some of the typical examples, as discussed above, are: child marriage, FGM, gender identity and sexual orientation. Furthermore, refusing to subscribe in part or in full to any aspect of the family, community or State sanctioned or promoted religion may also engage the Refugee Convention in the context of religion *or* political opinion.

In the case of political opinion, UNHCR and the literature supported the view that children can exercise political agency. There are instances where political opinion has been relied upon in refugee decisions. However, the literature has been critical of the approach taken by decision-makers in attributing the ability to act with agency in the context of this convention ground. As argued herein, failing to see children as capable of forming views or exercising their agency does not comply with the mandate provided by the CRC.

There are very few published cases dealing with this area of child refugeehood. There is more information and cases relating to the religion ground perhaps due to the link with protection rights (and nexus with the particular social group in many cases) for example in the case of FGM or child marriage.

The analysis in this section emphasised, somewhat, the relationship between CRC rights and refugee determinations, despite the absense of a formal framework for determining child claims. The approach in the decisions in relation to this category is nevertheless inconsistent, consistent with the other two categories. This is the least-developed rights category in refugee law. This may be due to the low number of claims from young people for one reason or another or the reluctance on the part of the decision-maker to attribute participation rights to children in the context of asylum (consistent with the divide that exists in the wider children's rights discourse as discussed in Chapters 2 and 3). The overarching themes in these discussions on case law are that all violations point back to the sociological understanding of childhood, which is now encapsulated in Article 6 of the CRC as illuminated by the Committee, *and* that a children's rights approach would assist in providing consistency, structure and increased visibility in the case of child refugee determinations.

Conclusions

Refugee law, among other areas of law, has challenged society's conceptualisation of children. Refugee law is at its foundation a protection mechanism and children have long been considered objects to protect. In this way refugee protection seems an obvious complement to a new, yet robust children's rights regime. The concept of children has since evolved in rhetoric, literature and law. Children are now rights holders in their own right as well as vulnerable persons requiring protection. They are people who possess rights relating to their own protection *and* rights that relate to their own beliefs, opinions and will. Children are subjects of law. Children are depicted as autonomous actors in society within the ever-increasing literature on the topic. However, it is the day-to-day lived experiences of children around the globe that shows that children are universally neither treated as individuals in need of protection nor children with autonomous rights and free will. For example, the CRC protects the child's right to practise their religion and express their beliefs. However, this right is often limited by the beliefs of the child's family. Alternatively, and more generally, the CRC protects the child's right to have their views heard and taken into consideration when decisions related to them are being determined. However, there are very few satisfactory examples of this. The child's voice in the courts or indeed asylum procedures is often limited by laws relating to capacity, the views of the parents and/or an insufficient system for guardians *ad litem* or legal representation.[248] There is also an unease where qualification as a refugee is concerned between the two regimes (international children's rights law and international refugee law) as discussed in Chapter 5 and demonstrated in this chapter. This unease has been insufficiently dealt with in literature, policy, law and decision-making in the case of children.

UNHCR and the Committee have dealt with the relationship between the two regimes and have even paved the way for the wide acceptance of the term *child-specific persecution* and the content therein. The guidance provided by both inter-governmental organisations highlighted that there are clear convergences between the two legal regimes and both suggested how the Refugee Convention could be interpreted in the case of children. Beyond international guidance, very little research exists that has looked at the characteristics of a positive experience of childhood, the rights embedded in international law that aim to enforce that experience *and* its intersection with refugee protection. The guidance and literature available at present has tended to analyse children's rights through the lens of refugee law. This means children's rights that have an obvious nexus with a convention ground *or* rights that relate to a procedural element of the determinations process are most often analysed. There are only limited examples of literature, policy, law and jurisprudence looking at the qualification of children as refugees through a children's rights lens.

Part I sought to elaborate on four provision rights sub-categories associated with childhood in the refugee context, namely: the right to family, the right to the highest attainable standard of health and an adequate standard of living and the right to education. All four rights were provided for in the CRC and they can also be found in the literature and law that preceded the CRC. The main finding in Part I related to the disconnect between social and economic rights and persecution. This is a challenge that exists across the board in respect of asylum determinations. It has affected cases submitted by adults as well as children. Part I showed that cases involving children's provision rights, which are heavily grounded in social and economic rights, were uncommon and instances where a breach related to non-discrimination and was State-sponsored or tolerated were favoured. Rights that were merely not provided for (for example healthcare) were deemed not to have a link with the Refugee Convention. Part I also showed that the CRC was explicitly relied upon as guidance in the interpretation of the Refugee Convention in the case of provision rights (albeit infrequently). It also showed that children were sometimes considered objects and sometimes subjects of the law. However, largely, the applicants were considered objects who required third party intervention to enable them to access their rights to family, health, an adequate standard of living and education. Part I also showed that although development or Article 6 were not mentioned in the case law (with the exception of *D. v. Refugee Appeals Tribunal*) the decisions were all 'forward looking' and mentioned rights that corresponded with the Committee's interpretation of Article 6 that comprised: 'physical, mental, spiritual, moral, psychological and social development'.[249]

Part II elaborated on protection rights deriving from the CRC as outlined in Chapter 2. This section looked primarily at the right to be protected from (1) exploitation including labour and trafficking, (2) forced military recruitment and participation in armed conflict including indiscriminate violence and torture and (3) involvement in illicit activities and gangs. In addition, Part II looked at the role of the family in protecting/persecuting the child. It was established in Part II that protection rights were the most developed in case law, guidance and literature. This is consistent with the historical and contemporary trajectory and development of international children's rights law, including in the context of refugee law. Part II also showed that the social and economic circumstances of the child, those reflected in the provision rights set out in Part I, make children more vulnerable to protection rights violations. Part II also brought to light the fact that the CRC was at times explicitly relied upon in the interpretation of the Refugee Convention in respect of protection rights.

Part II showed that children were most often viewed as objects of protection in the context of refugee law and where they were viewed as subjects exercising their agency, it tended to work to their disadvantage. For example, protection from involvement in illicit activities is a CRC and ILO right, yet in refugee law it has at times been interpreted to be a voluntary choice, even at the age of 14. The literature on the topic suggested that where agency enters into the protection sphere the outcomes were more likely to be negative. Development and Article 6 did not arise in protection rights cases either. However, some of the case law, for example in the case of the possibility of re-trafficking, the judgments were also 'forward looking'. They considered the child's access to rights or a livelihood, for example in the case of minors with no known family members in the country of origin, into the future, which reflects the modern understanding of childhood – a process of growth and development. In addition, the case law also referred to rights that corresponded with the Committee's interpretation of Article 6, as outlined above.

Part III elaborated on participation rights deriving from the CRC as outlined in Chapter 3, but with a focus on the religion and political opinion convention grounds. There is very limited case law and literature on child agency specific to persecution. In the case of adults, as Chapter 4 highlighted, there has been a tendency to rely more on political persecution in refugee law generally. However, the literature and case law suggests that in the case of children where there is a nexus with the political opinion ground or any case where agency is prominent are less common and less likely to have positive outcomes. This may be due to the fact that an analysis of claims where the violations stem from participation rights involves a subjective assessment by a third party to determine if the child is indeed capable of forming and expressing political opinions or other views.

Part III showed that child cases are dealt with differently. Children were subjects of the law in relation to participation rights. The link to development was less clear in these cases. This is likely due to the fact that decision-makers are hesitant to attribute agency to children and they are not likely to see agency as *part* of childhood. Protection and provision rights, or social and economic rights, were dominant in case law and the literature. Breaches of civil and political rights were infrequently considered in the case of children. This is the opposite of the trend in adult refugee cases. It is difficult to draw out the links between development and this area of case law as these aforementioned cases largely focused on whether or not the child had capacity to exercise their agency, not whether or not it was their right to do so. In other words, the case law did not therefore deal with the substantive issue of qualification, but rather focused on the child's ability to exercise their agency. However, some of the CRC rights, such as the rights to identity and to practice one's religion, overlap with the Committee's interpretation of Article 6 and therefore must form part of any children's rights approach.

Despite being part of the wider discourse on childhood from the seventeenth century, child agency in the rights sphere is still only in its infancy.

A children's rights approach

A conceptualisation of the child refugee is therefore someone who is likely an object of law, a particularly vulnerable person requiring protection, whose situation may be worsened or who may be more likely to fear persecution based on their social and economic circumstances. It may then be said that in terms of prioritising rights within the CRC in the interpretation of the Refugee Convention, protection rights rank highest, followed by provision rights and finally participation rights. There is guidance and there is a clear move generally to focus on agency in the case of children in all disciplines, but children who exercise said agency are looked upon with trepidation within asylum procedures as described by Bhabha and Crock.[250]

Some of the case law discussed in this chapter referenced the CRC. This shows that children's rights, although the regime developed years after the establishment of the refugee framework, have begun to influence refugee law nonetheless. This has been a slow process and it is likely that these types of refugee cases will continue to grow. Despite inconsistencies, child-specific applications have been successful. This indicates an expansion of the area of refugee law to encompass developments in the area of children's rights law, most recently in the case of participation rights. This shows that the Refugee Convention is capable of accommodating applications by children and that a children's rights approach is possible and indeed advisable given the variations in outcomes in case law and approaches to child refugee law.

A children's rights approach to the interpretation of the Refugee Convention would lead to greater consistency in determinations. International children's rights law would be considered as part of the assessment as to whether or not a particular rights violation amounted to persecution. The 'persecution barometer' would therefore comprise international children's rights law.

Children's rights should form part of the decision making process to ensure that any analysis of the threshold for persecution considers their most basic rights, while recognising that the rights violation must not only amount to persecution, but must be characterised by differential impact on the basis of discrimination. And, as argued throughout this book, Article 6 should form the foundation of this evaluation in line with the interpretation of the right to survival and development provided by the Committee:

> Article 6: the child's inherent right to life and States parties' obligation to ensure to the maximum extent possible the survival and development of the child. The Committee expects States to interpret "development" in its broadest sense as a holistic concept, embracing the child's physical, mental, spiritual, moral, psychological and social development. Implementation measures should be aimed at achieving the optimal development for all children.

Furthermore, a children's rights approach would encompass both social and economic rights and civil and political rights reflecting all the rights contained within the CRC. Protection rights therefore might not be privileged over other rights violations in the application of a children's rights approach to the interpretation of the Refugee Convention. It may also minimise the reliance on Article 3 (best interests) as a catch-all right.

Notes

1 Jacqueline Bhabha, *Child Migration and Human Rights in a Global Age* (PUP 2014) 208.

2 Graca Machel, *Impact of Armed Conflict* (UN 1996) paras 1 and 250. <www.un.org/ga/search/view_doc.asp?symbol=A/51/306> accessed 15 July 2016.

3 Jacqueline Bhabha, 'Demography and rights: women, children and access to

asylum' (2004) 16 *International Journal of Refugee Law* 227.

4 European Migration Network, *EMN Annual Report on Immigration and Asylum* (EMN 2016) 5 and 27.

5 Jacqueline Bhabha, *Child Migration and Human Rights in a Global Age* (PUP 2014) 207.

6 Michelle Foster, *International Refugee Law and Socio-Economic Rights: Refugee from Deprivation* (CUP 2007) 35.

7 Jacqueline Bhabha, *Child Migration and Human Rights in a Global Age* (PUP 2014) 207.

8 See *INS v. Cardoza-Fonseca* 480 U.S. 421, 49 at note 22 (1987). See also: Jacqueline Bhabha, 'Demography and rights: women, children and access to asylum' (2004) 16 *International Journal of Refugee Law* 227.

9 International Protection Act 2015 Section 15.3 Application for Protection (Ireland).

10 See, for example: Catherine Cosgrave and Liam Thornton, 'Immigration and Asylum Law' in Children's Rights Alliance and the Law Centre for Children and Young People, *Making rights real for children: A Children's Rights Audit of Irish Law* (Children's Rights Alliance 2015) 175.

11 Jacqueline Bhabha, *Child Migration and Human Rights in a Global Age* (PUP 2014) 210.

12 *Ibid*, 224.

13 *Ibid*, 228–229.

14 *Ibid*, 207.

15 Jacqueline Bhabha, 'Demography and rights: women, children and access to asylum' (2004) 16 *International Journal of Refugee Law* 227.

16 Satvinder Singh Juss, 'Refugee Law and the Protection of Children fleeing Conflict and Violence in Afghanistan' (2013) 18 (2) *Journal of Conflict & Security Law* 303.

17 See, for examples of child cases and literature: UN High Commissioner for Refugees, *The Heart of the Matter – Assessing Credibility when Children Apply for Asylum in the European Union* (UNHCR 2014).

18 Anne Marie Ambert, 'Sociology of sociology: The place of children in North American sociology' in Patricia Adler and Peter Adler, *Sociological Studies of Child Development* (Vol 1, JAI Press 1986) 11–31.

19 Convention on the Rights of the Child 1989, Preamble and Articles 20 and 22.

20 *Ibid*, Article 24.

21 *Ibid*, Article 27.

22 *Ibid*, Article 3.1.

23 Universal Declaration of Human Rights 1948, Article 16.3. See also: International Covenant on Civil and Political Rights 1976, Article 23; International Covenant on Economic and Social Rights 1976, Article 10; Convention on the Rights of the Child 1989, Preamble.

24 UN Committee on the Rights of the Child, *General comment No. 6 (2005): Treatment of Unaccompanied and Separated Children Outside their Country of Origin* CRC/GC/2005/6 para 40.

25 UN High Commissioner for Refugees, *Handbook and Guidelines on Procedures and Criteria for Determining Refugee Status under the 1951 Convention and the 1967 Protocol relating to the Status of Refugees* (UNHCR 2011) para 183.

26 1951 Convention and 1967 Protocol relating to the Status of Refugees, IV. B.

27 Bhabha noted that it is just that principle that has resulted in a tendency for accompanied children's asylum claims to be subsumed within family applications. Jacqueline Bhabha, *Child Migration and Human Rights in a Global Age* (PUP 2014) 221.

28 United Nations High Commissioner for Refugees, 'Guidelines on International Protection: Child Asylum Claims under Articles 1(A)2 and 1(F) of the 1951 Convention and 1967 Protocol relating to the Status of Refugees' HCR/GIP/09/08 22 December 2009.

29 UN Committee on the Rights of the Child, *General comment No. 6 (2005): Treatment of Unaccompanied and Separated Children Outside their Country of Origin* CRC/GC/2005/6 para 39.

30 *Ibid*, para 27.

31 Alice Farmer, 'A Commentary on the Committee on the Rights of the Child's Definition of Non-Refoulement for Children: Broad Protection for Fundamental Rights' (2011) 80 *Res Gestae* 45.

32 *Chen She Hai (an infant) by His Next Friend Chen Ren Bing v. Minister for Immigration and Multicultural Affairs* [2000], 201 CLR 293 (Austl.).

33 See, Jacqueline Bhabha and Mary Crock, *Seeking Asylum Alone – a Comparative Study: Unaccompanied and Separated Children and Refugee Protection in Australia, the UK and the US* (Themis Press 2007).

34 Home Office, *Asylum Policy Instruction: Discretionary Leave* (Version 7, Home Office 2015) <www.gov.uk/government/uploads/system/uploads/attachment_data/file/460712/Discretionary_Leave_2__v7_0.pdf>.

35 *AA (unattended children) Afghanistan CG [2012] UKUT 00016 (IAC).*

36 See Chapter 3.

37 International Covenant on Economic and Social Rights 1976, Article 12.

38 Universal Declaration of Human Rights 1948, Article 25.

39 Convention on the Rights of the Child 1989, Article 24.

40 Committee on the Rights of the Child, General Comment No. 7 *Implementing child rights in early childhood* CRC/C/GC/7/Rev.120 September 2006 para 34.

41 United Nations High Commissioner for Refugees, *Guidelines on International Protection: Child Asylum Claims under Articles 1(A)2 and 1(F) of the 1951 Convention and 1967 Protocol relating to the Status of Refugees* HCR/GIP/09/08 22 December 2009 para 12.

42 See *Case of the Yean and Bosico Children v. The Dominican Republic*, IACtHR, 8 Sep. 2005 where two girls of Haitian origin were denied the right to nationality and education because, among other matters, they did not have a birth certificate.

43 For example, *Case of the "Juvenile Reeducation Institute" v. Paraguay*, iaCtHR, 2 Sep. 2004. In this case, the Inter-American Court of Human Rights found that failure to provide basic health services to marginalised groups amounted to a breach of the right to life as articulated in Article 4 of the American Convention on Human Rights. American Convention on Human Rights 1969, Article 4.1 Right to Life: Every person has the right to have his life respected. This right shall be protected by law and, in general, from the moment of conception. No one shall be arbitrarily deprived of his life. This case also reflected the use of the CRC. A former advisor to UNICEF and an expert on children's rights was consulted and the CRC was referred to throughout. The rights relevant to children and this case as contained in the American Convention on Human Rights, in particular Article 19 (Every minor child has the right to the measures of protection required by his condition as a minor on the part of his family, society, and the state), were also referred to in testimony. The CRC was not referred to in the decision, but it was in the Concurring Opinion of Judge A.A. Cançado Trinidade (para 9).

44 United Nations High Commissioner for Refugees, 'Guidelines on International Protection: Child Asylum Claims under Articles 1(A)2 and 1(F) of the 1951

Convention and 1967 Protocol relating to the Status of Refugees' HCR/GIP/09/08 22 December 2009 13.

45 Convention on the Rights of the Child 1989, Article 24.

46 *RRT Case No. N94/04178*, N94/04178, Australia: Refugee Review Tribunal, 10 June 1994.

47 Convention against Torture and Other Cruel, Inhuman or Degrading Treatment or Punishment 1984.

48 See: Katharine Williamson, 'AIDS, Gender and the Refugee Protection Framework' (2004) RSC Working Paper No. 19 *Refugee Studies Centre*. *N v Secretary of State for the Home Department* [2005] 4 All ER 1017 (this case dealt with [European Convention on Human Rights] ECHR Article 3).

49 United Nations High Commissioner for Refugees, *Guidelines on International Protection: Child Asylum Claims under Articles 1(A)2 and 1(F) of the 1951 Convention and 1967 Protocol relating to the Status of Refugees* HCR/GIP/09/08 22 December 2009 31.

50 Convention on the Rights of the Child 1989, Article 24.3.

51 UN High Commissioner for Refugees, *Handbook and Guidelines on Procedures and Criteria for Determining Refugee Status under the 1951 Convention and the 1967 Protocol relating to the Status of Refugees* (UNHCR 2011), details a number of circumstances where health may play a role in defining persecution. The first instance relates to the 'religion' ground.

52 *Matter of Dennis Reyes-Diaz* (EOIR Aug. 2, 2001) (unpublished); *Matter of Brus. Wilson Fuentes-Ortega*, A78-677-043 (BIA Nov. 6 2002); *Matter of Santos Ramon Zepeda Campos* (IJ Dec. 28, 2000) (Phoenix, Arizona) *Matter of Aurelio Mauricio Lopez* A78-677-018 (BIA Nov. 28 2001) (unpublished) in Jacqueline Bhabha, *Child Migration and Human Rights in a Global Age* (PUP 2014) 227.

53 *RRT Case No. 1101038*, [2011] RRTA 307, Australia: Refugee Review Tribunal, 14 April 2011 at 79.

54 For a compilation of recent FGM cases, see: International Refugee Rights Initiative Rights in Exile Programme, 'FGM/C Case Law and Other Legal Documents' <www.refugeelegalaidinformation.org/fgmc-case-law-and-other-legal-documents> accessed 16 July 2016.

55 See: Save the Children, *Outcomes for Children from Household Economic Strengthening Interventions: A Research Synthesis* (Save the Children 2015); Save the Children, *Towards the end of child poverty* (Save the Children 2015).

56 See: UNICEF, *The State of the World's Children 2016: A fair chance for every child* (UNICEF 2016).

57 Convention on the Rights of the Child 1989, Article 27.

58 See: Ridge Tess, 'Childhood poverty and social exclusion' (2004) 14 (2) *Children, Youth and Environments*; Phil Agulnik, *Understanding social exclusion* (OUP 2002); Tim Butler and Paul Watt, *Understanding Social Inequality* (Sage 2007); Alberto Minujin and Shailen Nandy (eds), *Global Child Poverty and Well-being: Measurement, concepts, policy and action* (Policy Press 2012).

59 Malcolm Langford et al. (eds), *The Millennium Development Goals and Human Rights: Past, Present and Future* (CUP 2015); Luis Ongay, 'Glocalists in Tijuana: youth, cultural citizenship and cosmopolitan identity (2010) 8 (4) *Children's Geographies* 373; Marilyn Fleer, Marianne Hedegaard and Jonathan Tudge, 'Constructing childhood: global-local politics and practices' in Marilyn Fleer, Marianne Hedegaard and Jonathan Tudge (eds), *Childhood Studies and the Impact of Globalisation: Practices at Global and Local Levels* (Routledge 2009); Jo Boyden and Joanna de Berry, 'Introduction' in Jo Boyden and Joanna de Berry, *Children and Youth on the Front Line: Ethnography, Armed Conflict and Displacement* (Falmer 1997); Tim Butler and Paul Watt, *Understanding*

Social Inequality (Sage 2007).

60 UN Committee on the Rights of the Child, 'Fifty sixth session Consideration of Reports Submitted by States Parties Under Article 44 of the Convention Concluding Observations of the Committee on the Rights of the Child: Afghanistan' CRC/C/AFG/1 4 February 2011.

61 UN Committee on Rights of Child, 'The Consortium for Street Children & War Child, NGO Shadow report for Afghanistan' 59 in *AA (unattended children) Afghanistan CG [2012] UKUT 00016 (IAC)* paras 57–59.

62 *Ibid.*

63 In *Fadele Emanuel, Fadele Kehinde, Fadele Taiwo, Fadele Victor v United Kingdom* and *Nona v. Netherlands No. 113078/87 1990* [European Court of Human Rights] ECtHR, the ECtHR dealt with children being returned to living conditions that were not deemed sufficient for the child's safety and well-being. The applicants referred to various rights including the child-specific right, Article 2 of Protocol 1 to the ECHR on the right to education. *Z and others v United Kingdom Application no. 29392/95* ECtHR 2001 also dealt with children living in inadequate conditions (and abusive conditions), the Court found that States must 'provide effective protection, in particular, of children and other vulnerable persons and include reasonable steps to prevent ill-treatment of which the authorities had or ought to have had knowledge' (para 73). However, these assessments dealt with Article 3 of the ECHR and not refugee protection.

64 *Cheung v. Canada (Minister of Employment and Immigration)*, [1993] 2 F.C. 314, Canada: Federal Court of Appeal, 1 April 1993.

65 *Ibid.*

66 *Chen Shi Hai* 201 C.L.R. 297.

67 Brian Edstrom, 'Assessing Asylum Claims from Children Born in Violation of China's One-Child Policy: What the United States can Learn from Australia' (2009) *Wisconsin International Law Journal* 169.

68 See Chapters 2 and 3.

69 The Convention on the Rights of the Child 1989 primary protects the right to *primary* education. See Chapter 2.

70 Glenn Mower, Jr., *The Convention on the Rights of the Child: International Support for Children* (Greenwood Press 1997) 34.

71 UN High Commissioner for Refugees, *Handbook and Guidelines on Procedures and Criteria for Determining Refugee Status under the 1951 Convention and the 1967 Protocol relating to the Status of Refugees* (UNHCR 2011) para 54.

72 *Ibid.*

73 United Nations High Commissioner for Refugees, *Guidelines on International Protection: Child Asylum Claims under Articles 1(A)2 and 1(F) of the 1951 Convention and 1967 Protocol relating to the Status of Refugees* HCR/GIP/09/08 22 December 2009, para 12 'Alongside age, other identity-based, economic and social characteristics of the child, such as family background, class, caste, health, education and income level, may increase the risk of harm, influence the type of persecutory conduct inflicted on the child and exacerbate the effect of the harm on the child'.

74 UN Committee on economic, social and Cultural Rights (hereafter 'CesCR'), General Comment No. 11: Plans of Action for Primary Education (Art. 14 of the Covenant), e/1992/23, 10 May 1999 guidelines para 14.

75 See *RRT Case No. V95/03256*, [1995] RRTa 2263, Australia, RRT, 9 Oct. 1995, www.unhcr.org/refworld/docid/4b17c13a2. html, where the Tribunal found that 'discriminatory denial of access to primary education is such a denial of a fundamental human right that it amounts to persecution'. at 47.

76 *RRT Case No. V95/03256*, [1995] at 41.

77 *Ibid*, at 37.
78 *Ibid*, at 36.
79 *Ali v. Minister of Citizenship and Immigration*, iMM-3404-95, Canada, iRB, 23 sep. 1996.
80 General Comment No. 5 (2003) General measures of implementation of the Convention on the Rights of the Child (arts 4, 42 and 44, para 6) para 12.
81 Judicial review of negative decision delivered by the Refugee Appeals Tribunal.
82 *D. [a minor] v Refugee Appeals Tribunal & Anor* [2011] IECH 431 at 7.
83 *Ibid*, at 17.
84 *Ibid*, at 24.
85 *Ibid*, at 23.
86 *Brown v. Board of Education of Topeka* 347 US 483 (1954) in *Ibid* at 18.
87 See: Separated Children in Europe Programme, 'Newsletter No. 43 – Summer 2015' (Defence for Children, NL 2016) 5051.
88 Michelle Foster, *International Refugee Law and Socio-Economic Rights: Refugee from Deprivation* (CUP 2007). See also: Inter-American Commission on Human Rights *Andrea Mortlock Case* in Human Rights Watch, *Returned to Risk: Deportation of HIVE-positive Migrants* (Human Rights Watch 2009) 10.
89 *RRT Case No. V95/03256*, [1995] RRTa 2263, Australia, RRT, 9 Oct. 1995, see above.
90 *D. [a minor] v Refugee Appeals Tribunal & Anor* [2011] IEHC, see above.
91 Convention on the Rights of the Child 1919, Article 12.
92 UN Committee on the Rights of the Child, *General comment No. 6 (2005): Treatment of Unaccompanied and Separated Children Outside their Country of Origin* CRC/GC/2005/6.; United Nations High Commissioner for Refugees, 'Guidelines on International Protection: Child Asylum Claims under Articles 1(A)2 and 1(F) of the 1951 Convention and 1967 Protocol relating to the Status of Refugees' HCR/GIP/09/08 22 December 2009 para 12.
93 United Nations High Commissioner for Refugees, *Guidelines on International Protection: Child Asylum Claims under Articles 1(A)2 and 1(F) of the 1951 Convention and 1967 Protocol relating to the Status of Refugees* HCR/GIP/09/08 22 December 2009 para 20.
94 *Ibid*, para 23.
95 *Ibid*, paras 26, 27.
96 *Ibid*, para 32–33.
97 *Ibid*, para 44.
98 *Ibid*, para 52.
99 *Matter of Chen*, 20 I. & N. Dec. 16, 19 (BIA 1989).
100 *Gomez-Guzmen v. Holder*, no. 11-3006, 2012 WL 2161636, at *3 (6th Cir. June 15 2012).
101 *Gomez-Guzmen v. Holder*, no. 11-3006, 2012 WL 2161636, at *3 (6th Cir. June 15 2012).
102 International Labour Organization, Minimum Age Convention 1973 (No. 138, Article 3).
103 Convention on the rights of the Child 1989, Article 19.
104 *Matter [name not provided]* (IJ Mar. 13, 1998) (Chicago, Ill.) (IJ Zerbe) in Jacqueline Bhabha, *Child Migration and Human Rights in a Global Age* (PUP 2014) 225.
105 European Asylum Support Office, *Newsletter – March 2014* 7 <www.easo.europa.eu/sites/default/files/public/EASO-Newsletter-March1.pdf> accessed 10 September 2016.
106 UNHCR, *Guidelines on International Protection: The application of Article 1A(2) of the 1951 Convention and/or 1967 Protocol relating to the Status of*

Refugees to victims of trafficking and persons at risk of being trafficked HCR/GIP/06/07 7 April 2006.

107 United Nations High Commissioner for Refugees, *Guidelines on International Protection: Child Asylum Claims under Articles 1(A)2 and 1(F) of the 1951 Convention and 1967 Protocol relating to the Status of Refugees* HCR/GIP/09/08 22 December 2009 para 15.

108 See: *SZBFQ v. Minister of Immigration* [2005] FMCA 197 and *Matter of M-J-*, CGRS Case No. 364 (China), BIA 30 March 2001.

109 United Nations High Commissioner for Refugees, 'Guidelines on International Protection: Child Asylum Claims under Articles 1(A)2 and 1(F) of the 1951 Convention and 1967 Protocol relating to the Status of Refugees' HCR/GIP/09/08 22 December 2009 11.

110 *Bian v. Canada (Minister for Citizenship and Immigration)*, IMM-1640-00, 11 Dec. 2000.

111 *Ibid*, at 46.

112 *Ibid.*

113 See also: *Zhu (L.W.) v. Canada (Minister of Citizenship and Immigration)*, IMM-2746-00, 13 Aug. 2001.

114 See, for example: *A B v. Secretary of State for the Home Department*, no. CC/64057/2002, 18 Deb. 2003.

115 *Ogbeide v. Secretary of State for the Home Department* (Unreported, IAT, Appeal No. HX/08391/2002, 10 May 2002) in Michelle Foster, *International Refugee Law and Socio-Economic Rights: Refugee from Deprivation* (CUP 2007) 285.

116 *Y.C.K. (re)* [1997] CRDD No. 261 No. V95-02904.

117 See for extensive analysis of human trafficking in international law including in the context of criminal law: Anne Gallagher, *The International Law of Human Trafficking* (CUP 2010) 122, 184, 209, 270, 358.

118 Convention on the Rights of the Child 1989, Article 38.

119 Graca Machel, *Impact of Armed Conflict* (UN 1996) paras 1 and 250. <www.un.org/ga/search/view_doc.asp?symbol=A/51/306> accessed 15 July 2016.

120 *The Application of the Convention on the Prevention and Punishment of the Crime of Genocide (Bosnia and Herzegovina v. Serbia and Montenegro* [2007] ICJ Rep. 43, para 291.

121 Human Rights Watch, 'Afghanistan: Taliban Should Stop Using Children as Suicide Bombers' 31 August 2011 <www.hrw.org/news/2011/08/31/afghanistan-taliban-should-stop-using-children-suicide-bombers> accessed 4 May 2016.

122 Graca Machel, *Impact of Armed Conflict* (UN 1996) paras 1 and 250. <www.un.org/ga/search/view_doc.asp?symbol=A/51/306> accessed 15 July 2016 paras 44–48.

123 *Ibid.*

124 United Nations High Commissioner for Refugees, 'Guidelines on International Protection: Child Asylum Claims under Articles 1(A)2 and 1(F) of the 1951 Convention and 1967 Protocol relating to the Status of Refugees' HCR/GIP/09/08 22 December 2009 paras 19–23.

125 See, for example: *O (a minor) v. Refugee Appeals Tribunal and Minister for Justice, Equality and Law Reform* [2010] IEHC 151.

126 Quaker United Nations Office, *Former Child Soldiers as Refugees in Germany* (Quaker United Nations Office and terre des homes 2013) 22.

127 See: Jacqueline Bhabha, *Child Migration and Human Rights in a Global Age* (PUP 2014) 207.

128 Quaker United Nations Office, *Former Child Soldiers as Refugees in Germany*

(Quaker United Nations Office and terre des homes 2013).

129 The 1951 Convention relating to the Status of Refugees does not apply to three categories of persons. Article 1D states that persons already in receipt of protection through the United Nations Relief and Works Agency for Palestine are excluded from the provisions contained within the Convention. Additionally, Article 1E excludes persons who can avail of protection in another jurisdiction other than their country of origin where they are already resident. Lastly, Article 1F excludes any person believed (where there are serious reasons to believe) to have: committed a war crime or a crime against peace or humanity; committed a serious non-political crime prior to applying for protection or been found guilty of committed acts contrary to the principles of the United Nations.

130 See: *Moreno v. Canada (Minister of Employment and Immigration)* [1994] 1 FC 298; *Negusie v. Holder*, 555 U.S. 511 (2009).

131 See: United Nations High Commissioner for Refugees, *The Exclusion Clauses: Guidelines on their Application*, December 1995, reprinted in *Refugee Law in Context: the Exclusion Clause* 19, 22 (Peter J. van Krieken (ed.), 1999); United Nations High Commissioner for Refugees on Child-Soldiers, reprinted in *Refugee Law in Context: the Exclusion Clause* 43, 44 (stating that '[t]he exclusion clauses do not distinguish between adults and minors').

132 See Sir Guy Goodwin-Gill, *The Refugee in International Law* (2nd edn, OUP 1996) 18–20.

133 See Sir Guy Goodwin-Gill, *The Refugee in International Law* (2nd edn, OUP 1996) 256–257.

134 France – CNDA, 20 December 2010, Mr. N., n°10004872. www.asylumlaw-database.eu/en/case-law/france-cnda-20-december-2010-mr-n-n%C2%B010004872

135 General Comment No. 5 (2003) General measures of implementation of the Convention on the Rights of the Child (arts. 4, 42 and 44, para 6) para 12.

136 Child as juvenile approach as discussed in Jacqueline Bhabha, *Child Migration and Human Rights in a Global Age* (PUP 2014) 227.

137 United Nations High Commissioner for Refugees, 'Guidelines on International Protection: Child Asylum Claims under Articles 1(A)2 and 1(F) of the 1951 Convention and 1967 Protocol relating to the Status of Refugees' HCR/GIP/09/08 22 December 2009 para 29.

138 See Jacqueline Bhabha, *Child Migration and Human Rights in a Global Age* (PUP 2014) 233.

139 See also: Galya Ruffer, 'Gang-Based Asylum Claims' <www.refugeelegalaidinformation.org/gang-based-asylum-claims> accessed 16 July 2016.

140 Mathew Happold, 'Excluding Children from Refugee Status: Child Soldiers and Article 1F of the Refugee Convention' (2002) *American University International Law Review* 17 (6) 1131.

141 USAID, *Central America and Mexico Gang Assessment Report* (Bureau for Latin American and Caribbean Affairs Office of Regional Sustainable Development 2006) 15.

142 Refugee protection requires the person in need of protection to be out of the country. This means children *in*-country and *in* gangs would not qualify as refugees.

143 Jeffrey Corsetti, 'Marked for Death: The Maras of Central America and Those who Flee Their Wrath' (2006) 20 (3) *Georgetown Immigration Law Journal.*

144 Jacqueline Bhabha, *Child Migration and Human Rights in a Global Age* (PUP 2014) 235.

145 Nicolás Rodríguez Serna, 'Fleeing Cartels and Maras: International Protection Considerations and Profiles from the Northern Triangle' (2016) 28 (1)

International Journal of Refugee Law.

146 Matter of S-E-G 24 I&N Dec. 579 (BIA 2008).

147 Matter of E-A-G 24 I&N Dec. 591 (BIA 2008).

148 Jacqueline Bhabha, *Child Migration and Human Rights in a Global Age* (PUP 2014) 235.

149 *Decision A7-00299*, 2007 CanLII 47735 (IBR), Canada: Immigration and Refugee Board of Canada 31 May 2007.

150 *Ibid*, pp. 5–6.

151 Clare Mulley, *The Woman who Saved the Children: A Biography of Eglantyne Jebb, Founder of Save the Children* (Oneworld Publications 2009, 2011 ebook reprint).

152 *Elgafaji v. Staatssecretaris van Justitie* (C-465/07; 17 February 2009) [2009] 1 WLR 2100.

153 Directive 2011/95/EU of the European Parliament and of the Council of 13 December 2011 on standards for the qualification of third-country nationals or stateless persons as beneficiaries of international protection, for a uniform status for refugees or for persons eligible for subsidiary protection, and for the content of the protection granted (recast) A 'person eligible for subsidiary protection' is defined in Article 2: 'a third-country national or a stateless person who does not qualify as a refugee but in respect of whom substantial grounds have been shown for believing that the person concerned, if returned to his or her country of origin, or in the case of a stateless persons, to his or her country of former habitual residence, would face a real risk of serious harm…' Serious harm is defined in Article 15: Serious harm consists of: (a) the death penalty or execution; or (b) torture or inhuman or degrading treatment or punishment of an applicant in the country of origin; or serious and individual threat to a civilian's life or person by reason of indiscriminate violence in situations of international or internal armed conflict.

154 As discussed in Chapter 4.

155 Convention on the Rights of the Child 1989, Article 37.

156 Universal Declaration of Human Rights 1948, Article 5.

157 International Covenant on Civil and Political Rights 1966, Article 7.

158 See, for example: Quentin Dignam, 'The Burden and the Proof: Torture and Testimony in the Determination of Refugee Status in Australia' (1992) 4 (3) *International Journal of Refugee Law* 343. However, recently there has been a move towards considering torture within complementary regimes, see: Jane McAdam, 'The European Union Qualification Directive: The Creation of a Subsidiary Protection Regime' (2005) 28 (2) *International Journal of Refugee Law* 461.

159 Convention on the Rights of the Child 1989, Article 37.

160 Jacqueline Bhabha, *Child Migration and Human Rights in a Global Age* (PUP 2014) 210.

161 United Nations High Commissioner for Refugees, 'Guidelines on International Protection: Child Asylum Claims under Articles 1(A)2 and 1(F) of the 1951 Convention and 1967 Protocol relating to the Status of Refugees' HCR/GIP/09/08 22 December 2009 para 33.

162 GH v RAT [2015] IEHC 583 at 21.

163 *Ibid*, at 11.

164 *Matter of Juan Carlos Martinez-Mejia* A 76 312 250, 5–6 (BIA Jan. 20, 1999).

165 See, for example: Sweden – Migration Court (Administrative) 17 March 2011, UM 206-11 and *LQ (Afghanistan) v. Secretary of State for the Home Department* [2008] UKAIT 00005.

166 *HK and Others (minors – indiscriminate violence – forced recruitment by Taliban*

– contact with family members) Afghanistan CG [2010] UKUT 378 (IAC).

167 *HK and Others (minors – indiscriminate violence – forced recruitment by Taliban – contact with family members) Afghanistan CG [2010] UKUT 378 (IAC).*

168 UN High Commissioner for Refugees, *UNHCR Eligibility Guidelines for Assessing the International Protection Needs of Asylum-Seekers from Afghanistan* HCR/EG/AFG/10/04 (UNHCR 2010) 39. Updated in 2013: UN High Commissioner for Refugees, *UNHCR Eligibility Guidelines for Assessing the International Protection Needs of Asylum-Seekers from Afghanistan* HCR/EG/AFG/13/01 (UNHCR 2013).

169 *AA (unattended children) Afghanistan CG [2012] UKUT 00016 (IAC)* at 133.

170 See, for example: Home Office, *Asylum Policy Instruction: Discretionary Leave* (Version 7, Home Office 2015) <www.gov.uk/government/uploads/system/uploads/attachment_data/file/460712/Discretionary_Leave_2__v7_0.pdf>. See also: Samantha Arnold, et al., *Durable Solutions for Separated Children in Europe* (Irish Refugee Council 2016) 43.

171 Convention on the Rights of the Child 1989, Article 9.1; Article 19.

172 Convention on the Rights of the Child 1989, Article 19 read in line with Article 5.

173 As discussed in Chapter 2.

174 *Bueckert v. Canada (*Minister of Citizenship and Immigration) [2011] FC 1042; *Aguirre-Cervantes v. INS,* 242 F. 3d 1169 (9th Cir. 2001) (opinion vacated on rehearing en banc and remanded, 273 F.3d 1220 (9th Cir. 2001); and *Secretary of State for the Home Department v. Fatemah Firouz Rinjbar*, Immigration Appeal Tribunal, no. HX/70912/94, 28 June 1994.

175 *[Names Not Provided] v. Minister* [2011] Immigration Board of Canada – Refugee Protection Division, RPD File No. VA9-01475, VA9-01476, VA9-01477, VA9-01478, VA9-01479, para 13 (Can.).

176 Discussed in Chapter 3.

177 Self-determination is defined in International Covenant on Civil and Political Rights Adopted and opened for signature, ratification and accession by General Assembly resolution 2200A (XXI) of 16 December 1966 entry into force 23 March 1976, in accordance with Article 49 in *Article 1.* 1 All peoples have the right of self-determination. By virtue of that right they freely determine their political status and freely pursue their economic, social and cultural development.

178 See: Heaven Crawley, "No one gives you a chance to say what you are thinking": finding space for children's agency in the UK asylum system' (2009) *Area* 1.

179 1951 Convention relating to the Status of Refugees, Article 1A(2).

180 Further reading on the right of the child to seek asylum, see Ciara Smyth, *European Asylum Law and the Rights of the Child* (Routledge 2014).

181 See also Jacqueline Bhabha, *Child Migration and Human Rights in a Global Age* (PUP 2014) 227.

182 Convention on the Rights of the Child 1989, Article 13.

183 *Ibid*, Article 14.

184 *Ibid*, Article 15.

185 *Ibid*, Article 16.

186 *Ibid*, Article 30.

187 UN High Commissioner for Refugees, *Handbook and Guidelines on Procedures and Criteria for Determining Refugee Status under the 1951 Convention and the 1967 Protocol relating to the Status of Refugees* (UNHCR 2011) paras 46–47.

188 However the *Council for Alien Law Litigation* could not establish whether or not the applicants were Somali. The decision was to quash the original the

Office of the Commissioner General for Refugees and Stateless Persons decision and send it back to them for further investigation as to the applicants' nationality. *Council for Alien Law Litigation, 24 June 2010, Nr. 45.395*. Summary provided by the European Database of Asylum Law. <www.asylumlawdatabase.eu/en/case-law/belgium-–-council-alien-law-litigation-24-june-2010-nr-45395> accessed 17 September 2016.

189 UN High Commissioner for Refugees, *Handbook and Guidelines on Procedures and Criteria for Determining Refugee Status under the 1951 Convention and the 1967 Protocol relating to the Status of Refugees* (UNHCR 2011) para 42.

190 Convention on the Rights of the Child 1989, Article 14.

191 See, for example: *D.A. (infant) (Pakistan) -v- Minister for Justice Equality and Law Reform* [2015] IEHC 208. The Irish High Court arguably implicitly accepted that a claim on the basis of religious persecution can be advanced on behalf of minors.

192 UN High Commissioner for Refugees, *Handbook and Guidelines on Procedures and Criteria for Determining Refugee Status under the 1951 Convention and the 1967 Protocol relating to the Status of Refugees* (UNHCR 2011) para 42.

193 *Ibid*, para 43.

194 *Ibid*, paras 42–44.

195 International Refugee Rights Initiative: Rights in Exile Programme, 'FGM/Case law and other legal documents' <http://refugeelegalaidinformation.org/fgmc-case-law-and-other-legal-documents> accessed 10 September 2016.

196 Jacqueline Bhabha and Wendy Young, 'Not Adults in Miniature: Unaccompanied Child Asylum Seekers and the New U.S. Guidelines' (1999) 11 (1) *International Journal of Refugee Law* 109.

197 UN High Commissioner for Refugees, *Handbook and Guidelines on Procedures and Criteria for Determining Refugee Status under the 1951 Convention and the 1967 Protocol relating to the Status of Refugees* (UNHCR 2011) para 44. See also: UN High Commissioner for Refugees, *Guidelines on International Protection No. 6: Religion-Based Refugee Claims under Article 1A(2) of the 1951 Convention and/or the 1967 Protocol relating to the Status of Refugees* (UNHCR 2004) HCR/GIP/04/06.

198 UN High Commissioner for Refugees, *Handbook and Guidelines on Procedures and Criteria for Determining Refugee Status under the 1951 Convention and the 1967 Protocol relating to the Status of Refugees* (UNHCR 2011) para 44.

199 Jacqueline Bhabha and Wendy Young, 'Not Adults in Miniature: Unaccompanied Child Asylum Seekers and the New U.S. Guidelines' (1999) 11 (1) *International Journal of Refugee Law* 109.

200 Comfort Momohed, *Female Genital Mutilation* (Radcliffe 2005) 5–7

201 Convention on the Rights of the Child 1989, Article 19.

202 See, generally: Louis Mikhail, Child Marriage and Child Prostitution: Two Forms of Sexual Exploitation (2002) 10 (1) *Gender and Development* 43–49.

203 Convention on the Rights of the Child 1989, Article 24(3); International Covenant on Civil and Political Rights 1966, Article 23; International Covenant on Economic, Social and Cultural Rights 1966, Article 10; Convention on the Elimination of All Forms of Discrimination Against Women 1979, Article 16.

204 UNICEF, *Child Marriage and the Law: Legislative Reform Initiative Paper Series* (UNICEF 2008).

205 *Ibid*.

206 *Ibid*.

207 Kate Halvorsen, 'Asylum Decisions on Child Applicants Report on 4-Country Pilot Project' (Ministry of Local Government and Modernisation 2004) 23.

208 *Ibid.*
209 NS (social group) Afghanistan CG (forced marriage) at 43.
210 *Ibid*, at 45.
211 *Matter of [name not provided]* A76-512-001 (Oct. 18, 2000) (Chicago, IL) (Zerbe, IJ) in Jacqueline Bhabha, *Child Migration and Human Rights in a Global Age* (PUP 2014) 225.
212 Jacqueline Bhabha, *Child Migration and Human Rights in a Global Age* (PUP 2014) 225.
213 General Comment No. 5 (2003) General measures of implementation of the Convention on the Rights of the Child (arts 4, 42 and 44, para 6) para 12.
214 For example: In Sweden, the Migration Court of Appeal in UM 3363-10 & 3367-10 (9 March 2011) granted a young couple subsidiary protection on the basis of the female's avoidance of forced marriage and the ensuing harassment both parties endured. Summary from the European Database of Asylum Law <www.asylumlawdatabase.eu/en/case-law/sweden-migration-court-appeal-9-march-2011-um-3363-10-3367-10> accessed 10 September 2016.
215 Jacqueline Bhabha and Wendy Young, 'Not Adults in Miniature: Unaccompanied Child Asylum Seekers and the New U.S. Guidelines' (1999) 11 (1) *International Journal of Refugee Law* 101; *Matter of Timnit Daniel and Simret Daniel*, A70 483 789 & A70 483 774, U.S. BIA, 31 Jan. 2002 (unpublished, non-precedent setting decision).
216 Spain – Supreme Court, 17 June 2013, No. 3186/2013.
217 Directive 2011/95/EU of the European Parliament and of the Council of 13 December 2011 on standards for the qualification of third-country nationals or stateless persons as beneficiaries of international protection, for a uniform status for refugees or for persons eligible for subsidiary protection, and for the content of the protection granted (recast), Article 10.1(d).
218 See, for example: Jenni Millbank, 'From Discretion to Disbelief: Recent Trends in Refugee Determinations on the Basis of Sexual Orientation in Australia and the United Kingdom' (2009) *International Journal of Human Rights* 13 (2/3); Nicole LaViolette, 'Sexual Orientation, Gender Identity and the Refugee Determination Process in Canada' (2014) *Journal of Research in Gender Studies* 4 (2) 68; Mary Kapron and Nicole LaViolette, 'Refugee Claims Based on Sexual Orientation and Gender Identity: An Annotated Bibliography' (2014) *Ottawa Faculty of Law Working Paper* No. 2014–2015.
219 UN High Commissioner for Refugees, *Handbook and Guidelines on Procedures and Criteria for Determining Refugee Status under the 1951 Convention and the 1967 Protocol relating to the Status of Refugees* (UNHCR 2011) paras 42 and 43.
220 *Ibid*, para 50.
221 *Ibid*, para 50.
222 Susan Hazeldean, 'Confounding Identities: The Paradox of LGBT Children under Asylum Law (2011) 45 *University of California, Davis* 373.
223 The fact that he was a child was not part of the decision. This may be because he was over the age of 20 when the decision was finally successfully overturned.
224 Hernandez-Montiel v. I.N.S. 225 F.3d 1084 (9th Cir. 2000); Susan Hazeldean, 'Confounding Identities: The Paradox of LGBT Children under Asylum Law (2011) 45 *University of California, Davis* 373.
225 Sanchez-Trujillo v. INS, 801 F.2d 1571, 1576 (9th Cir. 1986) and Matter of Acosta, 19 I&N Dec. 211 (BIA 1985) in *Hernandez-Montiel* v. I.N.S. 225 F.3d 1084 (9th Cir. 2000) at C. See Chapter 5. *Matter of Toboso-Alfonso*, 20 I. & N. Dec.) 819 (B.I.A. 1990) and *In re Tenorio*, No. A72 093 558 (EOIR Immigr. Court July 26 1993) were also referred to.
226 Lambda Legal Defense and Education Fund, Hernandez-Montiel v. INS*: Final*

Victory! (July 5, 2001) in Julia Blanche Meister, 'Orientation-based Persecution as Grounds for Refugee Status: Policy Implications and Recommendations' (2014) 9 (1) *Notre Dame Journal of Law, Ethics and Public Policy* 275.

227 Susan Hazeldean, 'Confounding Identities: The Paradox of LGBT Children under Asylum Law (2011) 45 *University of California, Davis* 373.

228 Convention on the rights of the Child 1989, Article 19.

229 *Ibid*, Article 19.

230 *Ibid*, Article 8.

231 *Ibid*, Article 13.

232 UN High Commissioner for Refugees, *Handbook and Guidelines on Procedures and Criteria for Determining Refugee Status under the 1951 Convention and the 1967 Protocol relating to the Status of Refugees* (UNHCR 2011) para 45. See also para 80.

233 *Ibid*, para 45. See also para 82.

234 *Ibid*, para 45.

235 *Ibid.*

236 For example in *Mr. N., n° 10004872*, the CNDA found that the applicant had a well-founded fear of persecution based on imputed political opinions linked to his former role as a child soldier in the DR Congo. The applicant was abducted by rebels (Congrès national pour la défense du people, CNDP) at age 15. He was drugged, tortured, trained and forced to fight. He was unable to escape and was forced to commit crimes against civilians. He learned that his father had been killed and his other family members had fled upon return home. He received death threats based on his involvement in the fighting and eventually fled. *CNDA, 20 December 2010, Mr. N., n•10004872.*

237 As established by the CRC and interpreted by UNHCR.

238 UN High Commissioner for Refugees, *Handbook and Guidelines on Procedures and Criteria for Determining Refugee Status under the 1951 Convention and the 1967 Protocol relating to the Status of Refugees* (UNHCR 2011) para 45.

239 *Ibid.*

240 Jacqueline Bhabha and Wendy Young, 'Not Adults in Miniature: Unaccompanied Child Asylum Seekers and the New U.S. Guidelines' (1999) 11 (1) *International Journal of Refugee Law* 109–111.

241 *AA (unattended children) Afghanistan CG [2012] UKUT 16 (IAC) (01 February 2012)* para 136.

242 Jacqueline Bhabha and Wendy Young, 'Not Adults in Miniature: Unaccompanied Child Asylum Seekers and the New U.S. Guidelines' (1999) 11 (1) *International Journal of Refugee Law* 109–110.

243 Sandy Ruxton, 'Separated Children Seeking Asylum in Europe: a Programme for Action (Separated Children in Europe Programme 2000). See also: *Salaam v. INS*, 229 F.3d 1234 (9th Cir. 2000). The board in this case refused refugee protection believing that the applicant was too young to be a leader (at 18) in a political organisation in Nigeria.

244 Germany – Federal Administrative Court, 24 September 2009, 10 C 25.08. Summary in English provided by the European Database of Asylum Law. <www.asylumlawdatabase.eu/en/case-law/germany-federal-administrative-court-24-september-2009-10-c-2508#content> accessed 17 September 2016.

245 Kate Halvorsen, *Asylum Decisions on Child Applicants: Country Pilot Project (Norway)* (Regjeringen 2004) 34.

246 *Ibid.*

247 Jacqueline Bhabha, *Child Migration and Human Rights in a Global Age* (PUP 2014) 232.

248 See, for example: Martine Goeman et al., *Core Standards for Guardians of Separated*

Children in Europe (Defence for Children, the Netherlands 2014) 20–22.

249 General Comment No. 5 (2003) General measures of implementation of the Convention on the Rights of the Child (arts 4, 42 and 44, para 6) para 12.

250 Jacqueline Bhaba and Mary Crock, *Seeking Asylum Alone – a Comparative Study: Unaccompanied and Separated Children and Refugee Protection in Australia, the UK and the US* (Themis Press 2007) 106.

7 Conclusions

Abstract

This chapter reflects on which violations of children's rights amount to persecution, whether or not the Refugee Convention provides a satisfactory framework for the determination of child refugee applications and whether or not children's rights approach to the interpretation of the Refugee Convention is possible and, in this regard, what the main trends are.

Introduction

The conceptualisation of children and childhood within refugee law and refugee literature was analysed in this book. The suitability of the Refugee Convention as a framework for the interpretation of child claims and to what extent a children right's approach to the interpretation of the Refugee Convention is possible were also analysed. The catalyst for this research was the rapid growth in children's rights discourse following the publication of the Convention on the Rights of the Child (CRC). The universal acceptance of the CRC, as a formula for childhood globally insofar as it represents the status quo in 1989, was also a motivating factor. However, it was the developments that followed the adoption of the CRC, where cross-pollination between the two areas of law began with increasing frequency, which provided the impetus to address the hypothesis that a children's rights approach to the interpretation of the Refuge Convention is indeed possible and perhaps needed. Developments prior to, but more definitively post, the adoption of the CRC, indicate that a children's rights approach is possible and is somewhat developing. The application of refugee law in the case of children brought with it conceptual, procedural and interpretive challenges, however.

Dichotomies

As set out in Chapter 1, there has traditionally been a dichotomy between refugee law and children's rights. In fact, as established in Chapters 3 and 4, there were concurrent developments in both areas of law at the international level from the 1920s that dealt with the theme of international protection. However, rather than incorporating children or explicitly referring to children in refugee law or arrangements, children were addressed in the context of either one-off administrative arrangements, such as the *Kindertransport* in the 1930s or the 1924 Declaration of the Rights of the Child. The latter primarily drafted with children affected by war and conflict in mind, a category of refugees often thought to be *prima facie* in contemporary discourse.[1] During this time, children were invisible within refugee discourse. However, recent developments in guidance, literature and case law to some extent show the interconnectedness of the two modern legal regimes. Nevertheless, contemporary literature deals primarily with children's rights as they relate to procedure and social and economic needs unrelated to qualifying as a refugee. There is a tendency to deal with refugee children in research and guidance holistically, with qualification forming only a small piece of the work. The focus remains on access to social and economic rights in the receiving country and procedural and other safeguards. There is, in fact, limited research on the qualification of refugee children, which deals with the interpretation of persecution as it relates to children. References in guidance and law to 'child-specific forms of persecution' are only recent.

Considering these insights, this research looked to unpack the reasons for the dichotomy and the invisibility of children within refugee discourse by examining the developmental paths followed by children's rights law and refugee law. The research undertook to identify and explain areas where there was overlap and where there was no overlap. The purpose of this exercise was to demonstrate the existing relationship between the two regimes and potential for a children's rights approach to expand in light of established guidance and the principles of treaty interpretation discussed in Chapter 5. The number and proportion of children seeking asylum is growing. Alongside this growth is the growing acceptance that children have agency and can exercise that agency in a variety of ways, which affects the way they are conceived of in law, including refugee law. In theory the increase in number and the growing acceptance of the notion that children have rights *in their own right*, and not just as dependents within a family unit, should result in more claims for refugee protection from children, which should in turn lead to a narrowing of the gap between the two legal regimes. This was the impetus for this research.

A children's rights framework

Chapters 2 and 3 formed the foundation of the research in terms of conceptualising the child outside of refugee law. The purpose of these chapters was to ensure that the analysis of refugee law that followed was cognisant of the wider children's rights framework and the childhood status quo as had developed over centuries, but solidified by the CRC. Childhood as constructed in

Chapters 2 and 3 was defined as a period of growth and maturation where intervention was required to ensure protection from harm, which would interrupt or affect the child's development as reflected in Article 6 of the CRC. Children as conceptualised in Chapters 2 and 3 were thus vulnerable. However, these two chapters also established that, based on a wave of literature arising from the seventeenth and eighteenth centuries and later the Civil Rights movement in the US and the codification of rights contained in the CRC, children had an evolving capacity to participate, make decisions and otherwise interact with the societies around them. Chapter 3 therefore established that children are rights holders and have rights that can be violated relating to their innate vulnerability, but also as a result of their own actions, behaviours and decisions. This chapter established also that adults and States have a role in ensuring access to many rights based also on the aforesaid understanding of children.

Invisibility in refugee law

Despite the rapid development of the children's rights framework and a near-universal acceptance of the legal norms associated with childhood, no such understanding existed in refugee law prior to the adoption of the CRC. In fact, as established in Chapter 4, children were largely invisible in early refugee arrangements. There was very little overlap between the two legal regimes historically. Furthermore, there is very little literature that considers children in refugee law prior to the CRC. However, with the advent of the CRC, it would follow that refugee law would begin to engage with the children's rights framework. However, at least in the contemporary and well-regarded literature on the topic, such as contributions made by Hathaway and Goodwin-Gill, there is very little discussion on the interpretation of the Refugee Convention in the case of children. The contemporary literature that deals with child refugees is often related to social and economic rights in the context of procedures and welfare, with only some exceptions. Nevertheless, as a result of the lack of work on child refugees and the lack of any significant correlation between the development of the two regimes and their interplay overtime, a conceptualisation was emerging. This was reinforced by the onslaught of soft law guidance emerging from the United Nations High Commissioner for Refugees (UNHCR) and the Committee on the Rights of the Child as discussed in Chapter 5.

A bourgeoning children's rights approach to the interpretation of the Refugee Convention

The insights from soft law guidance and the ever-growing children's rights literature base showed that a children's rights approach to the interpretation of the Refugee Convention was not something completely new and was something that was to some degree developing. In their guidance materials,

UNHCR referred to the CRC and the Committee on the Rights of the Child referred to the Refugee Convention. Both referred to the UDHR. The UDHR, the foundation of both conventions, paved the way for a children's rights approach in that refugee case law, guidance and literature accepted in theory and in practice that the UDHR must form part of the canon of rights interpreted alongside the Refugee Convention. The CRC emerged much later than the UDHR, the International Covenant on Civil and Political Rights (ICCPR), and the International Covenant on Economic, Social and Cultural Rights (ICESCR), but it nevertheless forms part of the global human rights framework. The interpretation of the Refugee Convention utilising the CRC is however a more recent development. This is due to the fact that the CRC entered into force over 40 years after the UDHR and over a decade after the ICCPR and ICESCR.

Some child refugee cases dealt with in the higher courts (national high and supreme courts and international or supra-national courts) have referred explicitly to the CRC in their judgments as highlighted in Chapters 5 and 6. Legal practitioners have also referred explicitly to the CRC in their representations in child refugee cases. These references have also made their way into higher court judgements. In recent years, direct references to child-specific rights deriving from *inter alia* the CRC, the UDHR and the ICESCR have been referred to in child refugee cases as established in Chapter 6. There is limited case law generally, however, on the interpretation of the Refugee Convention in the case of children.

Limited case law

It is established that two factors have influenced the availability of case law; both relate to the child's innate vulnerability and dependence on adults. In the first instance, child refugee claims are typically subsumed within or connected to the head-of-household's application. Secondly, very few numbers of separated children make their way to Global North countries to seek refuge, though they represent a significant proportion outside receiving regions such as North America and Europe. This number is on the rise, but the proportion of separated child applicants remains small. This book does not discuss the reasons there are few separated children arriving to Global North destinations, nor why they may not seek asylum when they do find themselves in Europe or North America, for example. This fact is useful merely to illustrate one of the reasons for the low numbers in applications.

The low number of applications from children presents a challenge to this research. It is difficult to gauge what assessment is undertaken when arriving at a decision as to the well-foundedness of the fear of persecution of a child if they are only considered within a larger claim. States' and decision-makers' moving away from assessing child claims in the context of an overarching family or head-of-household claim may serve to further develop a children's rights approach. However, we can see that at least procedurally, rights relating to family unity are prioritised. Access to more case law or first instance decisions relating to children would be useful for further development of a children's rights approach. There was nevertheless sufficient case law and analysis in the literature to draw some conclusions as to the current state-of-play of the conceptualisation of child refugees.

A children's rights barometer for persecution: present-day case law

Chapter 6 examined case law relating to the children's rights framework, more specifically the conceptualisation of childhood, developed in Chapters 2 and 3. It was evident that the most widely used approach to categorise rights contained in the CRC, the Three Ps Approach, was also a useful framework in the context of refugee law. The analysis showed that rights considered to be categorised as provision, protection and participation were indeed violated to the extent that they amounted to persecution in the context of refugee law. Children were recognised as refugees on the basis of a violation of provision rights. The right to access education as set out in every human rights treaty under the aegis of the United Nations (and beyond) is one such example. This section also established that provision rights relating to the highest attainable standard of health (unless amounting to inhuman or degrading treatment) and an adequate standard of living were not as well as developed as standalone grounds and were often linked to other rights violations, in particular protection rights. This somewhat reflects the reluctance to interpret social and economic rights violations in the context of the Refugee Convention, which also exists in the wider discourse.

Some violations of protection rights were also considered to amount to persecution. This category of children's rights was the most developed in refugee case law. Several rights, such as the right to be protected from trafficking, torture and abuse, including domestic, have appeared in case law. Chapter 6 concluded that children in refugee discourse are most often considered in terms of their innate vulnerability and need for protection. Although there is a reluctance to acknowledge that social and economic rights violations amount to persecution, the protection rights case law established that there is nevertheless recognition of the role social and economic circumstances, in particular poverty, have on other violations that amount to persecution. In other words, it is acknowledged that children from disadvantaged circumstances are more vulnerable to persecution, for example, trafficking or military conscription or gang recruitment.

Violations of participation rights were less prevalent in the case law than provision and protection rights. Part III in Chapter 6 considered rights relating to autonomy or instances where children exercised their agency. The likely reason for particularly limited case law in this area of rights is due to the two factors addressed above: child claims are often subsumed within adult claims and the small number of separated children applying for refugee protection relative to the number of separated children globally. This analysis nevertheless showed that some violations of children's participation rights did amount to persecution. The most common cases involving children who exercised their agency related to views or transgressions that ran contrary to societal norms. These rights violations ranged from involvement in anti-government movements to expressing a desire not to be forced to marry. Other examples related to sexual transgressions such as one's sexual orientation, gender identity or engaging in pre-marital sexual activities. One challenge identified in Chapter 6 was the trepidation with which officials approach these cases. Bhabha described child-specific attitudes, such as suspicion, condescension and patriarchal views, to 'non-conforming adolescents' as contributing to the inconsistent interpretation of refugee law in the case of children. This is a point of procedure so outside the scope of the present research, but it is revisited below. Overall, civil and political rights were less prominent in the case law and literature than social and economic rights even in the context of *qualification*. This is in contrast to trends in adult claims.

A particular convention ground

All refugee claims must have a nexus with a convention ground in order to satisfy the refugee definition. Although participation rights were interpreted in the context of the religion and political opinion convention grounds, no other section of the book sought to explicitly draw a parallel between the convention grounds and the children's right or rights which were violated. However, it was acknowledged in Chapter 5 that child claimants most often invoked the particular social group ground. Indeed, most case law referred to in respect of provision and protection rights were considered within the frame of the particular social group ground. Chapter 5 sought to link children's rights discourse and the particular social group ground from the outset, before considering the relevant case law as there was considerable conceptual overlap. Children's rights and childhood studies discourses place the child within a social group, namely children, who have a role in a particular society. Childhood was described as having certain attributes in Chapter 2, which shows that the social group both exists based on those innate characteristics, most notably innocence, and that the group is visible by others in the society. These are the two criteria refugee applicants who invoke the particular social ground must normally satisfy. Indeed, there is a wealth of guidance and case law that supports the relevance of the particular social group ground in the context of child refugee law.

The other grounds, race, nationality, religion and political opinion were referred to where relevant. However, the main objective of the research was to examine instances where violations of children's rights amounted to persecution. The convention grounds nevertheless serve to embed children's rights violations in refugee law. To take an example, in the case of the child who would be prohibited from accessing education on the basis of nationality, he could be conceptualised as a child (and thus inherently part of a social group) and someone who suffered discrimination based on nationality. For the purposes of this research, it is the violation of the right to education that was important, not the convention grounds as the main question asked herein was which children's rights violations may amount to persecution.

The findings

Children are recognised as refugees on the basis of child specific forms of persecution. This assertion is buttressed by expansive guidance, literature and some jurisprudence. The case law to date shows a willingness to engage with children's rights in the interpretation of the Refugee Convention. However, the limited case law reaching higher courts and the number of cases involving a violation of a fundamental children's right, which is determined not to amount to persecution, for example protection from forced gang involvement as discussed in Chapter 6, shows that the approach to date is inconsistent. There is inconsistent utilisation of and reference to the CRC in refugee case law. This may be due to the lack of authoritative guidance in the national and international contexts, which would require consideration of one treaty in the interpretation of another (assuming they are relevant).

In addition, it was found that violations of protection rights are most prevalent in refugee case law databases and literature. This indicates that the *child-as-vulnerable-and-in-need-of-protection* conceptualisation is dominant in this area of law, consistent with the children's rights status quo. However, there are indications that refugee law is evolving alongside the wider children's rights discourse in light of developments around child agency. This is evidenced by guidance, literature and case law on children's abilities and right to exercise their agency in the context of religion and politics, for example, to the extent that they may put, or find themselves, at risk of persecution. These developments are new. The conceptualisation of children in refugee law to date remains paternalistic in its application. This is not surprising as it is consistent with the wider children's rights law framework.

Paternalism in refugee law is also due in part to best interests assessments as discussed in Chapter 3. The best interests principle requires a subjective and third party assessment of the best interests of the child. Although the child has a right to participate in this process and this is confirmed by the Committee on the Rights of the Child, the processes through which the best interests are determined are often criticised for being informed by decisions made by adults *for* children rather than adults *in partnership* with children.[2] Because Article 3 is the right most commonly referred to in refugee discourse there is a tendency to favour the paternalistic approach. The more nuanced rights relating to active citizenship, like freedom of expression, for example, may be overlooked.

The introduction of a children's rights approach would perhaps bring refugee law more in line with the CRC. The Three Ps Approach to the interpretation of the CRC established that there are three sides to children's rights: provision rights, protection rights and participation rights. This research also established that these three categories represent the universal understanding of childhood, an understanding based on the principle of development. No one set of rights is seen to be more important than the others in pursuit of 'optimal' development. It is therefore possible to suggest that participation rights carry the same weight. In applying this approach in the context of refugee law, the result should be more consistent. Protection rights would not be prioritised over participation rights in the consideration of a claim utilising a children's rights approach. Children would not be disadvantaged by the perception of or the act of exercising their agency. A children's rights approach may mitigate this risk.

The questions

This conclusion raises a number of questions as to the development of a children's rights approach to the interpretation of the Refugee Convention.

Primarily, however, it challenges the existing children's rights paradigm in that the interpretation of the Refugee Convention to date only uneasily deals with the matter of child agency. Although this research does not deal with matters of procedure, the conceptualisation herein challenges what Bhabha refers to as 'child-specific attitudes'.[3] Some research looks at this aspect of procedure, in particular credibility, but more research is required to fully grasp the impact attitudes have on the grant of status. It is not just further study that will correct this perception or correct the tendency to view children as incapable of holding political views in their own right, it is consistency in the approach of the law and specifically a children's rights approach. In the context of applying a human rights approach to the interpretation of the Refugee Convention, Foster suggested that clear and authoritative guidance on the application of human rights law in the interpretation of the Convention and in unpacking the meaning of persecution would facilitate a more expansive interpretation taking into account the wealth of literature and case law on violations of social and economic rights in the context of persecution.[4] The same can be said of a children's rights approach.

This book sought to analyse how children are conceived of in refugee law and in what instances would a violation of a children's right amount to persecution in current practice, specifically in the Global North. However, discussions on deficit childhood in Chapter 2 raised some questions around the universality of the children's rights law framework with the CRC as the bulwark. Chapter 5 referred to a resistance to incorporate the best interests principle in the context of refugee law due to the fear that it may mean children's claims would be weighted differently in that officials would have to make a welfare- and/or rights-based assessment comparing two jurisdictions rather than using the existing, albeit developing in the context of children, interpretation of the definition of refugee. There is a fear that broadening the scope for interpretation of the Refugee Convention may result in more children, and perhaps a significant proportion of the world's children, becoming eligible for protection on the basis that their children's rights as contained within the CRC are not satisfied and/or regularly violated.

The Refugee Convention does not, however, allow for such flexibility, as in it cannot encompass all violations of children's rights as they must be deemed to amount to persecution with a link to a convention ground. The rights violations must not only amount to persecution, but must be characterised by differential impact on the basis of discrimination. There is nevertheless scope for expansion consistent with the laws of treaty interpretation and in line with the object and purpose of the treaties. There is an abundance of guidance on the ways in which the Refugee Convention may consider CRC-based rights. At the fore are recommendations and laws that require a lowering of the threshold of persecution; for example, witnessing rather than experiencing a form of violence, or a more generous application of the benefit of the doubt. However, as said throughout this book, these are matters of procedure.

Moving forward

Considering the findings and the conclusions, a number of paths of research would be recommended to continue to build upon a children's rights approach to the interpretation of the Refugee Convention. Firstly, a reverse approach to the structure of this book would provide an additional avenue through which we could conceptualise the child refugee. A reverse approach would put refugee law first and children's rights second. The analysis would thus stem from the refugee legal framework and deal with the convention grounds and how child's claims are dealt with in relation to the 'link'. This approach was not chosen as the objective was to assert a more child-centred conceptualisation of childhood before deconstructing rights, which may be violated and perhaps amount to persecution. This statement was qualified by the word 'more' as the CRC, which forms the basis of the international legal framework was not drafted in consultation with children, but is nevertheless closer to a child-centred framework than the refugee framework given that children are not explicitly mentioned as persons eligible for qualification within the Refugee Convention.

Secondly, this research and the project described above would also be complemented by an in-depth analysis of the procedural challenges faced by children seeking asylum in order to ascertain the extent to which refugee determinations are affected by factors like credibility or 'child-specific attitudes'. It is not sufficient to conclude here with a conceptualisation of childhood based on children's rights and an examination of the instances where a violation amounts to persecution. The objective and subjective analyses of the different elements of a child's claim must be considered. For example, how is the child's right to have their voice heard, or participate, in determination proceedings? This question is particularly pertinent in those instances where the child is subsumed and at times indistinguishable in the adult's claim. Another point raised throughout is how a refugee decision-maker may make a subjective assessment as to the capacity of a child to exercise their agency by expressing views contrary to the religious, political or societal status quo. These factors impact upon the child's ability to access asylum procedures and their ability to substantiate a claim and thus must form part of this discourse. Indeed, a wealth of literature is already available on this aspect of child claims, but it does not deal with a children's rights approach to the interpretation of the convention with a view to examining the qualification of child refugees. As noted throughout, safeguards and child welfare dominate the discourse on child refugees and asylum seekers.

Thirdly, there is insufficient case law available at the international level. It would be a worthwhile endeavour to focus on one or more countries as case studies to analyse their administrative decisions and lower court decisions, as well as a more exhaustive evaluation of higher court decisions that deal with children qualifying or applying to qualify for refuge. This research provides a general overview of the literature and the case law available and widely accessible to researchers via the most common refugee law databases and literature. However, the findings are inconclusive as the case law, which is limited, does not illustrate significant trends.

Conclusions

The hypothesis set out in Chapter 1 was that the Refugee Convention is capable of accommodating claims from children and that in fact there is already jurisprudence, guidance and literature that support a children's rights approach to its interpretation. To complement the children's rights approach, this research set out to establish a conceptualisation of child refugees and asked which children's rights when violated amount to persecution. The hypothesis is supported by the findings in that a children's rights approach is possible and indeed there is evidence that it is already developing. The conceptualisation of the child refugee that emerged was one of innocence and vulnerability, yet there are indications that autonomous rights are increasingly the subject of refugee determinations. This is consistent with developments in children's rights and children and childhood studies generally.

Notes

1 UNHCR define '*prima facie refugee*' as a person recognised as a refugee, by a State or UNHCR, on the basis of objective criteria related to the circumstances

in their country of origin, which justify the presumption that they meet the criteria of the applicable refugee definition. See: UNHCR, *Master Glossary of Terms Rev. 1* (2006) 17 <www.unhcr.org/cgi-bin/texis/vtx/refworld/rwmain/opendocpdf.pdf?docid=42ce7d444> accessed 12 May 2016.

2 See: Jane Fortin, *Children's Rights and the Developing Law* (3rd edn, CUP 2009).

3 Jacqueline Bhabha, *Child Migration and Human Rights in a Global Age* (PUP 2014) 207.

4 Michelle Foster, *International Refugee Law and Socio-Economic Rights: Refugee from Deprivation* (CUP 2007).

Index

For Product Safety Concerns and Information please contact our EU representative GPSR@taylorandfrancis.com
Taylor & Francis Verlag GmbH, Kaufingerstraße 24, 80331 München, Germany

www.ingramcontent.com/pod-product-compliance
Ingram Content Group UK Ltd.
Pitfield, Milton Keynes, MK11 3LW, UK
UKHW011009180926
475701UK00004B/648
9780367280819